THE LADY
IN MEDIEVAL
ENGLAND
1000–1500

1. Effigy of Lady Joan Beauchamp, Worcester Cathedral (detail)

THE LADY
IN MEDIEVAL
ENGLAND
1000–1500

PETER COSS

WRENS
PARK

A Sutton Publishing Book

First published in the United Kingdom in 1998 by
Sutton Publishing Limited · Phoenix Mill
Thrupp · Stroud · Gloucestershire · GL5 2BU

This edition published in 1999 by Wrens Park Publishing, an imprint of
W.J. Williams & Son Ltd

British Library Cataloguing in Publication Data
A catalogue record for this book is available from the British Library.

ISBN 0-905-778-367

Title page photograph: Lady's head, St George's Chapel capital, Worcester Cathedral

Typeset in 11/12 pt Ehrhardt.
Typesetting and origination by
Sutton Publishing Limited.
Printed in Great Britain by
Redwood Books Limited,
Trowbridge, Wiltshire.

Contents

For my mother and sister

List of Illustrations

Acknowledgements

I would like to thank all those who have given advice and encouragement in the preparation of this book. I am particularly grateful to Mr Adrian Ailes, Dr William Aird, Dr Padma Anagol, Dr Rowena Archer, Ms Jean Birrell, Dr Paul Brand, Dr David Crook, Professor Archie Duncan, Professor Brian Kemp, Dr Helen Nicholson, Professor Pauline Stafford, Dr Henry Summerson and Dr Garthine Walker. I would also like to thank Dr Lindy Grant and Mr Geoffrey Fisher of the Conway Library, Courtauld Institute of Art, and Ms Rachel Watson and Ms Sue Groves of Northamptonshire County Record Office for their help and kindness during my visits. I am very grateful to Mr Simon Eager, Mr Richard Griffiths of Malvern and Mr M.W. Smith of Durham for their photographs, and once again to Mr David Hill of Stourbridge for his heraldic illustrations.

I owe special thanks to Mr Martin Stuchfield, honorary secretary of the Monumental Brass Society for his kindness in supplying photographs from the Malcolm Norris Collection at short notice. I would also like to take this opportunity of recording the characteristic generosity of the late Dr Norris in bringing a number of hand-holding effigies to my attention at the beginning of this project. Ms Jaqueline Mitchell and Ms Sarah Fowle of Sutton Publishing saw the work through to publication in a friendly and efficient manner. And, finally, my wife, Angela Coss, provided not only the index but help, advice and criticism at all stages of the work. It owes a very great deal to her.

Illustrations were supplied by or reproduced by the kind permission of the following: The British Library (Plates 2–12, and Figs 4, 12–15, 18–19, 26, 29–30, 45, 48, 62, 64, 66, 72, 74, 77); Mr David Hill (Plate 13); The Burrell Collection, Glasgow Museums and Art Galleries (Plate 1); Mr Richard Griffiths (title page photograph and Figs 1, 28, 34); The Pierpont Morgan Library, New York (Fig. 2); The Public Record Office, Kew (Crown Copyright) (Figs 5, 9, 61, 65, 68); The Conway Library, Courtauld Institute of Art, University of London (Figs 10, 20, 25, 27, 31–2, 41, 49–50, 57, 63, 70, 76, 80); F.H. Crossley and Maurice H. Ridgway (Fig. 25); The British Museum (Fig. 11); The Dean and Chapter, Durham Cathedral (Figs 16–17); The Master and Fellows of St John's College, Cambridge (Fig. 33); The Royal Commission on the Historical Monuments of England (Crown Copyright) (Fig. 36); The Malcolm Norris Collection, Monumental Brass Society (Figs 42–3, 52–3, 56, 58–9); Mr Simon Eager (Fig. 51); Mr Charles Stopford-Sackville (Fig. 60); The Huntingdon Library, San Marino, California (Figs 75, 79). While every effort has been made to acknowledge all copyright holders I would like to apologise should any omissions have been made.

CHAPTER 1

Introduction

In 1466 the Pastons produced their famous account of their ancestry and claim to gentility.[1] Ostensibly at least, it was a very male-centred account, stressing lordship, lineage and heraldry. The Paston women were alluded to only as proof of the capacity of the male Pastons to marry well, to proclaim their links with other gentry, and to announce their ability to provide sufficient dower for their wives to live comfortably after their deaths:

> Also they shewed how that their ancetors (ancestors) had in old time and of late time married with worshipfull gentlemen [sic], and proved by deeds of marriage and by other deeds how their ancetors had indowed their wives. . . . and made open by evident proofe how they and their ancetors came linealy descended of right noble and worshipfull blood and of great lords sometime liveing in this our realme of Ingland.

Agnes Paston, the only lady mentioned by name, is identified as 'wife to the said William Paston, father to the said John, William, and Clement, [who] in title of her dower, is in possession of bondholders and also of bondmen, whose ancetors have been bondmen to the ancetors of the said John Paston sithen (since) the time that no minde is to the contrary.'

And yet, as many commentators have shown, the apparent implications of statements like this are in large measure belied by the Paston letters themselves. Principally, though by no means exclusively, through the central figure of Margaret Paston – one of the best known of all medieval ladies to the twentieth century – they show not only the diversity but also the sheer vitality of the lady's role. They reveal, furthermore, a surprising degree of mutuality in the marriage relationship, with lord and lady both giving and receiving respect from each other. Something of their capacity to act in concert is revealed in a letter of June 1465 when John Paston wrote to his wife having had word from his bailiff, Richard Calle, that one Master Philip had entered his manor of Drayton in the Duke of Suffolk's name and intended to similarly enter the manor of Hellesdon.[2] Calle sought advice. John's advice – addressed to his wife – was:

> that ye comfort my tenants and help them till I come home, and let them wet (know) I shall not lose it . . . ye be a gentilwoman, and it is worship for you to comfort your tenants; wherefore, I would ye might ride to Hellesdon and

Drayton and Sparham, and tarry at Drayton and speak with them, and bid
them hold with their old master till I come.

She was to tell them of the failure of a previous Suffolk claim on the manor and
to impugn Master Philip, saying that it were shameful, especially for a priest, to
set a lord on to such an untrue course as this. She was to tell them that she had
written of the situation to her husband and that it was as yet too early to expect a
reply – a lie intended presumably to buy time – and also to let them know that as
soon as John Paston returned home he would see them. She was to emphasise
that the perpetrators of this action would never acquire Paston's respect or
compliance. Moreover, she was to make much of those who had been Paston
'well-willers', seek the support of neighbours, and generally 'fynd all othir menis
that ye kan to plese the pepill'. John's advice to his wife, however, went beyond
the giving of comfort to more practical considerations. She was to point out to
the tenants that even if Suffolk did have title to the lands, which he did not, he
would have no right to seek rent from them until Michaelmas and she was to
make it clear to them that she would demand from them every penny that they
owed. Finally, if any entry was made at Hellesdon, she was to 'shuff him owt and
set sum man to kepe the place if ned be'. To be sure, the letter implies John
Paston's primacy in directing the family affairs and in offering his wife guidance
but, if it gives a false impression at all, this lies in exaggerating John Paston's
resolution in attending to the needs of his estates rather than the lady's ability to
handle the tenantry and the practical defence of the family's interests, which
Margaret's earlier history at Gresham had already proved. Above all else,
Margaret Paston reveals herself as devoted to the interests of her marital family.
Caister Castle, the most spectacular of the Paston gains from the Fastolf estates,
she referred to as 'the finest flower in *our* garland' (author's italics). Her role in
support of the Pastons' position, moreover, went beyond the maintenance of
household and family and of the defence of its estates in the narrow sense. The
correspondence shows her active in the treating and negotiations that lie behind
and around local court cases, parliamentary elections, and alliances generally. She
treated with sheriffs, undersheriffs, members of the peace commission and the
like. In short, the traditional division of responsibility between public and
private, between external and internal affairs, is brought sharply into question
when confronted by this evidence.

The letter also introduces us to the language of gentility. John Paston reminds
Margaret that she is a gentlewoman and as such she can expect to command
respect. The letters, in fact, abound in the language of gentility. We hear it, for
example, in marriage negotiations when Margaret writes to her opposite number,
the mother of John Paston III's intended bride: 'to the right worshipful and my
very good lady and cousin Dame Elizabeth Brews'.[3] Should the negotiations fail,
and Margery Brews not be secured, Margaret will be 'as sory for hyr as for eny
gentylwoman leveing (living)'.[4] We hear it in Richard Calle's letter to Margery
Paston: 'myn owne lady and mastres (mistress) and be-for God very trewe wyff'.[5]
We hear it in letters from servants: 'Right reverend and worshipful mistress,
I recommend me unto your good mistressship' and even 'To my right noble and

worshipful mistress, my Mistress Paston'.[6] And we hear it in the perhaps tongue-in-cheek letter from Thomas Danvers to John Paston II: 'Ye be the best cheser of a gentellwoman that I know'.[7]

These extracts from the Paston letters give rise to several lines of inquiry which constitute the themes of this book. The most basic question, though not a facile one, is to seek the meaning that contemporaries attached to the term 'gentilwoman'. Was there a clear, medieval definition? Or, to ask the question in a different way: how was the lady perceived within secular society, that is to say both by herself and by her male counterparts? Another, linked, question is to ask whence came the lady and how did she evolve? These are simple questions, but they are by no means easy to resolve.

There are two further fundamental questions, however, which together provide the main focus for this book. The first is to ask how precisely women related to, and participated within, the culture of gentility, a culture which at first sight, at least, appears to be full of essentially male preoccupations: martial prowess, public reputation and so on. The second question is an extension of the first: how did lord and lady co-exist in medieval society; by what means did they successfully co-inhabit their world; and, how closely were their lives intertwined?

In raising these issues I am guided principally by one of the insights of the American feminist historian, Joan Kelly. For her 'the social relations of the sexes' was a primary object of study:[8] 'Embedded in and shaped by the social order, the relation of the sexes must be integral to any study of it.'[9] Although the social relations between the sexes surfaces explicitly within historical writing from time to time, it has largely been subsumed within gender history. The notion of gender entered into women's history during the 1970s as a means of highlighting the fact that female subordination was not natural but socially and culturally constructed. Recently it has begun to give rise to perceived problems.[10] From the point of view of the present book, the most significant of these is the tendency to objectify or reify gender. It is a problem which is perhaps inherent, although not intended, within definitions. The temptation is first of all to construct composite yet homogeneous categories of male and female gender and then to proceed to observe their manifestations and their collisions within social reality. The dangers are obvious and two-fold. One is that it is not individuals who interact in this at all but categories.[11] The second is that such stereotypes tend to be either based upon normative and paradigmatic models produced within society, which may be partial and are certainly ideological, or derived from psychoanalysis, most especially from the Lacanian/Freudian variety which is essentially ahistorical.[12] My objective is to attempt to counteract this tendency by placing the 'lived experience' of ladies at the centre of the stage. Gender constructions are significant only as societal expectations. Gerda Lerner's description of gender in action comes closer to actual social relations: 'It is a costume, a mask, a straitjacket in which men and women dance their unequal dance.'[13]

A second tendency within both feminist and gender history of the Middle Ages, for which I hope to offer something of a corrective, is the deep-seated desire to discover a specific female social space and hence a specifically female cultural role within history. This approach is derived essentially from the idea of separate spheres, once very popular within women's history but now under fire.[14] It is ironic that this male ideology was taken over with such enthusiasm by feminists, the difference being that in the feminist construction the woman ceased to be passive but active, even dynamic, within her own private – as opposed to public – sphere. To be sure, the dichotomy between public and private surfaces, largely among male writers, in many historical societies, but at best it only partially conforms to reality. Hence Linda Kerber, for instance, argues that 'separate spheres' should be regarded as a rhetorical device.[15] As Joan Kelly put it succinctly: 'Woman's place is not a separate sphere or domain of existence but a position within social existence generally.'[16] The search for a separate social space, although an understandable and legitimate line of enquiry, is none the less in danger of misrepresenting reality.

Needless to say, the study which follows does not set out to deny the subordination of woman to man in past societies, nor to minimise either the force or the destructive power of misogyny, but only to emphasise that the lives of men and women were integrated, for good or ill, and to examine that integration. It seems to me that the concept of patriarchy, meaning the institutionalisation and idealisation of male dominance, should be retained. The advantage is that it denotes a situation which arose historically – at the very dawn of civilisation, it would seem – and which has persisted through time, but which is nevertheless subject to change in both form and intensity.[17] Embedded in ideas as well as institutions, patriarchy is inherited by both men and women. With this historical constancy in mind, we can observe shifts within the relationships between the sexes without expecting to detect any great sea change. Misogyny, too, is subject to reformation, as for example in the wake of the Reform movement within the Western Church during the eleventh and twelfth centuries.

These considerations provide the inspiration for this book. It will begin with a broad consideration of the position, status and image of the lady in England during the eleventh and twelfth centuries, concentrating upon continuity as well as change. It will then move to examine the spread of gentility in medieval England, focusing especially on female participation within a predominantly chivalric culture. It will then proceed to a detailed examination of the social relations between the sexes, beginning with the visual representation of the ladies and of the relationship between ladies and lords, and moving on to analyse their affective relations before turning to causes and expressions of antagonism. This will be followed by a study of verbal representations and the problem of the internalisation of values presented in the predominant modes of discourse. At this point we will be in a position to understand more fully the role of the lady in the society of medieval England.

Like its companion volume on the Knight in the medieval period, this book is intended both as a work of synthesis and as an essay in interpretation. I have drawn upon the work of many scholars as well as my own research, and I have relied heavily upon their expertise in specific areas. As the book is designed to be fully accessible to the general reader, as well as to the professional scholar, I have confined my citations as far as possible to works that are available in print, both primary and secondary sources. I have avoided citing unpublished theses and the like. The work is not intended as a bibliography of all that is written on the subject and the reader should be clear that the work is specifically a book on the lady and is not intended as a general work on women in medieval society. I have, however, indicated where I think there are significant gaps in our knowledge and where I believe further work needs to be done.

CHAPTER 2

The Origins of the English Lady

It is necessary to begin with an obvious truth. The existence of the lady is dependent upon both the fact and the concept of nobility. At the apex of European societies of the early Middle Ages were groups described by Latin writers as *illustres*, *primates*, *proceres*, *primores*, *principes*, *magnates*, *maiores*, *optimates* and the like.[1] As David Crouch has written, 'The perception of this dominant group was universal in society. The group intermarried within itself: it had wealth, power and access to the rulers – where there were such – who had raised themselves to dominance over provinces and kingdoms.'[2] In other words, European societies had a nobility, a *nobilitas*.

As with much social terminology the term 'nobility' is not used entirely consistently and hence it is not without its problems for historians. It is also used as an adjective and actions as well as people may be noble (*nobilis*). Even a city or a castle could be described as noble. It is true, moreover, that the social level at which people were called noble varied, according to the writer and across time and place. None the less, it was used in preference to refer to the most elevated of social groups. And it was applied with reference not only to present position but also to ancestry and descent. Orderic Vitalis, born in England but writing from Normandy, refers to the men of non-noble descent (*ignobilis*) whom Henry I had raised to positions of power 'as it were, from the dust'.[3] Although there can be little doubt that he was echoing a widely held view of 'new men', it is equally well known that Orderic was exaggerating the extent of their rise. These men were already established landowners, lords in their own right – but they were not of noble descent as it would have been understood by contemporaries in England and Normandy.

As Crouch reminds us, the French equivalent of noble is *gentil*, a word derived from the Latin *gens*, meaning 'family' or 'stock'.[4] Women as well as men enjoyed nobility through ancestry. In writing down the dower settlement which Duke Richard III of Normandy made on his wife, the scribe refers to the 'nobility' of her lineage.[5] A person's nobility came from both sides of the family. None the less, a woman's social rank often depended upon her husband. From her husband, for example, a woman might acquire the dignity of countess. In the wake of the

Conquest the continental word count (*comes*) was equated with the pre-Conquest Anglo-Danish term earl or, to use its Scandinavian cognate, *jarl*. Although the word *eorl* was much used in the tenth century to denote a man of high birth, a noble man, it came in the time of the Danish King Cnut to apply to those provincial governors who replaced the traditional 'ealdormen', and indeed surpassed them in the breadth of their power and also, generally, in rank. It was quite natural that earl and count should become equated; indeed, there are signs that this was already happening before the Conquest in the reign of Edward the Confessor.[6] With the count came the countess (*comitissa*), the wife of an earl. Well known on the continent, this usage did not appear in England until after the Norman Conquest. Its failure to figure in Anglo-Saxon and Anglo-Danish England probably reflects the fact that the distinction between private and public dignity had not dissolved here to the extent that it had on the continent. In Domesday Book the Latin *comitissa* is, in effect, projected back into pre-Conquest England. Both Judith, the Norman widow of the Anglo-Danish Earl Waltheof, for example, and Godiva, the widow of Earl Leofric, were called countesses by the Domesday clerks. Examples can be found in the twelfth century where women referred to themselves as 'once countess' (*quondam comitissa*) after the death of their husband. However, for the most part they continued to retain the dignity in widowhood.

It remains significant, however, that the dignity of countess was dependent upon a husband's, or late husband's, rank. A startling, if rather unusual, example of this is the description of Bertha, the wife of Ranulf de Glanvill, Henry II's great justiciar, on one occasion as *vicecomitissa*.[7] Ranulf, early on in his career, was Sheriff of Yorkshire. The Latin for sheriff is *vicecomes* (i.e. the continental viscount). The term *vicecomitissa* can only be translated by a rather awkward term like sheriffess; 'viscountess' would give entirely the wrong impression of its meaning. But she clearly has a status which is a reflection of her husband's.

This is explicitly stated in the romance of *Erec et Enide* by the great French writer, Chrétien de Troyes. The count of Limors has abducted Enide and forced her to marry him. He tries to console her by pointing out that this will make her 'a countess and a lady'.[8] It has to be said that she was not impressed. But what was meant by a lady? The term could be used in a very elevated sense. During the civil war between King Stephen and the Empress Matilda, daughter of Henry I and claimant to Stephen's throne, the term 'Lady of England' was used to describe her position at a critical juncture.[9] Stephen had been captured at the Battle of Lincoln on 2 February 1141 and Matilda was now manoeuvring her way towards the crown. When she met the powerful papal legate, Henry of Blois, Bishop of Winchester, on 2 March, she swore to consult him on all important matters, if he would 'receive her in holy church as his lady'. He duly obliged, receiving her in fact as 'Lady of England'. At the subsequent church council held at Winchester she was accepted as 'Lady of England and Normandy'.[10] The title was an ambiguous one, probably intended as a recognition of her right to the throne. It was not entirely unprecedented, however. Queen Adeliza had been called the same, before her coronation, as wife of Henry I.[11] It is clearly meant to convey the idea of an uncrowned, or perhaps more explicitly not-yet-crowned,

2. High-born ladies could be generous patrons. The Crucifixion scene from the Weingarten Gospel book shows Countess Judith, its donor, as a penitent before the cross

ruler. Moreover, it distantly echoes the position of King Alfred's powerful daughter, Aethelflaed, wife of the ealdorman of Mercia, who was *hlaefdige Myrcena* or 'lady of the Mercians', and was similarly a ruler without a crown.[12]

These phrases can be explained in part by the lack of terminology to cover such situations. But the word lady, *domina* in Latin or *hlaefdige* in Anglo-Saxon, is merely the female equivalent of lord, *dominus* or *hlaefdig*, and its more normal use is in that sense. This, for example, is the sense in which it is used in Domesday Book. At Eardisland, Herefordshire, a manor belonging to the earl of Mercia, the reeve 'had the custom . . . that on the arrival of his lady at the manor, he would present her with 18 *orae* of pence, so that she would be well disposed'.[13] And then there is the evidence of Asa, who held three small pieces of land in the East Riding of Yorkshire which were the subject of a dispute in 1086. The jurors testified that Asa held her land 'separate and free from the lordship and power of Bjornulfr her husband, even when they were together, so that he could neither give it, sell it or forfeit it. After their separation, she withdrew with her land and possessed it as its lady (*ut domina*)'; in other words, one might say, she held the land as its lord in her own right.[14] What this conveys about Asa's status is ambivalent. Should we consider her as noble? Almost certainly, not.

None the less, given that nobility was a matter of perception it was also fluid. It was no doubt for this reason that we find it being used, in eleventh- and twelfth-century France and England, in comparative and superlative senses. A man, or indeed, a woman may be *nobilior* (more noble) or *nobilissimus* (most noble) and these terms could be used to describe their rank as well as their actions. If a person could be considered more noble, then by implication another could be considered less noble. It is logical in this society that a lesser nobility should have emerged.

What can we say then of the status of the lesser landowning families of eleventh- and twelfth-century England? Domesday Book indicates that England in 1066 was inhabited by four or five thousand secular landholders, most of whom would no doubt have been described as thegns. One way of approaching the question of their status in the community is by examining their residences.[15] In an eleventh-century tract known as the 'promotion law' we are told that:

> if a ceorl prospered so that he had fully five hides of his own land, church and kitchen, bell house and burh-geat, seat and special office in the king's hall, then was he thenceforward entitled to the rank of thegn.

It has been convincingly argued that this tract conveys the principal marks of thegnly status, even if what the writer has in mind is neither the average *ceorl* (usually translated as peasant but probably indicating here a minor official or such like figure) nor the average thegn. The reference to royal service suggests that what is intended is a royal thegn not a middling thegn who served another lord. Apart from the reference to the land being the thegn's own, which seems to refer to land held by charter (bookland) rather than, for example, lease land, the most significant item here is the *burh-geat*. *Burh* means fortification and the *burh-geat* (the gate of the *burh*), therefore, indicates a fortified manor house. The gatehouse would be the most important feature of a fortified enclosure surrounding the manor house. The bell-tower may also suggest a church tower forming part of a lord's enclosure or *burh*. These features fit well with the excavations of the manor houses at Goltho in Lincolnshire and Sulgrave in Northamptonshire. Both show a large hall with bank and ditch. At Sulgrave, dating from the early eleventh century, there are also associated buildings including what appears to have been a kitchen as well as a church.

A thegnly residence of this type is indicated in a writ of Edward the Confessor dated between 1042 and 1046 by which he confirmed to Westminster Abbey the estate granted by Azur Swart (the Black) and his wife Aelfgyth. This was the *burh* of Wennington in Essex, with its four hides of land, church and churchsoke, together with land called 'At the Lea'. This last was probably in the neighbouring vill of Alveley, i.e. Aelfgyth's *leah*, which contains the name of Azur's wife, Aelfgyth.

The reference to churches in all of this is of great significance. Increasingly during the tenth and eleventh centuries ancient, largely royal, estates were broken up into smaller units and given by charter to king's thegns. Here the thegns built their residences and often reorganised the settlement to suit the new arrangement, creating nucleated villages and associated field systems. Estate churches were constructed to serve both the lord and his family and the peasant tenants where nucleation had occurred. The church would often be in close proximity to the manor house. This was in fact a long-drawn-out process across the tenth to twelfth

3. Iffley, Oxfordshire, a twelfth-century village church. Juliana de St Remy, lady of the manor, gave this church to Kenilworth Priory in 1189

centuries.[16] The period from *c.* 1050–*c.* 1150, in particular, has been described as a time of a 'Great Rebuilding' of ordinary churches.[17] By the latter date the vast majority of later medieval churches already existed. By 1200 the parish system had crystallised and church and society adjusted to these changes.

An early snapshot of the sort of landowning society this produced is provided by a lease of Church Tew in Oxfordshire in 1050–2. It was leased by the Abbey of St Albans to Tova, widow of Wihtric. The manor was a large one of sixteen hides, according to Domesday Book. South-eastwards of the settlement lay the church and beside it, until *c.* 1800, was the manor house, more or less where it had stood, no doubt, in Tova's time. Thirteen thegns are named in the witness list to the lease, many of them presumably Tova's friends and neighbours from the surrounding settlements.[18]

Members of this Anglo-Saxon thegnly class and their post-Conquest successors obviously enjoyed considerable status in society, notwithstanding the fact that it was by no means a monolithic class and that there were considerable differences in terms of landed base. A lesser nobility was coming into being. Much tension existed around the issue of nobility or gentility, especially in the twelfth century. Among the marks of noble status was the use of the locative surname, *x de* (of) *y*. It was a feature which came to characterise the landed classes, although it was never universal. One of the counties which has received detailed treatment in terms of surname development is Oxfordshire. The Oxfordshire portion of the 1279 Hundred Rolls, the great incomplete survey of landholding held in that year, shows 59 per cent of all lords of manors bearing locative surnames. The return of tenants by knight service, both tenants-in-chief of the Crown and subtenants, in 1242–3 indicates that 66 per cent of military tenants in the same county held surnames derived from places.[19] This, however, was the result of a long process, which was not complete even by 1200. The outlines of this process, however, are clear enough. At the time of Domesday Book many, although not all, tenants-in-chief either already possessed hereditary surnames, or held names that were to become hereditary thereafter.[20] Some surnames, indeed, were already hereditary in Normandy. Other families of baronial or substantial knightly rank can be shown to have developed hereditary names during the first half of the twelfth century. By the close of the century these names were being borne by younger sons as well as heads of families. The evidence is relatively sparse and the chronology uncertain but it is clear that a substantial proportion of knightly sub-tenants had developed hereditary surnames by the end of the century. If we take the honour of Wallingford as an example, 48 of its 63 military tenants in Oxfordshire, Berkshire, Buckinghamshire and Gloucestershire can be shown to have had hereditary surnames by 1200.[21] More work needs to be done to attempt to establish precise dating but it may well be the case that many knightly families developed hereditary, and especially locative, names only in the mid- to late twelfth century. In some cases, the adoption of a locative name was delayed until the thirteenth century.

It is hardly to be doubted that in England as in France the locative surname was a matter of prestige, adopted unless a pre-existing surname already carried considerable social clout, and that it moved down the social scale.[22] It indicated initially either the possession of a castle or *caput* (head) of an honour or, as it moved downwards, residence in and lordship over a settlement. Given the prestige that was attached to surnames it is not surprising to find that when men married heiresses from more illustrious families, their sons sometimes took their mother's name in preference to their father's. For example, when Robert de Stafford III, grandson of the Domesday lord of Stafford, died his heir was his sister Millicent, married to Harvey Bagot. Their son took the name Stafford.[23] In such cases a lady might retain her maiden name, as did Roese de Verdon, heiress to the manor and castle of Brandon in Warwickshire and descendant of Lesceline, daughter of Geoffrey de Clinton, Henry I's chamberlain. Though she married Theobald le Boteler, when Roese died in 1247 their son succeeded to the estate as John de Verdon.[24] And when Robert Fitz Meldred of Raby married Isabel, daughter of Geoffrey de Neville of Burreth, a distant cousin of Hugh de Neville, the powerful Angevin forester, such was the prestige of the Neville name that their son, Geoffrey, took his mother's name and so founded the branch of the Neville family at Raby from which Warwick the Kingmaker later descended.[25]

Most scholars of the nobility and of chivalry believe that a major change took place during the second half of the twelfth century, a change which the great French medievalist Georges Duby referred to as the fusion of the aristocracy.[26] At the heart of this social change lay the refinement of chivalry and its adoption as an ideology of exclusion by the high aristocracy of northern France. Romance literature points to the development of a clearer class consciousness within aristocratic circles towards the end of the twelfth century, investing knighthood with strong and exclusive moral and social values. The works of Chrétien de Troyes, produced around the 1170s and early 1180s, are especially significant here. Among the manifestations of this change were the increased significance attached to knighthood by the greater men, with particular emphasis upon the ceremony of dubbing, the development of heraldry, and on the part of lesser men the use of the hitherto reserved title *dominus* in their charters. Developments in France were mirrored in England, at least as far as many of the essential features are concerned. Heraldry belongs to a highly aristocratic world. Prompted initially perhaps by the tournament, heraldry began to take on an hereditary form from the 1140s. It was disseminated downwards from the highest families during the later twelfth and early thirteenth centuries through associations of service and land tenure, although much of this process is obscure. It is first evidenced in the seals that accompanied land transactions. Knighthood became more exclusive during the later twelfth and early thirteenth centuries with a resultant thinning of knightly ranks, partly at least as a response to increasing costs. By the 1230s and 1240s it was becoming the norm to separate off knights from other witnesses to charters, only the knights and the greater lords, who were also knights, carrying the designation *dominus* or sir. This was paralleled by the dissemination of the words *domina* and *dame*.

A family's nobility was manifested in its actions. Among the most prestigious acts was the foundation of a religious house. The founder's descendants functioned as a monastery's patrons, a position which conferred not only spiritual benefits but also material ones.[27] A religious house became a focus for burial, for family loyalty and local prestige.[28] It gave rights of entry into religion for members of the family, for instance, and it involved an expectation of hospitality. It was the monastic patronage of great lords and courtiers that was most in evidence in Anglo-Norman England. In this, as in much else, they tended to follow fashion, moving from the Benedictines, for example, to the new orders such as the Cistercians and the Augustinian canons. Where the great men led, their tenants followed, giving land, churches and tithes. Thus when Gilbert (de Clare) of Tonbridge (d. 1117) endowed the priory of Stoke-by-Clare in Suffolk, his 'barons' were entreated to follow suit. Roger of Gyney, for example, gave two-thirds of his tithes at Haveringland and Whitwell, Norfolk, and of his land in the city of Norwich together with the Church of St Clement there. Geoffrey of Blavenni, a knight of Gilbert's elder brother, Roger fitz Richard, gave lands at Birdbrook, Essex, when he became a monk. Gilbert de Clare, Earl of Hertford (d. 1152) and his brother Earl Roger (d. 1173) were buried there.[29] In the second half of the twelfth century patronage came increasingly from lesser families, and in their own right. The Augustinian house at Cirencester in Gloucestershire, for example, was now receiving property from local landowners such as Richard Murdac, Ansfrid Thorel and Constance Musard.[30] Some middling and lesser landowners founded houses themselves. In Warwickshire, Ralph le Boteler founded the Abbey of Alcester, William Burdet the Priory of Alvecote and Robert de Pillarton the Priory of Pinley.[31] Whether one's ancestors had endowed monasteries was still considered an important ingredient of gentility in the fifteenth century, as the Paston evidence shows.[32]

But nobility was also a matter of manners. The French writer on love, Andrew the Chaplain, believed there was a certain air (*natura*) which great men possessed and which lesser men tried to copy or acquire.[33] Although women shared in this sense of quality, there does not appear to have been much that was gender specific denoting a lady. If a woman behaved nobly in Anglo-Saxon England she was said to behave *earlic*, 'like an earl'. Her status was derived from her husband and from her family and she was expected to behave accordingly.

With this in mind, let us examine the situation of the lady during the eleventh and twelfth centuries. How much freedom of action did she enjoy, and how was she treated by her male counterparts? The long-held view that the Anglo-Saxon period constituted a golden age for women, even for noble women, has been seriously questioned in recent years.[34] It is certainly true that the evidence of laws, charters and wills, especially when taken at face value, allows them considerable rights and freedom of action.[35] The wills of later Anglo-Saxon England make it abundantly clear that no exclusive preference was given to men as heirs. Wulfgeat, for example, left his property to his wife, his two daughters and a kinswoman despite the fact that he had a grandson. He asked his lord, 'for the love of God', to be a friend to his wife and daughter.[36] According to a law of Cnut, in the absence of a will a man's property is to be divided justly between his widow, his children and his close kin. The wills, moreover, are evidence not only for the rights of women to inherit, but also for their right to bequeath their lands as they themselves wished. As many as a quarter of the surviving Anglo-Saxon wills are by women, and a number of others are by husband and wife jointly. As a result of these rights, the divisions of property within families must have been subject to considerable variation.[37]

4. *The will of an Anglo-Saxon lady, Wynflaed, favouring her daughter Aethelflaed* (c. 950)

These women bequeathed considerable amounts of land. Wynflaed's will, for example, which dates from around 950, includes provision for her son and grandson, but shows a distinct preference for her daughter Aethelflaed, whose name recurs throughout the will.[38] She receives her mother's personal jewellery and 'the estate at Ebbesborne and the title-deed as a perpetual inheritance to dispose of as she pleases'. Eadmaer, on the other hand, who appears to be her son, receives an estate but effectively as a life interest: 'If Aethelflaed survive [Eadmaer] she is to succeed to the estate at Faccombe'. Various women of unknown relationship to the testator receive movable goods. Ceolthryth, for example, gets a mancus of gold and some valuable clothing, while Cynelufu gets 'her share of the untamed horses'. But Aethelflaed is the favoured legatee, getting 'everything which is unbequeathed, books and such small things'. None the less, there are also gifts to male kinsmen and provision is made for male dependants, both free and unfree. The will of Wulfwaru in the late tenth century left an estate divided between her elder son and younger daughter. They were 'to share the main residence between them as fairly as they can so that each of them shall have a reasonable part of it'.[39]

A famous inheritance quarrel occurred in Herefordshire in the early eleventh century. One Edwin sued his own mother for a piece of land. She was furious: 'she became very angry with her son . . . in the manner appropriate to an eorl (a noble)'. She then proceeded to make a grant of the land before witnesses: 'Here sits Leofflaed, my kinswoman, to whom I leave both my land and my gold, my furnishings and my clothing and all that I own.' The mother then demanded that this be reported to the shire court. Turning to the men present, she told them to 'act like thegns' and to tell the meeting that she had left her property to Leofflaed 'and not a thing to my son'. For added security, however, Leofflaed's husband had the details written down.[40]

The evidence is quite clear then that people had the right to bequeath land as they saw fit. At the same time, laws and private agreements reveal the financial side of marriage.[41] The key feature was the *morgengifu*, the 'morning-gift', which the prospective husband paid not to the father or to the kin, but to the woman herself. A considerable amount of property could be involved, both in money and land. What is important is that the wife had control over it herself. Thus she could sell it, bequeath it or even give it away. Although marriage agreements were drawn up by kin, it is clear that the girl herself had a say. A late tenth-century text on the betrothal of a woman speaks in terms of the obligations of a bridegroom and of the counter obligations of the bride's kin. The marriage has to be 'agreeable to her'. In addition to the morning-gift, the bridegroom must specify the property he will leave her should she survive him. A law of the Kentish King Aethelbert had stated that a woman could walk out of a marriage that did not please her, and that if she took the children with her she was entitled to half of the property. This provision does not figure in later laws but one consistent feature is that a wife should not be held responsible for her husband's crimes, and should not be vulnerable, therefore, in terms of her property.

It was natural, given the degree of financial independence of a wife, that women would become involved in lawsuits over land. In the case of Wynflaed versus Leofwine it was said that she had received the estates of Hagbourne and

Bradfield from Aelfric in return for the estate at Datchet. Wynflaed was required to prove her ownership. This she did, with the support of many people. Of the twenty-four who were named, no fewer than thirteen were women. The text continues: 'and many [other] reliable thegns and women, though we cannot now recount them all'.[42] The law codes also show us widows being treated humanely. Aethelraed's code of 1008 stipulates that a widow should remain unmarried for a year and then make her own choice. Cnut echoes this, but adds: 'if she chooses a husband within the year's space she is then to forfeit . . . all the possessions which she had through her former husband'. By implication she retains any property that is her own. The widow's right to choose is equally emphasised by Cnut: 'A widow is never to be consecrated a nun too hastily and neither a widow nor a maiden is ever forced to marry a man whom she herself dislikes.'[43]

There are some obvious problems in taking much of this material at face value. Flexibility over inheritance could just as easily work for as against a woman. Around the year 1000 the great Midland noble, Wulfric Spott, left the bulk of his property to his brother and nephews and to Burton Abbey, by-passing his own daughter. It may well be that surviving wills give something of a false impression. It could be argued that men were less under pressure to leave wills when they had sons to inherit and that daughters were in a more vulnerable position, needing the extra security of a written document. The case of the Herefordshire woman who disinherited her son in favour of her kinswoman in Cnut's reign has to be seen in its full context.[44] On looking more closely we see strong male interests at work. The woman was not herself in court. Thegns came to her from the Herefordshire shire court and she made her statement by proxy. Leofflaed, the kinswoman to whom she granted the land, was the wife of Thurkil the White. In the shire court it was he who had spoken on the claim. He then rode to Hereford to have the case recorded in the Herefordshire Gospel Book from where the evidence comes. In 1066 the land in question was held by him and by the clergy of Hereford. The court proceedings would have been presided over by the Bishop of Hereford and by the Danish earl. Thurkil is a Danish name. It looks very much as though we have here one of the Danish king's men marrying an English wife. It also looks as though the normal expectations of an English son were being overridden, possibly under political pressure. It would be unwise to assume that all English women possessed the social power to act similarly, whatever the flexibility of the laws of inheritance.

To take another case, Aethelgifu tells us in her will that her husband left her property with the right to grant it or to bequeath it to whomsoever she wished. Notwithstanding this, Eadhelm, who was her husband's sister's son, seized the estate of Standon. Aethelgifu appealed to the king, and Eadhelm returned the land 'against his wishes'.[45] If this shows a woman's position being protected by the king, it also suggests how vulnerable in practice a woman's tenure could be. The king was prepared to guarantee women's wills, but he did so for payment. Other women may not have been as fortunate as Aethelgifu. Equally, the laws of Cnut forbidding the marrying off of widows and demanding that women consent to marriages imply that some at least were being married without their consent. Moreover, this comes in a section dealing with the abuse of power and, indeed, these laws can be seen as a political agreement between king and nobles, rather like Henry I's Coronation Charter in 1100. It is hard to avoid the suggestion that there was already 'an established practice of royal intervention in noble marriage'.[46] And, again, Cnut's pronouncement that the morning-gift should be forfeited if a widow marries within a year suggests that women's property rights were not as absolute as some sources suggest. The eleventh century in general was a time of considerable social upheaval and instability. One wonders just how much the ancient laws of Aethelbert could have counted for in these circumstances.

Another source for the situation of eleventh-century women is of course Domesday Book. Interpretation of Domesday Book in this, as in many other respects, is fraught with difficulty. None the less, it yields some interesting insights. The bald facts are as follows.[47] At the time of the death of King Edward the Confessor, some 350 women held landed estates in England. These estates were valued at a little over £4,750 and amounted to around 3,500 hides, that is to say about 5 per cent of the total hidage, although the figure drops to 3 per cent if we take out the lands of Queen Eadgyth and Godgifu, the Confessor's late sister. Anglo-Saxon society was extremely hierarchical. In reality, some thirty-six noble women held the bulk of this property. They include figures like Eadgifu, the wife of Wulfweard the White, chamberlain in the households of two queens, and Aethelgyth, wife of Thurstan, who held one of the largest female interests. Aethelgyth's property amounted to some 60 hides, valued at £120. Thurstan's will tells us that he gave his bride numerous estates in Norfolk as a marriage payment and Domesday Book reveals her interest in eleven manors there. Her Norfolk property was concentrated in Clackclose Hundred where there were about 165 men under her commendation and soke. She also held six manors in Essex, again it seems from her husband's family, and two in Suffolk. One of these latter, Shimpling, appears to have been hers by inheritance from Thurketel of Palgrave or his wife, Leofwynn.

The size of Aethelgyth's interest, however, was an exception. Female property-owning in 1066, as revealed by Domesday Book, was dominated by members of the families of the great earls, the *eorlisc* families, and most notably the family of Earl Godwine. About half of all the property was held by just three women: Queen Eadgyth, Earl Godwine's daughter; Godwine's widow, Gytha; and Earl Harold's 'Danish wife' or 'concubine', Eadgifu the Fair (*pulchra*). Altogether the property of women of the great *eorlisc* families accounts for about 80 per cent of the hidage and 85 per cent of the value of all the property held by women. It very much looks as though much of this property was held by them as deliberate acts of family policy. Most particularly, about 15 per cent of the land held by the Godwine family was in the hands of its women, a stark contrast with the 3 per cent of lay land held by all other women. Gytha, Godwine's widow, held estates in Sussex directly of the king and other estates in Somerset and Devon which she undoubtedly acquired after her husband's death. It has been plausibly suggested that this was part of Earl Harold's strategy to ensure the loyalty of thegns in areas that were not directly under his own control.

Another of Earl Harold's most staunch supporters was the mysterious Eadgifu the Fair. Quite apart from her status as his concubine, she appears to have been influential in her own right. By 1066 she held land across seven counties with an assessed value of £400. In addition to her demesne property she enjoyed the commendation of, and soke over, people in nearly seventy-five villages. Much of her Lincolnshire land and her property in the East Riding of Yorkshire may have been her own family inheritance, but many of her estates in Cambridgeshire, East Anglia and Wessex seem to have derived from Harold and his influence. Once again, we find that people were tied to her through personal commendation and by socage, indicating that this woman exercised lordship in her own right. Eadgifu's relationship with Harold was a longstanding one – she bore him six children. Variously described as *pulchra, faira, bella* and Eadgifu the Rich (*dives*) she seems to be identical with Eadgyth Swanneshals (Edith Swan-neck) who held property in Norfolk.[48] Harold clearly endowed her with land beyond what was customary and it may well be that this too was part of a general family strategy

The women of the house of Leofric were also well endowed with property, although not on the scale of the family that had surpassed them. Godiva (or Godgifu), wife of Earl Leofric, had land amounting to 80 hides valued at £120. Most of her demesne properties were concentrated in Warwickshire and Worcestershire.[49] In addition, however, she held the strategically important estate of Newark in Nottinghamshire and it may well be that she had acquired this, the 'key to the north', around the time of her husband's death in 1057 as a means of consolidating her family's position in Mercia. While the role these women exercised is an interesting phenomenon in its own right, it has to be seen in the peculiar political context of mid eleventh-century England when power was slipping from the royal house into the hands of the *eorlisc* families. These women were certainly not the norm among noble women in late Anglo-Saxon England. The property in the hands of women in 1066 was not wildly out of line with the 2 per cent in female hands in 1086, especially when one considers the peculiar conditions of the Conquest when the Conqueror had to satisfy so many male followers.

The loose and flexible inheritance system that prevailed at this time created, in effect, a 'pool' of actual and potential heirs. It is hard to believe that lordship did not impact upon inheritance in England as it did elsewhere.[50] In Normandy a well-known case is that of Mabel of Bellême. Her father, William Talvas, had the misfortune to have a disloyal son, Arnold. For some reason his other son, Oliver, was unsuitable as heir. He was supported by the family until he became a monk in old age, but he never succeeded to the estates. The Bellême estates passed to their sister, Mabel, who married Roger II of Montgomery, a man loyal to the duke. Given that noble women were among potential heirs – though they were not heiresses in the later sense when strict rules of inheritance operated – their marriage to incomers could provide social stability. Thus was the case, for example, when Cnut's Danish follower Siward married the daughter of the Anglo-Saxon house that had provided earls of Northumbria. Not only was Earl Siward the more secure but an extra legitimacy was added to his line. This factor operated on a grand scale following the Norman Conquest and the relentless dispossession of the English thegnage. Many a Norman married the daughter of a previous tenant. Thus Robert d'Oilli, castellan of Oxford, married the daughter of Wigot of Wallingford and thereby acquired her father's lands, while Geoffrey

5. *The lands of the late Countess Godiva, Warwickshire Domesday (1086). Few great ladies were holding extensive estates at this date*

de la Querche married Aelfgifu, 'heiress' of the Warwickshire thegn Leofwine. It may well be true that Archbishop Lanfranc's concern at the number of English women who were residing in nunneries without either having made profession or having been offered by their parents as oblates was partly due to pressure to release them as 'peace-weavers and channels of inheritance'.[51] If the Normans were marrying to gain legitimacy and to extinguish other claims by effectively 'inheriting' them, this may equally be what Thurkil the Dane had done when he married Leofflaed back in Cnut's Herefordshire.

The potential that lay in the claims of noble women could be political dynamite. A particularly strong example comes from the summer of 1093 when Edith, daughter of King Malcolm of Scotland and St Margaret, was residing at the nunnery of Wilton from whence, according to her father's plans, she was to marry Count Alan the Red, lord of Richmond. Marriage would have conveyed to him her claim to Lothian. Relations between the kings of England and Scotland,

6. An eleventh-century scandal: the mysterious Aelfgyva and a clerk (Bayeux Tapestry)

having eased a little, now foundered on this plan. Malcolm promptly went from their aborted meeting at Gloucester to Wilton to reclaim his daughter, tearing the veil from her head. The equally angry Count Alan then abducted one Gunnilda from the same nunnery, but died before he could marry her. She was no less than the daughter of Edith Swan-neck. Edith, as we have seen, had been a power in the land. As Eleanor Searle points out, her daughter was 'the heiress to whatever legitimacy remained of the old Danish war-lineage' – a fact of particular significance given that the honour of Richmond had an unusual number of Anglo-Danish tenants remaining on its estates.[52] Searle reminds us that the action of great lords, as of kings, was often prompted as much by solidarity with the collectivity of their vassals as by personal interests. Count Alan's actions in these matters should not be seen, therefore, as the strange passion of an old warrior in his mid-fifties as he switched his attention from one young woman to another, but as an expression of practical politics and as a reflection of the ideological force of the female participation in a loose and flexible inheritance system.[53] In the event Count Alan's brother 'succeeded not only to his estates but to his matrimonial plans'[54] and, as a result, Archbishop Anselm attempted to intervene, writing the girl what has been described as 'a bitterly physical letter, horrible to read, attempting to disgust her with the world and man's embrace'.[55] It is a reminder that a noble lady was not only subject to the matrimonial plans of ambitious warriors but at any turn could feel the full force of the misogynistic training of their monkish counterparts.

What, then, can we conclude about the position of the lady in late Anglo-Saxon, or more correctly Anglo-Danish, England? In a formal sense, she was clearly not without rights. In practice, however, this could be severely curtailed by the power of men. Much depended upon individual wealth and status and upon the family to which she belonged. The women of *eorlisc* and ministerial families counted for most. A few great women clearly had tremendous authority. It might be argued that the lady suffered through the increasing militarisation of society and by the growth of ties of vassalage. On the other hand, this should not be pushed too far. Domesday Book reveals the considerable lordship of figures like Aethelgyth and Eadgifu the Fair. Moreover, Mabel of Bellême in contemporary Normandy should give us pause. In addition to mothering nine children she was vigorous in defence of her inheritance. She travelled with a retinue of one hundred armed men. She was capable of seizing castles and poisoning her enemies. Orderic Vitalis describes her as 'a forceful and worldly woman, cunning, garrulous, and extremely cruel'. She was finally murdered, while resting after taking a bath, when four of her vassals rode at night into her castle at Bures and cut off her head. Her epitaph described her as, 'A shield of her inheritance, a tower guarding the frontier; to some neighbours dear, to others terrible. She died by the sword, by night, by stealth, for we are mortals all . . . Pray for her.'[56]

There were of course differences between England and contemporary Normandy, and sequentially between Anglo-Danish and Anglo-Norman England. The difficulty lies in knowing how different these societies were. The Normans do appear to have been more abreast of the transition in inheritance practices that was common to continental societies.[57] Inheritance was being progressively restructured

7. The victims of eleventh-century warfare: a woman and child flee from a burning house (Bayeux Tapestry)

around patrilineal descent. In Normandy, situations like that of Mabel of Bellême were becoming rare. Until the rules hardened in favour of primogeniture, the choice of an heir within a family had depended partly on the father or other male kin and partly on the lord, who needed to ensure that an inheritance went to a vassal who was both loyal and able. Thus land could pass with a daughter to a strong vassal, by-passing sons. The restructuring, however, put descent firmly in the male line, with the patrimony going to the eldest son. Younger sons were often given lands of acquisition. It may well be that this system was already gaining ground in Normandy before the Conquest. The tendency for the greatest families to associate themselves by name with their chief residence or castle (Roger of Montgomery, Roger of Beaumont, etc.) might well indicate this.[58] Hereditary succession by males certainly seems to have been well established in Norman England.[59] Descent went to a female only in default, as the sole means of preserving the lineage. She was not expected to succeed to her inheritance as a spinster, however, but to convey her lands to her husband and thence to her offspring. The lady's role was clearly subordinate, under the dominion of husband, head of family or lord. Meanwhile, on marriage a daughter received a marriage portion (*maritagium*) from her father and her dower from her husband. It is more a matter of trends, however, than of hard and fast rules. The *maritagium* was extremely variable, and the dower generally less than the one-third of the husband's property that later became the norm. It may well be that this system was already taking hold in England before the Conquest, although the evidence is scanty.[60]

What Domesday Book has to say about landholding in 1086 is revealing. There is less land in women's hands now than there had been in 1066. The tenants-in-chief in 1086 include only one great widow, the Countess Judith. Countess Godiva, widow of Earl Leofric, had recently died. Queen Matilda and fewer than ten wives of leading tenants held land which had presumably been given to them in dower. There were also daughters of two tenants-in-chief who were each holding a single estate, again presumably as marriage-portion. In addition, says J.C. Holt, there was 'a scattering of English ladies still with possessions of their own, the residue of an older society in which women had property in their own right. This last group was minute compared with what it had been in 1066. These women saw their time out enjoying a right which the Conquest had destroyed.'[61]

8. *The magnificent late Saxon tower at Earl's Barton, Northamptonshire. Countess Judith held an estate here*

That there was a general preference for daughters as heiresses over collateral males in early twelfth-century England seems clear. The situation was fraught with tension, not only in England but throughout the romance-speaking lands, and especially at the level of high politics.[62] After all, the civil war that followed the death of King Henry I in 1135 was between his daughter and nephew and their respective supporters. In general there were now far more heiresses. By 1130 more than twenty post-Conquest baronies had descended in the female line; by 1150 the number had risen to thirty. Normally, however, it was only one daughter or sister – usually the eldest – who succeeded. The Countess Judith, niece of the Conqueror and widow of Earl Waltheof, for example, left two daughters, Maud and Adeliza. Maud, the elder, inherited and married Simon de St Liz. Adeliza remained in the custody of her sister and brother-in-law until Simon married her to Ralph de Tosny. She was not landless but she had a much poorer deal. Who controlled the marriage of such women was a matter of great concern to kings and their tenants. The coronation charter of Henry I brought some regulation into the system:

If any baron or any of my men should wish to arrange a marriage for his daughter, sister, niece or cousin let him speak to me about it. But I will not take anything from him for this permission, nor will I forbid him to give her, save if he should wish to marry her to my enemy.

BASSET AND RIDEL

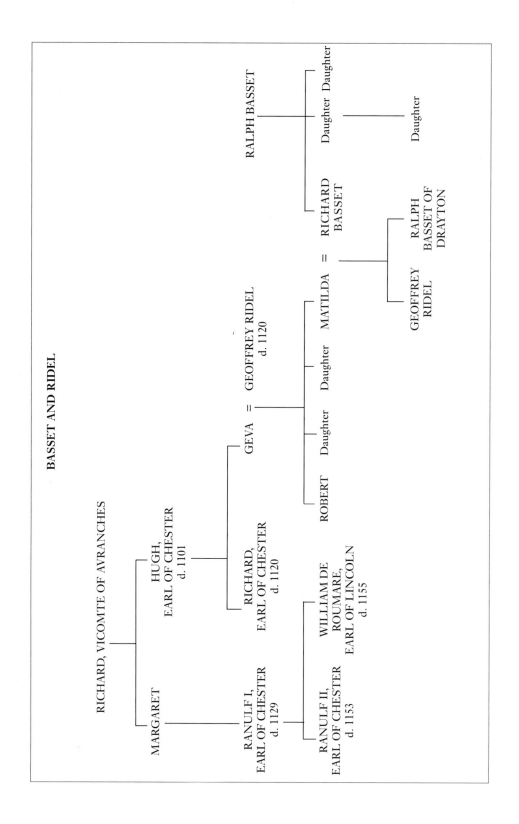

He goes on to promise to arrange the marriage of any orphaned heiress with the counsel of his barons. He also promised not to give widows in marriage against their wishes. The charter in fact distinguishes between childless widows and those with children. The latter were to retain custody of their land and children either in their own hands or the hands of relatives. This suggests that they were probably less likely to have to remarry.[63]

It is a fairly safe assumption that the previous king had taken payment for his approval of marriages. It is hardly surprising, either, that the promises of 1100 were not kept. The first surviving Exchequer Pipe Roll, for 1130, shows regular proffers to the king for the marriage and wardship of heirs. Widows fined, that is to say they paid, so that they should not be compelled to marry. One of the first great ladies who is known to have done so is Countess Lucy after the death of her third husband, Ranulf le Meschin, Earl of Chester, who died in 1129. She offered 500 marks that she should not take a husband for five years. She also offered an additional 100 marks that she might do justice in her own court among her own men. Widows could be an even more attractive financial prospect at this time, both to the king as dispenser of patronage and to those seeking it, as the later custom that a childless widow should return her marriage-portion to her husband's family had not yet come in.

Seen from this perspective the position of the twelfth-century lady looks an uninviting one. A good example of the way in which ladies were pawns in the interests of powerful and ambitious men comes from the years 1120–23 in a charter by which Henry I gave the daughter of Geoffrey Ridel to Richard Basset.[64] Richard was the son of Henry's famous servant, Ralph Basset, and the whole arrangement derives from the circle around the king and reflects the interconnections between royal servants and their ambitions for the future.[65] Geoffrey Ridel, another of the king's 'new men', had been drowned in the wreck of the White Ship in 1120. He died leaving his heir, Robert Ridel, under age. It was now arranged that Robert should marry the granddaughter of Ralph Basset, 'namely the daughter of one of his daughters by his wife' (*filiam cuiusdam filie sue de muliere*). Meanwhile, Richard Basset, Ralph's son, was to marry the daughter of Geoffrey Ridel and to hold the Ridel lands in wardship until Robert Ridel became a knight and married the Basset girl. At that point Richard Basset, having lost the income from the Ridel wardship, would receive £20 land from the royal demesne and four enfeoffed knights, in effect as a marriage-portion with his Ridel wife (*cum uxore sua in maritagio*). But if Robert Ridel should die without heir from his wife then Richard Basset and his heir by Geoffrey Ridel's daughter should have the entire Ridel lands. It was further provided that if the other daughters of Geoffrey Ridel had not been married during their brother's life and during Richard Basset's wardship, then Richard would provide for them, with the advice and discretion of the king. The whole arrangement reveals a deep concern for lineage. The Ridels would gain a dual marriage alliance with the Bassets and, at the same time, secure the best they could for the future should their blood be transmitted through a female. The king, moreover, had provided for yet another of his 'new men'. The family dimension is further illustrated by the statement that it was made at the request of Ranulf, Earl of Chester, and William his brother, Nigel d'Aubigny and others of Robert Ridel's kin, and of Geva his mother. Geva, widow of Geoffrey Ridel, was in fact the daughter of Hugh, Earl of Chester, and the land in question had come to the marriage through her.[66] She is the only woman in the witness list. Indeed, the plain fact is that none of the ladies directly concerned in this matter is mentioned in the document by name: not Geoffrey Ridel's daughter, Matilda, who was to marry Richard Basset, nor the other daughters of Geoffrey Ridel, nor the wife, daughters or granddaughter of Ralph Basset. Admittedly, there is some concern for the status and presumably the livelihood of the girls. The Ridel women are not to be mistreated. But the family strategies were entirely in the hands of the men. Moreover, the Earl of Chester's own barons were also party to the transaction, and the charter is famous for the interaction it reveals between the royal court and a great feudal honour.[67] Marriage at this level was a matter of political as well as social concern. In the event, this marriage was to give Richard Basset the barony of Weldon, Northamptonshire. The Northamptonshire Survey (1124–29) and the Leicestershire Survey (*c.* 1130) show that Richard acquired the barony soon after. He called his eldest son Geoffrey Ridel II.

Geva's appearance in the witness list is instructive. Women tend to be formally involved in transactions when the land in question has been transmitted through them. Gifts made by husband and wife jointly, to monastic houses for example, are often of property which the wife has brought to the marriage, and which her husband now formally controlled. Joint foundations of nunneries tend to obscure a woman's initiative. At least eight nunneries can be shown to have been founded on land which was either the wife's *maritagium* or her dower.[68] It was in the interests of the grantee that the wife should be associated with the gift in such circumstances, as title against any other claimants depended upon her.

In one important respect, the inheritance 'system' was modified by a ruling (*statutum decretum*), probably between 1130 and 1135. This ruling was as follows: 'where there is no son, the daughters divide their father's land by spindles, and the elder cannot take from the younger her half of the land without violence and injury'. It was a significant change and it was in operation, although again not exclusively, during the 1140s. No longer would the eldest female exclude the others. Little is known of the circumstances of the ruling but it can be seen to be in the interests not only of the Crown but also of the nobility. The division of baronies created additional opportunities for younger sons as the number of heiresses was increased. Moreover, at this time the flow of acquisitions from which younger sons were provided was drying up. Both sons and fathers stood to gain. Lords were also gainers from increased feudal incidents of marriage, wardship and relief (that is, payment to succeed to a fief). There were also advantages, of course, for the younger sisters who were likely to find better marriages and would be less reliant upon the charity of their fathers and brothers. The *statutum decretum* may have been the result of negotiations between the king and his greater male subjects, like the coronation charter of 1100, as the tenants-in-chief sought to promote their own interests and to safeguard their family strategies.[69] The greatest potential gainer, however, was the Crown.

Needless to say, what has been described as 'a vigorous marriage market under the direction of the Crown' continued into the time of the Angevins.[70] The

9. Northamptonshire widows and their lands: from the Rolls of Ladies, Boys and Girls, 1185

greater documentation available allows the historian to see the system in operation more clearly. In 1176 an inquiry into women in the king's gift was included in the articles of the eyre, the list of matters which the king's travelling justices were asked to investigate. The records of a similar inquiry survive for 1185 in the Rolls of Ladies, Boys and Girls (*Rotuli de Dominabus et Pueris et Puellis*). The justices received evidence of the value and annual yield of widows' lands, in particular, of their ages and of the age and sex of their children. The object was, of course, to gain maximum information which could profit the Crown. The return for Northamptonshire, for example, names eleven widows ranging in age from twenty to sixty years. Emma, widow of Hugh fitz Robert, was said to be forty years of age. She was the daughter of Henry Tiart and had formerly been the wife of Robert de St Paul, the king's chamberlain. She was holding dower lands in Oxfordshire from her first marriage, as well as her *maritagium* and dower in Northamptonshire. Her eldest son (*filius suus primogenitus*), Robert fitz Hugh, was just under age at twenty, and therefore in royal custody. No details are given of any other sons. However, she had six daughters: one aged eighteen, who was married, another aged seventeen, two who were nuns and two who were younger. She now faced the possibility of yet a third arranged marriage. Alice, widow of Thomas de Beaufou, was only twenty years of age. She had one son, aged three, who was at present in the custody of Nigel, son of Alexander, who was her uncle. Beatrice, widow of Robert Mauntel, king's sergeant, was thirty years of age. She had one daughter and three sons, the first born being ten years old. He was in the custody of Robert de Sauci, by gift of the king. All the others were with their mother. Margaret Engaine, aged fifty, had been 'in the gift of the lord king', as the roll puts it, for the last eight years. However, Geoffrey Brito had married her without the king's licence. This having been pointed out to the justices, Geoffrey was now obliged to show by what warrant (that is to say, by what authority) he had done so. The lady with the most children was the fifty-year-old Alice, widow of Fulk de Lisures, and sister of William Mauduit. She had two sons who were knights, two other sons, six daughters who were married and three others yet to be married.[71] None of this was any guarantee that she would not be remarried.

The Pipe Rolls, the records of the Royal Exchequer, show a steady stream of bids for the hands of heiresses and widows. Some of these came from relatives as they tried to keep control of marriages within their own families. The additional information supplied by the Fine Rolls in the reign of King John show this king, with severe financial problems, selling more readily than ever before. It now became relatively common for widows to bid for freedom from forced marriages. This tended to ensure the receipt of their inheritance and dower as well, and sometimes also included the custody and marriage of their children. This is also the time when royal grants of wardships and marriages begin to contain the provision that the heir or heiress should not be disparaged, i.e. married to someone of seriously inferior stock.[72] It is hardly to be doubted that the Crown was responding here to a matter of considerable concern to an increasingly lineage-conscious nobility. These developments were reflected in Magna Carta in 1215. Clause 6 forbids disparagement, while clauses 7 and 8 protect the widow's marriage portion, inheritance and dower, and stipulate that no widow shall be compelled to remarry provided that she gives security that she will not do so without the king's consent or the consent of whatever lord she holds her land from.[73]

Widowhood placed ladies in a potentially powerful position, which of course is why many of them were prepared to pay to retain their independence. Some remained widows for some considerable time. Margaret, widow of Henry de Beaumont, 1st Earl of Warwick, for example, was widowed in 1119 and was still living as a widow in 1156.[74] A widowed countess, with custody of her children, could exercise considerable authority. One such was Matilda, wife of Ranulf II, Earl of Chester. The daughter of Henry I's illegitimate son, Robert, Earl of Gloucester, she was not an insignificant figure even during her marriage. On Ranulf's death in 1153, leaving his son Hugh II aged only six, she seems to have become the controlling force in the great earldom. She retained the custody of her son, issued charters of her own as well as joint charters with him, and functioned as the chief witness to instruments issued in his name. She effected the transfer of the Augustinian priory from Calke to Repton, endowing the canons with Repton Church. She died, still a widow, in 1189.[75]

Widows were responsible for the foundation of religious houses, particularly nunneries.[76] Among them was Elstow in Bedfordshire, founded by Countess Judith, niece of William the Conqueror and widow of Waltheof, Earl of Huntingdon, who was executed in 1076. It may well be that this was an act of atonement for her part in the betrayal of her husband. She remained a widow. There is a tradition that she refused a marriage to Simon de Senlis, who married one of her daughters instead. Stixwould in Lincolnshire was almost certainly founded by Lucy, widow of Ranulf I, Earl of Chester, she who paid 500 marks to be allowed to remain a widow for five years. A charter of Lucy's, addressed to her sons, granted all her land in Stixwould, Thorp and Honington to the nuns. This was her own inheritance. She may have joined the community herself. A prioress called Lucy is mentioned in charters dated between 1160 and 1168. Among those who certainly did enter nunneries of their own foundation was Ela, Countess of Salisbury, who founded Lacock Abbey in Wiltshire in 1229. It may well be that such widows founded nunneries to ensure their future security, whether or not they ended their days there. Perhaps, too, they were an expression of their independence.

To some degree at least, contemporary perceptions of the lady can be extrapolated from charters and from records of the royal administration. For direct comment, however, we are reliant upon narrative sources. England in the twelfth century saw a proliferation of historical writing.[77] Not surprisingly, this writing participates in the construction of gender which is so marked a feature of the twelfth century in general. The explanation for this has been much debated. But whatever its specific causes, it is also symptomatic of an increasing emphasis upon demarcation and definition which is a feature of this age. This gender construction was heavily misogynistic and impregnated with Christian ideas of sin. Thus William of Malmesbury, for example, remarks that Robert of Arbrissel imposed a rule of silence on his nuns because without it women would be inclined to chatter. Orderic Vitalis, the Anglo-Norman chronicler, describes the vision of purgatory of the priest of Bonneval.[78] He saw a troop of women who 'seemed to the priest to be without number, riding in female fashion on women's saddles which were studded with burning nails . . . loudly lamenting the sins for which they endured such punishment. Indeed, it was for the seductions and obscene delights in which they had wallowed on earth that they now endured . . . agonies too many to enumerate.' Orderic denounced the degenerate courts of the Conqueror's sons, William Rufus and Robert Curthose, censuring both the women who tempted and the men who fell: 'courtiers, fawning, seek the favours of women with every kind of lewdness'.

The gender definition of the age puts considerable emphasis upon the exercise of public authority and upon military activity. The division into masculine and feminine characteristics has the effect of de-emphasising female activity. One expression of this is the concern by ecclesiastical authorities about effeminate

10. Man as judge, women as suppliants: the judgment of Solomon as depicted on a capital in Westminster Abbey in the early twelfth century

male behaviour. A stark expression of the effects of the resultant role definition is the appearance of the word *virago* to describe an active female, i.e. as a pseudo-man. This is how William of Malmesbury described the Empress Matilda. William wrote essentially as a partisan of the empress in the civil war between Matilda and King Stephen. The author of the *Gesta Stephani*, writing from the opposite stance, saw her as arrogant, haughty, overbearing and arbitrary. Her look was 'grim . . . her forehead wrinkled into a frown, every trace of a woman's gentleness removed from her face, blazing into unbearable fury'. At the same time she was quite capable of employing the range of women's allurements in the exercise of her power. By contrast, this author sees her followers as effeminate men, characterised by 'wanton delight rather than resolution of mind'.[79]

There is a contrast between how the twelfth-century writers portrayed powerful Anglo-Saxon women of the past and how they were portrayed at the time. The famous daughter of King Alfred, Aethelflaed, Lady of the Mercians, comes across from Old English sources as a woman accorded great respect, active in war and lordship. This was not lost to the twelfth-century historians, but for them she was another virago. Henry of Huntingdon wrote a tribute to her in verse, which he inserted at the appropriate point in his chronicle. For him she was 'a man in valour, though a woman in name'.[80] William of Malmesbury saw her in much the same way, as a woman who 'protected her own men and terrified aliens'. What was significant to them was the paradox between her feminine nature and her masculine achievements.[81] Aethelfryth, the wife of King Edgar, who murdered her step-son is seen by William of Malmesbury as alluring Edward with 'female blandishments' and for him her crime becomes a specifically female crime, 'the sin of an abandoned mother'.[82]

A more fulsome source for the role of contemporary queens and countesses is Orderic Vitalis, writing from the Norman monastery of St Evroult.[83] Women figure frequently as patrons and benefactors to the abbey, often in the company of their husbands and family. Family history constitutes in fact one of the main themes of his chronicle, as it does in many chronicles of the time. High-born women feature much as the companions and helpmates of their husbands. Queens are shown taking over in times of crisis. Thus, for example, when King Louis of France, in conflict with the Normans, was held captive at Rouen, Queen Gerberga negotiated his rescue and made peace. Most significantly, she is described as taking the place of her husband in acting with the advice of her magnates. The Conqueror's queen, Matilda, spent most of her time in Normandy where she functioned as regent. Another example is provided by King Stephen's wife, Matilda of Boulogne. In 1138 she called on her men to blockade Dover, taking action against Robert of Gloucester who had renounced his homage to the king in favour of Empress Matilda; in response her men ' gladly carried out their lady's commands, and closed the narrow straits to prevent the garrison receiving any supplies'. As Marjorie Chibnall says, 'Any great lady had to be ready to assume responsibility in her husband's time of need, and to defend her dower rights. Her interests and his were one.'[84] In some circumstances this could involve them in military action. When Robert Bordet, lord of Tarragona, had returned from southern Italy to Normandy to recruit more knights his wife, Sibyl, was left to defend the city: 'She was as brave as she was beautiful. During her husband's absence she kept sleepless watch; every night she put on a hauberk like a knight and, carrying a rod in her hand, mounted on the battlements, patrolled the circuit of the walls, and kept the guards on alert for the enemy's strategems.'

What is particularly significant is when and why ladies come in for censure. Problems seem to arise when women are seen to dominate their husbands. The chief manifestations of this seem to be high-handedness and pride. Symptomatic, however, is the ignoring of the advice of barons which a lady acting correctly is praised for relying on. Thus, Helwise, Countess of Evreux, ignored their counsel and relied on her own judgement: 'So she was heartily disliked for her woman's presumption by Robert, Count of Meulan, and other Normans, who abused her in the king's presence and incited him to hate her.' In other words, she was considered to have 'overstepped the bounds of a wife's normal duties'.[85]

The same features are found elsewhere in France, for example in the genealogical literature which is a prominent feature of the second half of the twelfth century in particular and which Georges Duby has exploited to such good effect over the years.[86] The clerical writers of these works show considerable resentment at the wielding of public power by women, and no doubt this resentment was found widely within aristocratic society. Where women can be shown to have 'overstepped', the full force of pent-up misogyny tends to spill out. But it is none the less true that women did exercise public power. There were those who wished to confine a woman's power to the domestic or private sphere. However, whether contemporaries liked it or not, there were women who in certain circumstances exercised considerable public power; this could be temporary, during their husband's absence, or permanent, normally in widowhood but occasionally as heiresses. This is why authorities such as St Bernard of Clairvaux accepted the existence of female rulers and offered advice. In essence this was to act upon the wise counsel of men.[87] What is also clear is that when women exercised power this tended to be considered as held in trust for male heirs.

Chroniclers in England tended to disapprove of men involving their wives directly in their fighting. A good example is the case of Petronilla, Countess of Leicester, who took part in her husband's rebellion against Henry II in 1173 and in the battle at Fornham near Bury St Edmunds. According to the verse chronicler, Jordan Fantosme, the Earl of Leicester held a council before seeking battle at which his wife was the first to speak in favour of action. 'The English', she said, 'are great boasters, but poor fighters'; they are 'better at quaffing great tankards and guzzling'. 'My lady,' replied the earl, 'now I hear you speaking out, I needs must take your advice, for greatly have I loved you.' The earl himself is portrayed as a powerful but foolish man. The height of his 'great folly' was to arm his wife (that is, to dress her in a hauberk) and to give her both shield and lance. Jordan's underlying views are clear from his accompanying portrayal of Earl Ferrers. He was 'a simple knight, more fitted to kiss and embrace fair ladies than to smite other knights with a war hammer'. In the event, Fornham was a disaster for the Earl of Leicester. 'My lady, the countess,' writes Jordan, 'has taken to flight and is found in a ditch in which she nearly drowns.' Her rings, he says, disappeared into the mud, and will not be found again in her lifetime. According to Jordan she now attempted to drown herself, but was pulled out of the mud. The message is perfectly clear. The rash counsel of ladies should not be heeded, nor should they participate in battle. Those who encourage these things will be rewarded accordingly.[88]

But we should not necessarily conclude that everyone shared Jordan's views. The fact remains that Petronilla did participate both in the giving of counsel and in the military action. Another fearless lady was Dame Nichola de la Hay, the hereditary castellan of Lincoln, who held her castle valiantly for the Crown against Prince Louis of France in 1217. She was much praised in the biography of William the Marshal. Written for his squire, this was a source close to the values of secular society. She is 'the good dame', 'whom God preserve both in body and in soul!' The French called her 'a very cunning, bad-hearted and vigorous old woman'.[89] If we hear less of women like these during the thirteenth century and after it is as much to do with relative domestic peace as a change in secular values. A Northamptonshire knight, Sir Thomas de Hotot, writing in the mid-thirteenth century, referred with obvious approval to a female ancestor who, while still a maid, felled a knight with one stroke of a spear back in the reign of King Stephen.[90] When the English brought domestic warfare to Scotland and the north in the late thirteenth and fourteenth centuries, there was no dearth of ladies able and willing to defend their positions. In 1338 William Montague, Earl of Salisbury, had to abandon the siege of Dunbar Castle after Agnes, Countess of Dunbar, had defended it for a full nineteen weeks. She was celebrated in verse as Black Agnes. Three years later, with William Montague himself a prisoner in France, his own wife, Katherine de Grandison, repulsed King David of Scotland from Wark-on-Tweed. So fearlessly did she hold the town, and offer comfort to the garrison, that a French chronicler called her one of the most valiant ladies of England, as well as one of the most beautiful.[91]

Wherever we turn, the role and status of a noble lady seem to revolve around her position as a wife. It is relatively easy to illustrate cooperation between lord and lady in twelfth-century England, but what can be gleaned from the sources in terms of affection? The attenuation of concubinage, the greater emphasis upon legitimacy which accompanied the stricter rules of inheritance, and the sacralisation of marriage in the twelfth century should all have brought the noble wife greater security.[92] But this did not necessarily bring her love. The idea that romantic love was an invention of the twelfth century has been seriously questioned.[93] Nevertheless, it became a central preoccupation of western literature as never before, giving us a new literary genre in the verse romance. No one today would seriously argue, I imagine, that romantic literature was a great liberating force for women, even noble women. Profoundly male-centred, it is ambivalent at best, narcissistic at worst.[94] None the less, it is possible that the behaviour of both men and women was affected by romance and the moral climate of which it was part. One thinks, for example, of the sympathetic view of female sexuality to be found in the *Lais* of Marie de France.[95] As is well known, twelfth-century culture placed increasing emphasis upon the individual. One expression of this was the momentous decision of the Church under Pope

11. Medieval romances were profoundly male-centred: on this Chertsey tile Iseult is depicted singing the songs which Tristan had devised

Alexander III to make free consent the test of a valid marriage. Moreover, it can be argued that the importance of the heiress in this period and the emphasis upon the stability of the marriage union made it more important than ever before that couples were compatible; affection if not love was a useful prerequisite for marriage.[96] This may well have affected male attitudes, if only out of self interest. But the ladies may have been affected even more. From the 1190s the Pipe Rolls show wards, including heiresses, buying the freedom to arrange their own marriages.[97] It may well be that in some instances at least this registered positive as well as negative intentions, i.e. that they had their own marriage partners in mind. J.C. Holt has shown that the idea of the disparagement of heirs which is found in Magna Carta was not invented by the baronial opposition but was first found on the Pipe Rolls in 1194 as a royal stipulation.[98] This being so, it is likely to have been in response to some form of social pressure. Maybe both young men and young women were becoming increasingly unhappy at marriage partners being foisted upon them willy-nilly. By the early thirteenth century English chroniclers are beginning to report female objectors to imposed marriage partners. But this should not be pushed too far. The notion of disparagement was essentially about lineage rather than romantic choice, whatever additional spin-off it may have had. And the fact that women were able to fine for avoidance of compulsory marriage was more a matter of regaining lost ground than an important stage in their emancipation. Even if more stress was being placed on a degree of affection before marriage at this time, it hardly means that love in marriage was something new. There are examples in Anglo-Saxon poetry of deep affection between man and woman. In *The Husband's Message* the man, in exile, asks the woman to remember their *freondscype* and to brave the perils of the sea so that they may be together once more. Both *The Wife's Lament* and *Wulf and Eadwacer* convey close and loving relationships.[99] Moving on to the early twelfth century we find an epitaph in which Orderic Vitalis describes Avice, lady of Auffay, as living in joy with her husband. In his own day, and before the love theme had blossomed in the literature of northern France and England, he speaks more than once of a man seeking a girl's hand in marriage because he loved her.[100]

Whether there had been a decline in the independence and power of noble women during the eleventh and twelfth centuries is much in contention and is difficult of resolution. The superiority in the sources for the twelfth century creates considerable difficulty. And while, on the one hand, there are good reasons to expect some degree of decline – the militarisation of social relations, the professionalisation of both Church and State with a heavier emphasis on the public role of men, the changes in inheritance patterns, stronger gender definition and misogyny – much of the evidence suggests that the practical status of noble women held up reasonably well.[101]

One suspects that many changes were more formal than real. If there was a decline in terms of freedom of action and independence, the lost ground was being made up by the end of the twelfth century. That there were many highly respected and powerful women throughout the period, however, is beyond doubt. The status of the lady was high, but it was heavily bound up with the status of men. The quality of the sources enables us to examine the varying relationships between lady and lord in greater detail across the succeeding centuries. It is both the changes and the continuities during these two centuries, however, that have collectively provided the starting point for the study which follows.

CHAPTER 3

Gentility and Social Position

During the course of the twelfth century a much stronger elite mentality was forged than ever before. One clear expression of status consciousness which is seen in twelfth-century sources is the language of deference.[1] Our awareness of this is largely due to the appearance of sources in the French vernacular which include conversation, so that it is possible to argue that it may well have existed in some form earlier. Nevertheless, its manifestations are striking. In particular, we find *dan* (from Latin *dominus*) or *sire* (from Latin *senior*) applied to men and *dame* (from Latin *domina*) applied to women. The Jerseyman, Wace, who wrote a *Roman de Brut*, a history of England, and a *Roman de Rou*, a history of Normandy, gives us examples of the diminutives *demoisel* (from Latin *domicellus*) and *demoiselle* (from Latin *domicella*) for young man and young woman respectively. *Demoiselle* ultimately gave rise, of course, to the English word 'damsel'. The *Roman de Rou* was commissioned by King Henry II during the 1160s. Likewise, Jordan de Fantosme, who wrote a verse chronicle of the war between England and Scotland in 1173–4 refers to many of the actors, largely magnates, as *dan*. There is evidence, however, of this usage descending the social scale. Jordan also describes Henry Blunt of London as *dan*. The Latin forms came to be widely diffused, perhaps reflecting vernacular usage. A charter of Walter fitz Robert giving a mill to the monks of Daventry around 1180 was witnessed by Lady (*Domina*) Margareta de Bohun and Lady (*Domina*) Matilda de Bohun, the grantor's wife.[2] The subsidy rolls of 1225 and 1232, records of royal taxation, give the title *domina* to propertied widows.

We can connect such developments with the appearance of a chivalric code of honour during the first half of the twelfth century. This can be seen in the chronicle of Orderic Vitalis, for example,[3] while the associated terminology of gentility – *chevaliers* and *gentils hommes* – can be seen in the contemporary *L'Estoire des Engleis*, written by Geoffrey Gaimar between 1135 and 1140.[4] Gaimar wrote for Constance, the wife of a lesser Lincolnshire landowner, Ralf fitz Gilbert. In his epilogue, Gaimar explains how his work came about. If the noble Lady Constance (*Dame Custance la gentil*) had not helped him, he writes, the work would never have been completed. She sent to Walter Espec, lord of Helmsley in

Yorkshire, for his copy of the work which Robert, Earl of Gloucester, had commissioned. This was, in fact, Geoffrey of Monmouth's recently written and highly influential *History of the Kings of Britain*. The sequence of borrowing of Geoffrey of Monmouth's work is interesting in its own right. Robert of Gloucester lent it to Walter Espec who in turn lent it to Ralf fitz Gilbert. Constance then borrowed it, Gaimar tells us, from her husband whom she dearly loved (*Dame Custance l'enprunant de son seignur k'ele mult amat*). The literary interest was the lady's but she had to go through her husband when it came to acquiring the necessary materials to indulge her interest. Gaimar tells us further that he hopes to write a history of Henry I which will be an improvement on the one that David has written. David appears to have written for Henry's queen, Adeliza of Louvain. Lady Constance paid a mark for a copy of this book which she often read in her chamber.

This episode is justly famous for the light it sheds on the literary interests of a twelfth-century lady. It also suggests that a minor landowning family of the early to mid-twelfth century had pretensións to gentility. It would be dangerous to make too much of this in terms of the gentility of the lesser landowners as such. After all, Ralf and Constance clearly had aristocratic associations. Moreover, they were related to the Clares. Gentility was long to be a matter of connections as well as intrinsic social merit. None the less, it is indicative of how a knightly family might feel and behave and of how they might be exposed to the latest fashions within aristocratic culture. The pretensions of lesser knights and their families help to explain the reactive comments by high-born aristocrats against rustic knights which seems to be a recurrent theme in the twelfth century.

It is doubtful though whether the idea of a fusion of the aristocracy, as proposed by Georges Duby, is the best way to comprehend what was happening, at least as far as England was concerned. It looks rather as though the greater families were seeking to hive themselves off from what we might call the lesser nobility as the latter were emulating their life style. One hint of this may be found in the romances of Chrétien de Troyes. A new title of *messire*, 'my lord' now makes an appearance as opposed to simply *sire* or *dan*. *Dan* becomes limited to addressing clergy, although *dame* continues to be used for the lady.[5] The result was the unintended one of forging a stronger elite mentality, which certainly was exclusive but which encompassed many more than the old, rather narrowly conceived nobility. By the early decades of the thirteenth century heraldry, for example, was available as an expression of status for all knights and knightly families; however, it remained confined to these strata until the fourteenth century. A new chivalric knightly class was born.[6]

On the face of it, at least, this new elite mentality was strikingly male-centred. One hardly need look further than the heavy emphasis upon knighthood itself. Of course, women participated strongly in aristocratic culture. Within the romances themselves they figure as appreciators of knightly prowess and beauty, as spectators to tournaments and other feats of arms, as inspirers of chivalric deeds and so on; but also as active exponents of courteous behaviour, of refined manners, of polite conversation and of gracious living. And they were, above all, partners in *fin amor*.

12. *The seal of Idonia de Hurst, lady of Broomhill, Kent, late twelfth century. Note the fashionable manches (long hanging sleeves) reaching almost to her hem*

How precisely did the ladies participate in this new elite culture and how did they relate to it? One way of approaching the way they perceived their world is through the evidence of their seals.[7] Ladies' seals were normally oval in shape rather than round as in male equestrian seals. Most often they portrayed the lady as a standing figure. In the case of queens they would be crowned, and holding the sceptre and orb. The earliest known in Britain is that of Matilda, queen of King Henry I, although this may be based upon a lost seal of the earlier Matilda, wife of William the Conqueror.[8] Aristocratic women were shown in fashionable dress, often with a lily in their right hand, a symbol of the Virgin Mary. Aristocratic status could also be conveyed by the carrying of a hawk or falcon in the left hand. Sometimes, in fact, the lady is depicted carrying both lily and hawk, as for example is Idonia de Hurst, lady of Broomhill, Kent. She is depicted in a full length and tight-fitting gown with manches (long hanging sleeves) and a heart-shaped brooch. She is holding the hawk by its jesses, the straps attached to the hawk's legs by which means the owner either holds the bird or lets it fly. This particular seal is of the late twelfth century, but the hawk-holding image was relatively common in the thirteenth. In an early and interesting variant on the standard image, Matilda, wife of Roger de Clare, Earl of Hertford, is depicted (c. 1170) receiving a hawk from an attendant.[9] Other ladies are shown with dogs. Matilda, daughter of Sir William de Hartshill, for example, has a small dog standing at her feet and another in her arms.[10] These images may be symbolic in certain ways – the dog, for instance, generally symbolises faithfulness – but it should not be forgotten that hawks and hounds played an important part in the recreational side of noble life. In the late fourteenth century, when the French noble, Sir Guy de Montigny, wrote a book of instruction for his young wife, he advised her: 'Think first of your hawk and your dogs, and only then of yourself.'[11]

However, ladies' seals soon came to contain heraldry, mirroring those of aristocratic males. Here the two branches of the Clare family, who were Earls of Hertford and Pembroke respectively, were among the first into the fray with their famous chevrons. The men were sealing heraldically from the 1140s onwards, while their multiple chevrons were refined down to three during the course of the twelfth century giving rise to their hereditary arms, *or, three chevrons gules*.[12] Their women followed suit. As early as the 1150s the seal of Rohese de Gant, wife of the Earl of Lincoln but daughter of Richard fitz Gilbert de Clare, displayed the chevrons, as indeed did the seal of her daughter, Alice, wife of Simon de Senlis, Earl of Northampton.[13] In the wider dissemination of arms, however, the generations from the late twelfth to the mid-thirteenth century were crucial. The earliest collections of coats of arms are those depicted by Matthew Paris, the famous chronicler of the Abbey of St Albans during the 1240s, and Glover's Roll, the earliest of our rolls of arms which dates from around 1253. Although these draw on earlier material, their appearance at this date is not without significance. Coats of arms were now widely diffused among knightly landowners, both high and low, indicating a growing participation in chivalric culture. Rules were already being developed as was blazon, the technical language of heraldry. In heraldry the surface of the shield is called the 'field' upon which figures or 'charges' are depicted. The accepted 'tinctures' comprise two metals (*or* and *argent*, that is gold and silver), five colours (*gules*, *azure*, *vert*, *sable* and *purpure*, i.e. red, blue, green, black and purple) and nine furs.

As the arms became hereditary and a matter of family honour they came to inhere in the women as well as the men. There can be no doubt that association through marriage played a major part in the dissemination of coats of arms during heraldry's first formative phase; in effect, the 'fields' and their 'charges' were carried through the women to be modified or 'differenced' in the arms of their men. Although much of this occurred well before the survival of rolls of arms in the thirteenth century, the process can be reconstructed in some cases using both rolls and seals and with the aid of genealogical knowledge. Two famous cases are the Clares, where a number of related families adopted the chevrons, and the Mandevilles.[14] In the latter case, members of six families can be shown to have derived their arms from those of Geoffrey de Mandeville, Earl of Essex, who died in 1144. They are, in addition to the Mandevilles: Vere, Say, Beauchamp of Bedford, Lacy and Fitz Richard. The Says were descended from Geoffrey's sister, Beatrice de Mandeville; the others owed their arms to Geoffrey's marriage to Rohese de Vere. The Earl of Essex himself bore the arms *quarterly or and gules* (that is, gold in the first and fourth quarters, red in the second and third). Roger fitz Richard, lord of Warkworth in Northumberland, for example, bore *quarterly or and gules, a baston sable*. (A *baston* or *baton* is a form of *bend* – the charge which runs diagonally across the shield – but which is cut short at the ends.) These arms were then borne by Roger fitz Richard's descendants.

The transmission of arms through kin can be shown in another example from the north-east of England. The Balliols, lords of Bywell and Barnard Castle, bore *gules, an orle argent*. The *orle* is a simple device but one that is not easy to describe in words. Known alternatively as a false escutcheon, it is a narrow border or *bordure* following the exact outline of the shield and in a different tincture from the main body of the shield. These arms were borne by John de Balliol, the regent of Scotland who died in 1268, but without doubt they go back to the twelfth century when they were adopted by the related Bertrams of Mitford. In the thirteenth century Roger de Bertram bore *gules crusily, an orle or*, arms which quite evidently derive from the Balliols.[15] [See colour plates]

Just as some men adopted the surnames of more illustrious wives, others absorbed the higher prestige of their wives' families by adopting their arms. One example is the famous Percy lion. Henry de Percy, lord of Topcliffe, Yorkshire, fought at Falkirk in 1298 and at Carlaverock in 1300 where he bore *or, a lion rampant azure*. In 1309 he purchased the barony and castle of Alnwick from Anthony Bek, Bishop of Durham, setting the family on its way to its future earldom and dukedom. The Percy lion is to be found throughout Northumberland and Durham. However, these were not inherited arms. In fact, they would seem to have been adopted from Henry's father-in-law, for the lord of Topcliffe had married Eleanor, daughter of Richard Fitz Alan, Earl of Arundel, who bore *gules, a lion rampant or*. The traditional Percy arms were, in fact, *azure, a fess of five fusils or*.[16] [See colour plates] They are evidenced from the early thirteenth century and almost certainly go back to the twelfth. To take another northern example, the Umfravilles of Prudhoe and Redesdale bore *gules crusily, a cinquefoil or*.[17] Ingram de Umfraville, a younger son, chose not to bear his brother's arms 'differenced', but rather a variant of the Balliol arms, viz. *gules, an orle ermine with a label of five points azure*. The reason is obvious: he was related by his marriage to the King of Scotland.[18]

Changing coats of arms can help to chart a family's rise. Ralph de Lumley was created the first baron Lumley in 1385, whereupon he turned his house into the castle which still stands, proudly, in County Durham.[19] Although the family later maintained that they came from illustrious Anglo-Saxon stock, in reality they were relatively minor knights of the Bishopric of Durham in the twelfth century. William de Lumley, in evidence during the last decade of the century, may well have been the man who first assumed the toponym as a surname. The Lumleys seem to have owed their rise to a sequence of propitious marriages as much as anything else. William de Lumley III married the daughter and co-heiress of Walter de Audre, who probably held the major estate at Lumley, allowing them to consolidate their property there, while his son, Sir Roger de Lumley, married Sybil, daughter and co-heiress of Hugh de Morwick of Northumberland. Whether these marriages had heraldic implications is unknown, but the marriages of the next two generations certainly did. Robert de Lumley I married Mary, daughter of Sir John Fitz Marmaduke of Horden. The Parliamentary Roll of Arms of *c.* 1308 shows Sir John bearing the arms *gules, a fess between three popinjays argent*, while Sir Robert de Lumley bears *gules, a fess between three popinjays argent and in the fess three mullets sable*, which are clearly the Fitz Marmaduke arms 'differenced'. [See colour plates] These are the earliest known Lumley arms, but they can hardly have pre-dated this marriage. As the family had long produced knights, it must have changed its arms. Robert died in 1308 and his son, Robert II, married Lucy de Thweng. The next arms that are known are those of Robert II's son and heir, Marmaduke de Lumley. He bore not the Fitz Marmaduke arms, however, but the Thweng arms, viz. *argent, a fess gules between three popinjays vert*. These became the Lumley family arms from then on. Marmaduke, it should be noted, bore the Thweng arms undifferenced because, with the extinction of the Thwengs, he became in effect the head of that line. The Thweng and Fitz Marmaduke arms were remarkably similar; this was because the Fitz Marmadukes had themselves adopted the Thweng arms 'differenced' upon an earlier marriage:

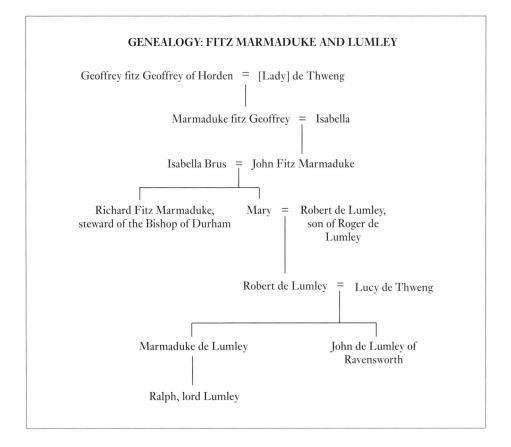

GENEALOGY: FITZ MARMADUKE AND LUMLEY

Geoffrey fitz Geoffrey of Horden = [Lady] de Thweng

Marmaduke fitz Geoffrey = Isabella

Isabella Brus = John Fitz Marmaduke

Richard Fitz Marmaduke,
steward of the Bishop of Durham

Mary = Robert de Lumley,
son of Roger de
Lumley

Robert de Lumley = Lucy de Thweng

Marmaduke de Lumley

John de Lumley of
Ravensworth

Ralph, lord Lumley

Like the Fitz Marmadukes before them, the Lumleys had adopted the arms of a more illustrious family into which they had married, and had effectively done so twice in successive generations.

By the thirteenth century it had become relatively common for married (or widowed) ladies to display their husbands' arms on their own seals. Nichola de Mundeville, for example, is shown holding a hawk by the glove in her right hand and a shield bearing her husband's arms in the left. The seal's legend gives the name of its owner: *Dame Nich(o)le de Mundevile*. Elizabeth, wife of Sir Hugh de Coleworth of Horndon, Essex, is shown in a long dress and fur-lined mantle, holding her husband's shield in her right hand and a hawk with bells and jesses, as more normally, in her left. Higher-born ladies, however, tended to display their father's arms as well as those of one or more husbands. Ela Basset, on a seal belonging to *c*.1250, displayed the arms of her late husband, Thomas, Earl of Warwick, and of her father, William Longespée. The former shield is held in her left hand, while the latter is placed opposite to her right. On the reverse, however, is the imprint of a counterseal. This gives the arms of her second, and current, husband, Philip Basset. There is, moreover, further decoration on the counterseal. The shield is depicted within a quatrefoil with lions above and below, a further

13. *The seal of Elizabeth de Coleworth of Horndon, Essex, thirteenth century. Her status is indicated by her fur-lined mantle, her hawk and her husband's shield*

allusion, no doubt, to her father's arms. The aristocracy of this period often used counterseals, usually engraved gems that were presumably worn on rings. Their original function seems to have been to counterseal documents sealed by the officials who were the custodians of their formal seals, but one can hardly doubt that they were aristocratic status symbols in their own right. They could be passed on from one generation to another. For example, Isabel, Countess of Gloucester (*c.* 1189–1217), the hapless bride who was to be repudiated by her husband, John Lackland (later King John), regularly countersealed with her father's small seal, a gem with an eagle and the legend 'Aquila sum et custos comitis' (I am the eagle and guardian of the earl).[20] Isabel had the legend altered to 'Ego sum aquila custos domine mee' (I am the eagle, guardian of my lady).

14. *The seal of Ela Basset, Countess of Warwick, c. 1250. She displays her late husband's shield in her left hand with her father's arms to her right*

15. *The counterseal of Ela Basset, Countess of Warwick. The arms are those of her current husband, Philip Basset*

16. The seal of Lady Agnes de Vesci,
c. 1254. Note her husband's arms on her
gown and on the shield in her right hand.
Her father's arms are to her left and, shown
less distinctly, on the lining of her mantle

17. The counterseal of Lady Agnes de Vesci.
She proudly displays the family arms of her
mother and her paternal grandmother

Sometimes seals can reveal much about a lady's identity and, indeed, sense of identity. For example, the lady Agnes, second wife of William de Vesci, lord of Alnwick, is depicted on her seal appended to a charter dating from after her husband's death in 1254, in a gown embroidered with the arms, the cross patonce, of her husband. Standing under a canopy, she is holding in her right hand a shield bearing the Vesci arms: *gules, a cross patonce argent*. On her left side is depicted her own family's arms: *vairy, or and gules*.[21] She was the daughter of William de Ferrers, Earl of Derby. Moreover, while the cross patonce is depicted on her gown, her mantle is lined with the Ferrers vair, signifying on her person the union of the two families. Her adopted family, however, clearly has precedence, both heraldically (it is shown on the dexter side as opposed to the sinister) and personally in that the cross patonce is nearer her body.

More interesting still, arguably, is the counterseal on the reverse, which illustrates pride in her own ancestry. Here is shown a tree from which hang three shields – due to damage to the seal, a fourth has been destroyed. One of them is once again her husband's cross patonce. One of the others, however, is from her mother, Sibyl, daughter of the great William the Marshal, Earl of Pembroke: *party or and vert, a lion rampant gules*.[22] Another represents her paternal grandmother, Agnes, sister and one of the co-heiresses of Ranulf III, Earl of Chester: *azure, three garbs or*. She was related, the counterseal reminds us, to two of the greatest (arguably, *the* two greatest) aristocrats of the early thirteenth century. One can only speculate as to whether the fourth shield was the Ferrers shield, representing her father once again, whether it represented her paternal grandmother or even, indeed, her mother-in-law. She was Margaret, illegitimate daughter of William the Lion, King of Scotland.[23]

Whatever the precise range of associations the lady was concerned to convey, however, she was certainly reminding the world of her illustrious kin. We should not assume too readily that she was making a form of feminist statement here, counteracting the formal association with her male kin depicted on the obverse seal. What in effect she was doing was supplementing her sense of identity, which was not restricted to husband and father. The most important point, however, is that her wider sense of identity is being transmitted through the male-orientated medium of heraldry. Her status was expressed – and necessarily so – through the dominant chivalric culture. This culture was ultimately male in inspiration, but it was a culture in which the aristocratic lady shared.

Even more up-front about her ancestry on the female side was Devorguila, wife and widow of John de Balliol. Her seal depicts her, in simple widow's garb, with wimple and veil, holding her husband's shield in her right hand and that of her father, Alan, lord of Galloway, in her left. Alongside her, however, but beneath these shields were two trees from which hang two further shields. They depict the *garbs* of the earls of Chester and the *piles* of David of Scotland, Earl of Huntingdon. They were the arms, in fact, of her maternal grandparents, David himself of the Scottish royal family and Matilda, sister of Ranulf III, Earl of Chester. On the counterseal these same arms are shown once again hanging from a tree, but below them there is a large shield on which the two arms of Galloway and Balliol are shown 'dimidiated'. Dimidiation involved the cutting in half of two shields in order to depict a relationship. Normally this meant taking the dexter half of the husband's shield and the sinister half of the wife's and putting them together to make one composite shield. Devorguila, however, reverses this and gives the Galloway lion precedence over the Balliol *orle*. And, once again, the *garbs* of Ranulf of Chester and *piles* of David of Huntingdon hang above it. She could hardly make it clearer that her status depended less upon her marriage to the Scottish regent than upon her own paternal and maternal kin.[24] Hugh de Balliol, son of John and Devorguila, seems to have shared his mother's sense of social position, at least in part. His own arms were *gules, an orle argent, with an escutcheon azure, a lion rampant argent crowned or*, representing his mother's arms. [See colour plates]

The depiction of relationships, however, was much more prominent on women's seals than on men's.[25] Dimidiation could produce some rather awkward results and by the early fourteenth century it had been generally replaced by impaling, by which the entire arms were placed side by side on a single shield, generally of course the man's on the left and the woman's on the right as seen by the observer.[26] In fact, more than one relationship can be shown in this way. Matilda, daughter of Thomas, lord Lucy of Egremont, was the wife of Henry Percy, Earl of Northumberland. She was also the widow of Gilbert de Umfraville, Earl of Angus. Her seal of 1381 depicts this. It is divided into three, *tierced per pale*. Umfraville is depicted dexter, Percy centre and Lucy sinister. She failed, however, to display the arms of her first husband, Richard Fitz Marmaduke.[27] Elizabeth de la Plaunche (d. 1423) did rather better. She managed to depict her paternal arms and those of her four husbands. She married, in succession, Sir John de Birmingham; Robert, lord Grey of Rotherfield; John, lord Clinton; and Sir John Russell. The shield on her seal is divided into five equal divisions with her paternal arms in the centre. However, the husbands have been re-ordered according to their social significance regardless of the chronology of her marriages. The arms are depicted in the order Grey of Rotherfield, Clinton, de la Plaunche, Birmingham and Russell.[28]

Yet another means of depicting multiple marriages was by placing four shields in a circle with their tips meeting at the centre of the seal. In this way Eleanor Mauduit, on a seal of 1325, showed that she was of the house of Clare, and that she had married Richard Fitz Marmaduke, Robert de Umfraville and Roger Mauduit.[29] Elaborate and often beautiful seals of the fourteenth century show not only delicate tracery but also lozenges and roundels in which multiple relationships can be indicated. The fine seal of Elizabeth de Burgh, who died in

18. The seal of Elizabeth de Burgh, d. 1360. Ladies' seals sometimes depicted their multiple marriages

1360, depicts the arms of her third husband, Sir Roger d'Amory, *barry nebuly of six*, between *three lions passant guardant* signifying her royal connections; her mother was the daughter of Edward I and Eleanor of Castile. A series of roundels depicted the arms of her earlier husbands, John de Burgh and Theobald de Verdon, together with the chevrons in respect of her father, Gilbert de Clare.

In short, there was considerable freedom as to which relationships might be shown and how. Margaret de Umfraville's seal, of 1328, depicted three shields. Two were for her parents, Thomas de Clare and Juliana Fitz Maurice, and were placed on the dexter and sinister sides of her seal respectively. They flanked a shield impaling the arms of her two dead husbands, Giles de Umfraville (d. 1303) and Bartholomew de Badlesmere (d. 1322).[30] There may well have been some male involvement in the choices women made; it would be surprising if there were not. But they must surely have played a major part in determining the content of their own seals.

19. The seal of Joan de Stuteville (1265–75). This unusual seal shows the lady riding side-saddle

Generally the distinction of oval seals for women was retained, although occasionally round, equestrian seals are found. A good example here is the seal of Joan de Stuteville (1265–75), whose fine seal shows her riding side-saddle holding not her husband's but her father's shield, signifying perhaps her status as sole heiress. It should not be forgotten, however, that the types of elaborate seals we have been discussing were largely the possessions of quite high-born ladies. The wives of many thirteenth-century knights, when they sealed heraldically, which was by no means invariably, used seals which simply depicted their husbands' arms.

That the marshalling of arms was important to women is indicated by the actions of Matilda, Countess of Northumberland. As we have seen, she had the arms of two husbands and her father impaled on her own seal. In 1369 she inherited the castle and honour of Cockermouth from her father. Her husband's heir was Henry Percy (better known as Hotspur), his son by his first wife. She declared that should she die without issue, Henry should succeed her, but on condition that he quarter the Percy arms with her own paternal arms of *gules, three luces argent*. This Hotspur duly did.[31] In fact, his father had already done so. Strictly speaking, if his wife were an heiress, a husband could bear a small shield or escutcheon of pretence at the centre of the shield until she inherited. Their descendants would bear the two coats of arms quartered, the paternal arms being in the first and fourth quarters. As time went on, further quarterings might well develop, although it was by no means obligatory to display them all.

Tombs and monumental brasses of women frequently depicted marshalled arms. The evidence of wills indicates that this was often by their explicit instruction. A late example is Margaret Paston's will of 4 February 1482:

Item, I wull that myn executours purveye a stoon of marble to be leyde alofte upon my grave within a yer next after my decesse; and upon that stoon I wulle have iiij scochens [i.e. escutcheons] sett at the iiij corners, whereof I wulle that the first scochen shalbe of my husbondes armes and myn departed [i.e. impaled], the ijde of Mawtebys armes and Berneys of Redham departed, the iijde of Mawtebys armes and the Lord Loveyn departed, the iiijte of Mawtebys and Sir Roger Beauchamp departed. And in the myddys of the seid stoon I wull have a scochen [sett] of Mawtebys armes allone, and under the same thise wordes wretyn: 'In God is my trust'; with a scripture wretyn in the verges thereof rehersyng these wordes: 'Here lieth Margaret Paston late the wife of John Paston, doughter and heire of John Mawteby, squier', and forth in the same scripture rehersed the day of the moneth and the yer that I shall decesse, 'on whos sowle God have mercy'.[32]

The primary function of heraldry was social display. It was not only on the field of battle and tournament, on seals and on funereal monuments that it was encountered. It was literally everywhere: on dress, for example, on domestic plate, on caskets and chests, on tiles, on wall paintings, in stained glass and on manuscripts. Female involvement in all of this was strong. The tiled pavement in the church of the Cistercian abbey of Hailes in Gloucestershire founded by Richard of Cornwall, the brother of King Henry III, includes the arms not only of Richard himself but also those of his three wives, Isabella Marshal, Sanchia of Provence and Beatrix von Falkenburg.[33] The last-mentioned lady was represented by the imperial eagle, also shown in the roundels which surround her figure in the donor portrait in stained glass. The lady died in 1277 and was buried in the Franciscan church in Oxford, where in all probability the glass originally resided. [See colour plates]

Impaling of arms can sometimes provide evidence for the possession and circulation of manuscripts. For example, Sir William Clopton and his wife, Dame Joan of Worcestershire, were owners of a manuscript which contained Robert Mannyng's *Handlyng Synne, Meditations on the Supper of our Lord*, Sir John Mandeville's *Travels*, a version of *Piers Plowman, La Estorie del Evangelie*, and *The Assumption of Our Lady*. The works suggest pious readers. Joan died in 1419 and a brass in Quinton Church commemorates her and her numerous acts of charity. It is not, however, the literary works that concern us here so much as three shields in the manuscript. One of them shows the Clopton arms impaled with those of Besford, Joan's family. The others depict the arms of her sister's husband and the arms of her mother-in-law's later husband. A close relationship is indicated between three gentry families. The actual relationship is through three ladies, but it is expressed heraldically through the men's arms, illustrating once again their close involvement in chivalric culture.[34]

Fashion is often closely allied to a spirit of exclusion. Heraldry is itself a major manifestation of this. As we have seen, the possession of a counterseal in the twelfth and early thirteenth centuries seems to have been a mark of high nobility. Another was to be commemorated in churches. Incised slabs acquired a new importance around the end of the twelfth century. For the very rich this gave way to sculptured effigies. The capacity to bear the expense of lavish commemorative tombs was increasingly a matter of individual and family pride. In churches noble families displayed their singular importance. The higher nobility, in particular, sported their elevated status in cathedrals and great churches, including monastic ones, especially those to which their families were benefactors. Lesser families had often to be content with demonstrating their status in their own parish churches. It was here that family chapels became increasingly significant during the later Middle Ages. But it was not only the possession of seals, tombs and the like which was important. Fashion was also reflected in their content. Aristocratic seals from the twelfth century, as we have seen, depicted ladies wearing the latest fashion in dress, the tight-fitting gown with long manches. The portrayal of fur-lined cloaks was another clear statement and long continued to be. One increasingly elaborate area of ladies' fashion was the headdress. For all that the male moralists said, *ad nauseam*, about headdresses as the epitome of female vanity, there can be no doubt that men were themselves implicated in using female dress as an expression of their own capacity to provide the latest fashions.[35] Let us take two examples from the fifteenth century, the age of the headdress *par excellence*.

The first is the sumptuous tomb of Richard Beauchamp, Earl of Warwick, set in his equally sumptuous Lady Chapel in St Mary's Church, Warwick. Sir William Dugdale described it as a 'magnificent tomb', 'inferior to none in England, except that of King Henry VII in Westminster Abbey'.[36] Richard died

20. Lady weepers from the sumptuous tomb of Richard Beauchamp, Earl of Warwick, d. 1439. Note the stylish dress and elaborate headdresses

in 1439, and his will dictated the details of his desired tomb. It included gilded latten images of fourteen lords and ladies 'in divers vestures' called weepers. Five are on each side, with two at each of the ends. Enamelled shields carry the arms of each weeper below the figure. The figures were to be constructed from wooden patterns. The choice of weepers was probably left to the executors, as was explicitly the case with the escutcheons, although they were undoubtedly constrained by protocol. The seven executors were all male. As to the figures, Henry, Duke of Warwick, the earl's son, and Cecily, his daughter-in-law, are at the head of the tomb, with the earl's daughter, Elizabeth, and her husband, Lord Latimer, at the feet. Five lords are on the south side of the tomb, and five ladies on the north. These are: Ann, the earl's daughter, wife of Richard Neville, the 'king-maker'; Margaret, the earl's daughter; Eleanor, the earl's daughter; Ann, wife of the Duke of Buckingham; and Alice, wife of the Earl of Salisbury. As one would expect, they are decked out exquisitely and in the latest fashions.[37]

The second example comes from Long Melford in Suffolk, where there are two startling brasses dating from around 1480. They are justly famous for their butterfly headdresses, representing the latest fashion of their day. The ladies are members of the Clopton family, and their brasses are among a series found in the

21. Brass of Margery Clopton, of Long Melford, Suffolk, exhibiting the butterfly headdress of the mid- to late fifteenth century

Clopton Chantry Chapel in Long Melford Church. The earliest brass is of William Clopton, son of Sir William Clopton, lord of Kentwell, who died in 1420 as, apparently, did two of his sisters. The latter were commemorated on a single slab, but only one figure now survives. This depicts the later version of the gown known as the houpeland, characterised by its very high waistline girded by a narrow belt and its copious sleeves reaching down to the knees. It also has a simple but seemingly unique headdress, which has been described as 'a wide flat cap, ornamented in front by a row of six five-pointed stars on a broad lattice work band, the whole resting on a wealth of curls'.[38]

The brasses that are of particular interest here, however, are those of Sir William's second wife, Margery, who died in 1424 and Alice Harleston, the last of Sir William's daughters by his first wife, who died in 1440.[39] In 1446 the manor was inherited by Margery's son, John, who must have been a mere infant when his mother died. It was he who commissioned the brasses, presumably when he was carrying out his extensive improvements to the church. Perhaps he had a particular affection for his half-sister, Alice. He is unlikely to have remembered what his mother wore. In any case neither of these ladies could possibly have worn the butterfly headdresses as they were the very latest fashion when the brasses were installed but were unknown at the earlier date. In other words, the headdresses are making a statement about the family's relationship to fashion, a statement which appears to be John's.

The heraldry is of interest too. Margery Clopton was the daughter of Helias Francys, esquire, of Norfolk. His arms were *gules a saltire between four crosses paty or*. There were shields at the four corners of the brass. The top dexter (now missing) depicted the Clopton arms (*sable, a bend argent cotised dancette or*), as was proper, and the top sinister the arms of the lady's family. The two shields at the bottom show Clopton impaling Francys. They are given twice, presumably to indicate that both families gain an alliance thereby. None of this is particularly remarkable. What is more interesting is the depiction of arms on the lady herself. On her kirtle she wears the arms of her own family. Her mantle, on the other hand, displays the Clopton arms.[40] This is the reverse of how the relationship was generally depicted on the earlier seals. One might wish to see in this a lady's preference for her own family were it not for the late date of the brass. It could perhaps be argued that she had left long-standing instructions. However, the situation is mirrored in the brass of Alice Harleston. She was married to John Harleston, esquire, of Essex. He bore quartered arms, viz. (1) and (4) *argent a fess ermine cotised sable* for Harleston, (2) and (4) *argent a chevron sable* for Denison. The brass shows Alice, once again, with her parental arms on her kirtle and her adopted arms on her mantle, as was the case with Margery.[41] If the thoughts that lay behind this belonged specifically to anyone, they belonged to John. The same feature is found, in fact, in the magnificent series of portraits in stained glass which adorn the first eight windows of the north aisle of the church. Of mid- to late fifteenth-century date, these too would appear to have been

22. *Brass of Alice Harleston, of Long Melford, Suffolk. As is the case with Margery Clopton, Alice's family arms are shown on the gown with her husband's arms on her mantle*

23. *Impaled arms: Clopton and Francys*

commissioned by John Clopton. Such changes can reflect shifts in fashion as much as individual choice. However, to show the husband's arms on the kirtle seems generally to have been more usual.[42]

The clothing that members of the various social strata should wear was from time to time the subject of sumptuary legislation.[43] The earliest was in 1337 when it was legislated by parliament that only knights and ladies should wear fur.[44] It has been argued that this may have been prompted, in part at least, by commercial or fiscal considerations; nevertheless, the social statement it contains is clear enough.

24. Marriage alliances were often depicted heraldically in stained glass: a portrait of Dorothy Clopton, wife of Thomas Curzon, from the north aisle at Holy Trinity Church, Long Melford, Suffolk, where a fine collection of mid- to late fifteenth-century stained glass is to be seen

There was – or there should have been – a clear social division, reflected in the apparel people wore. As we have seen this social divide is indicated by seals throughout the thirteenth century, when only knights and their wives sealed heraldically, and when the seal legends reserved the term lady (Latin *domina* or French *dame*) for knightly widows and wives. The records of national taxation, the subsidy rolls, retain this formal distinction between the knights and ladies and the other taxpayers right up to 1334, when assessment of individuals by nationally appointed assessors ceased. The Warwickshire subsidy rolls for 1332, for example, in addition to thirty-two knights, including the Earl of Warwick himself, refer to Lady Elizabeth de Clare, Lady Margaret de Stafford, Dame Alice de Astley and the lady (unnamed) of Whatcote, who was in fact Maud, widow of Sir Philip le Wolf.[45]

None the less, this distinction must in reality have been very difficult to maintain. Gentility ceased to be a matter only of the highest birth and knighthood if, indeed, it had ever been. There was the question of gentility by association, for example by service in a gentle household. The *Rules* of Bishop Robert Grosseteste, which were devised in 1240–42 for the Countess of Lincoln, for instance, advise: 'Order your knights and your gentle men who wear your livery (*Comaundez a vos chivalers e a vos gentis hommes ki vos robes pernent*) that they ought to put on that same livery every day, and especially at your table & in your presence to uphold your honour, and not old surcoats, and soiled cloaks, and cut off cloaks.'[46] Many household servants, both male and female, were in any case of knightly stock. There was the question of younger sons and daughters of knights, many of whom were not knights themselves nor married to knights. And through much of the thirteenth century there were increasing numbers of secular lords of manors who were not knights. Leaving aside the clergy, there were local administrators, some of whom were lay or in minor orders, living on the margins of gentility, and there were wealthy merchants and their wives. All of this must have produced uncertainty and perhaps tension around the issue of gentility. By the time of the great sumptuary act of 1363, the 'Statute Concerning Diet and Apparel', a major change had taken place within English society.[47] The crystallisation of the gentry as a social formation had begun to change perceptions of the social order.[48] People thought not only, as they had traditionally done, in terms of one family being of greater social value than another (of more illustrious ancestry and so on), but increasingly in terms of horizontal bands. The esquire had emerged as a social rank and the squirearchy, as it were, had been born as a social stratum, bringing with it the beginnings of a graded gentry. Esquires were now recognised heraldically, and sealed their documents armorially. The sumptuary law, in the words of its famous preamble, was occasioned by 'the outrageous and excessive apparel of divers people against their estate and degree, to the great destruction and impoverishment of the land'. It was essentially a product of the social dislocation which followed from the Black Death and the enormous loss of life this involved; but it also reflected the changes which had taken place within English society over decades which had led to the new gradation.

Knights and ladies were placed in a separate social category from 'squires and all manner of gentle men (*gentils gens*) below the estate of knight'. Within these categories, however, there was to be further differentiation according to income. Knights and ladies with an income from rent and land of between 400 marks and £1,000 per annum could wear more or less what they wished except ermine and 'letuse' and apparel embroidered with precious stones, apart from their headdresses. Knights with less than £200 per year were forbidden to use cloths valued at more than 6 marks and to use cloth of gold, gowns furred with ermine or miniver and apparel embroidered with precious stones. This was to apply to their wives and daughters, except again that they might use precious stones in their headdresses, and to their male children. The fact that the statute talks of wives rather than ladies at this point might well indicate a preference for a (very) restricted use of the latter term. Esquires with an income from land and rent up to 200 marks were to be differentiated from those esquires and gentle men with less than £100, and again what applied to the esquires applied to their wives, daughters and male children. Merchants and other townsfolk, like the clergy, were to be treated essentially according to the categories to which their income level corresponded. It has been rightly pointed out, therefore, that this statute was not aimed specifically at merchants.[49] The superiority of rural landowners was implicit and the level of movable goods on which urban income was to be estimated was perhaps pitched in terms of the landed income to which it was to correspond, but there was no discrimination against merchants and citizens such as applied to the lower orders.

How far the sumptuary law should be taken as a mirror of reality is a difficult question. Such legislation is, naturally, difficult to implement.[50] Many people were by this time, perhaps, somewhat surer of their own gentility but there remained considerable insecurity and tension around the issue. The sumptuary legislation itself had referred, rather vaguely, to esquires and all manner of gentle men below the estate of knight. Chaucer made great play with this matter in *The Canterbury Tales*, around the ambivalent figure of the Franklin, for example, and the Wife of Bath who denied the validity of the entire concept of gentility based upon birth.[51] The Statute of Additions of 1413 heralded the arrival of a further gradation within the gentry, that of 'gentleman', the social consequences of which took some time to work through.[52]

These are complex phenomena, and even now they are not wholly understood. Looked at from the point of view of the lady, however, what is clear is that a woman's social status continued to be defined in relation to a man's. The sumptuary law of 1363 makes this clear enough. The graded poll tax of 1379, whereby each person was taxed according to his or her status, reaffirms it. Here the term lady applies to the widows of all knights and of esquires who by their estate ought to be knights. This corresponds, in effect, to traditional usage. The number of men who declined to take on knighthood was greatly increasing at this time; the emergence of esquire as a social grade now gave them a cushion. Above this level we have countess, baroness and the female equivalent of the short-lived social category of banneret, *banresse*.[53] When we examine the surviving returns to the poll tax, we do indeed find widows paying at the rate appropriate to the status of their late husbands.

The widespread concern for gentility led to shifts in terminology. The term *dame*, which was carried over into English, ceased to have such exclusive connotations. In effect, it came to signify respectability. Having described his five proud London aldermen, dressed in their livery, Chaucer turns to their wives, who so enjoy being called 'madame' and heading the procession on feast days:

> It is ful fair to been ycleped 'madame',
> And goon to vigilies al bifore,
> And have a mantel roialliche ybore.   [royally carried]

Such women were at the apex of urban society. It was perhaps in this milieu, more than any other, that the word dame moved socially down. The term could also be used ambivalently, or even satirically. Chaucer's Wife of Bath was known as Dame Alice. The term lady, on the other hand, seems to have retained more cachet; although it also kept its traditional usage, it could be used, like lord, to signify members of the very highest strata of society. In *What the Goodwife Taught Her Daughter*, young girls were advised against rich robes and garlands and counterfeiting the lady, as if 'thy lord were a king'.[54]

Another product of this concern was a proliferation of courtesy literature and a growing interest in matters such as table manners. Most of the courtesy literature, which was composed from the twelfth century on, was written for men and boys, whether in Latin, French or English.[55] *What the Goodwife Taught Her Daughter* is an exception. It survives in five manuscripts and was probably quite popular. It is first found in a West Midlands manuscript composed around 1350. It was clearly circulating in London in the fifteenth century. It revolves around the household, and the young girl is pictured essentially as a future wife and mother. It is certainly true that such works circulated within urban society, and found a strong audience there. But there is no reason to believe that the audience was exclusively urban. In the earliest manuscript it is associated with *Urbain le Courtois*, a courtesy text addressed to boys. The fact that the one is in English rather than French does not necessarily indicate an audience from a different social milieu.[56] The culture of the first half of the fourteenth century was as yet trilingual, although the triumph of English was not far in the future. An early fifteenth-century manuscript containing the *Goodwife* came from rural Warwickshire. The popularity of such works reflects a general preoccupation with respectability and social values. Although there is undoubtedly an element of downward dissemination of values, there is no need to see in this the existence of a specific bourgeois ethos, in opposition to the values of the gentle. Indeed, the advice which the daughter is given is not strikingly different from that which the French knight, Geoffrey de la Tour Landry, gave his daughters.[57] There is the same emphasis upon piety, deference and restrained behaviour. The manuscript owned by the fifteenth-century London mercer, Roger Thorney, also contains courtly lyrics and texts.

The culture of the fifteenth-century, or for that matter fourteenth-century, merchant and his family is unlikely to have been very different from that of the rural gentry. The growing incidence of inter-marriage between the two would have counteracted any such cultural division in any case. It is dangerous to construct general arguments around specific cases, but the behaviour of Elizabeth Rich, the London widow who, in 1475, married Sir William Stonor, the head of a well-established gentry family, hardly suggests a different scale of values from his. With her contacts she was well placed to play a major part in his business affairs, but she was hardly one for thrift. In January 1480, shortly after the lady's death, William received a letter from a friend and relative, William Harleston, who commiserated with him, before proceeding to offer some advice:

> My Ryght reverent and worshipfull Neve (nephew), I an my wiff recommande us unto you with all our hertes. And I beseche almyghty God to have mercy on my lady your wiffes sowle, for verily she was a good woman and a well disposid; and I pray God send you no wersse than she was.[58]

The advice is that he can now break up his existing household with honour and worship, 'after the decesse of my good lady your wiff' and re-establish it sadly [i.e. soberly] and wisely with a convenient fellowship, so as to keep within his 'lifelode', that is, within his means. Thomas Betson, the London merchant and business associate who became Elizabeth's son-in-law had counselled her against extravagance: 'I wylle avyse you, madame, to remembre large expensez and be ware of them . . .'. Again, when her husband was sick in June of that year, he advised her ladyship to cause him to be merry and of good cheer and to put away all fantasies and unthrifty thoughts, for: 'A man may hurt hymselff by ryotouse meanes; it is good to be ware.'[59]

Elizabeth was also socially ambitious in the manner of the gentry. In October 1476 she wrote to her husband with great enthusiasm:

> And sur, you schall undyrstond that I have be with my Lady of Southfolke as on Thursday last was, and wayted uppon hyr to my lady the Kynges Modyr and hyrse, be hyr commaundment. And also on Satyrday last was I wayted uppon hyr thedyr ageyne, and allso ffro thens she wayted uppon my lady hyr Modyr, and browght hyr to Grenwyche to the Kyngis good grace and the quenyse: and ther I sawe the metyng betwyne the Kynge and my ladye his Modyr. And trewly me thowght it was a very good syght.[60]

She was mightily put out when she found that the Duchess of Suffolk was displeased because her two sisters-in-law, Mary Barantyne and Elizabeth Stonor, who were in the duchess's household, might not be kept on because of the manner in which they were arrayed, and made it known that it was a threat to William and to his family's reputation. If anyone was in danger of falling short of the courtly ethic of largesse it was the 'knightly' William Stonor rather than the 'bourgeois' Elizabeth Rich. And, to judge from his letter to his future bride, the very young Katherine Rich, Thomas Betson knew at least as much about the art of gracious wooing as John Paston III or even John Paston II, 'the best cheser of a gentellwoman that I know'.[61]

The fifteenth-century letters allow us to perceive the social position of the lady more clearly than is possible for previous centuries. As is well known, during marriage the lady's role tends to be masked. Their joint action is often subsumed under the husband's name. As widows, on the other hand, their social position comes into sharper focus. An indication of the quantity of land directly under the control of ladies in the thirteenth century comes from the government's inquiry of 1297 into all those who held £20 worth of land in the counties. The information was required for military purposes, the Crown seeking to impose cavalry service on all the lay landowners, whether or not they were knights. The Sheriff of Northamptonshire sent in a thorough return in which he named 97 knights, 41 sub-knightly armigers (potential men-at-arms), 30 women and 37 abbots and priors. Two of the women were also heads of religious houses, the Abbess of St Mary du Prée, outside Northampton, and the Prioress of Catesby. The remaining 28 constituted 17 per cent of lay landowners in the county.[62] Most of them were widows. They are not, of course, the entirety of landholding widows, since the sheriff was returning only those with £20 land. They tend to be widows of baronial and well-endowed knightly families. They could also be holding inherited land. Denise de Montchesny, for example, had succeeded to her lands only in July 1297. Born before 22 July 1283, her marriage was given by the king to Hugh de Vere, on condition that she married no one but himself.[63] It is not clear whether they were yet married in 1297. This situation was an abnormal one. Girls were not normally allowed to remain unmarried heiresses for long. Hence even where women were returned holding their own inherited land, this was normally as widows.

Two of the ladies were countesses: Alice de Lacy, Countess of Lincoln, and Joan de Clare, Countess of Fife. Two others are specifically called lady, another example perhaps of restricted usage of the term. Emmelina 'lady of Sutton' was Emmelina Longespée, who was still holding King's Sutton and Astrop in 1316. She was probably related in some way to the late Sir William Longespée, grandson of the Earl of Salisbury, who had died in 1257.[64] However, she was neither his widow nor his heir. The other lady was Clemencia de Vescy, 'lady of Foxton'. Clemencia, also known as Clemencia d'Avaugour, was a cousin of Queen Eleanor of Castile and was one of the many relatives the queen had brought to England.[65] A comfortable marriage was arranged for Clemencia, and the queen took no chances in ensuring that she was well provided for. She was married to

John de Vescy, son of William de Vescy, lord of Alnwick, and Isabel de Periton. On 27 August 1290 William enrolled a deed in the royal chancery on the expectation that his son, John, would endower Clemencia with land worth £200 per annum at the church door, that is to say at the marriage ceremony.[66] 'As', he says, 'he proposes to observe inviolably all the covenants and promises made to the queen,' he promised to deliver to her, in the event of John predeceasing her, £250 worth of land within three months of John's death, to be held by her in name of dower for the rest of her life. Should William himself be dead by then, he grants that Clemencia should have dower of this and of the entire inheritance. Foxton, which was Isabel's own inheritance, was not one of the manors specifically named in this agreement. Not long before this, however, William de Vescy and Isabel had already passed the manor of Foxton to their son. Hence on John's death, in 1297, Clemencia was holding dower here too.[67] The heir to Foxton was Isabel's son by her first husband, Adam de Welles, who died in 1311 leaving a widow, Joan. As Isabel herself was still alive, there were now three widows who needed providing for. Moreover, at some point, Isabel granted an annuity out of the manor of Foxton to her two daughters, Cecily and Aline. She finally died in 1314. Clemencia d'Avaugour lived until 1344. It is to be doubted if she was ever resident at Foxton. At one point she had leased her third of the manor to Adam de Welles. The occupation of dower lands, and indeed the lands of a lady's own inheritance, was not as simple a matter as might appear on the surface.

Some of these women were living, then, twenty years later. In addition to Clemencia, they include Emmelina Longespée, Margery Kiriel, Margery de Keynes, Margery de Whittlebury, Elena de Lucy and Margery de Meusse, all of whom were returned as lords of townships or parts of townships in 1316. Others had been holding their lands for some time in 1297. Christiana de Mareys (or *Marisco*) had been granted the manor of Overstone by the king, in exchange for other lands, in 1281. It was quite a profitable manor, for when she died, around 1312, her executors leased it for £50 per annum.[68] They had been instructed to hold the property for seven and a half years after her death. Alice, widow of John de Holecote, Isabella de Grey 'of Newbottle', Hawise de Greyley and Milicent de Montalt were all holding their estates at the time of the survey of knights' fees in 1284–5.

Not all dowers were acquired smoothly. Mabel Grimbaud was the widow of William Grimbaud, who was lord of Horton and Brafield on the Green. In 1284, however, William passed the manors to John de Kirkby, Bishop of Ely, who seems to have been the lady's brother. From him they passed to another brother, William, as heir, and he made a life grant to Henry Spigurnel. Mabel had to sue for her dower in both manors.[69] She lived until 1312.

Some of the ladies bore the same surnames as the male landowners who were returned by the sheriff, suggesting that these were either their sons or, at least, their husbands' heirs. These include Sara de Pavely (whose son, Sir Lawrence de Pavely, may be the knight depicted with his wife in effigy in the church at Paulerspury), and Eva Murdak of Edgecote, whose son, Sir Thomas Murdak, was later to be murdered at the instigation of his wife, Juliana, in 1316.[70]

25. Effigies were sometimes in oak: knight and lady of the Pavely family, Paulerspury, Northamptonshire

On occasions these women had to fight for their rights. Isabella de Paunton, for example, had to defend her right to the view of frankpledge of her tenants of the manor of Glaston in county Rutland before the royal justices in 1285.[71] They could also be exacting landlords. One of the free tenants of Christiana de Mareys, Walter de Mazun, complained that she had unjustly expelled him from his holding. It had been leased to him by the bailiff before she came on the scene and he had expended a great deal, he said, in improvements.[72]

These ladies were a significant feature of medieval society. They had a certain lifestyle to support and prestige to maintain. One of the ladies whose activities can be scrutinised in some detail is Elizabeth de Burgh, lady of Clare. Given the sheer abundance of the records which she has left behind, it is hardly surprising that she has received a good deal of attention from historians recently.[73] Not only are there fine estate records, including both accounts and 'valors', essentially statements of what the lady could expect from her estates, but also household accounts, which are impressive both in quantity and range, and her will which was drawn up in 1355.

Elizabeth was born in September 1295, the youngest daughter of Gilbert de Clare, Earl of Gloucester and Hertford and Joan of Acre, daughter of Edward I.[74] In 1308 she was married to John de Burgh, eldest son of the Earl of Ulster, in one of those double ceremonies which occurred among the nobility from time to time. Her brother, Gilbert, married the Earl of Ulster's daughter. With the death of Earl Gilbert at the Battle of Bannockburn in 1314, she became one of three heiresses and a rich prize. In 1316 she married Theobald de Verdon, who was alleged to have abducted her from Bristol Castle. Widowed again a few months later, she came under royal pressure to marry Roger d'Amory in 1317, after which the Clare estates were partitioned among the heiresses. In 1322 Roger d'Amory died in rebellion against the king, and Elizabeth was widowed for the third and final time. It was only after the fall of the royal favourite, Hugh le Despenser the younger, and the accession of Edward III in 1327 that Elizabeth was finally free to enjoy her own estates in peace. She never married again, and it is this second phase of her life, until her death in 1360, with which we are concerned here.

Her household account rolls offer an immediate entrée into her lavish lifestyle. Although the basic foodstuffs were supplied from her own demesnes, there were constant and considerable purchases of fish, wines, spices, cloths and furs from London suppliers and from fairs. Noble life centred upon the household, where the head of the household presided over a clearly delineated hierarchy. There was a strong element of theatre. At meal times Elizabeth presided in her 'great, thronelike chair', called a *cathedra*,[75] with all the members of the household playing their roles. There was a constant stream of guests to enjoy the quality of the food and the entertainment. Minstrels figure in her accounts, particularly in her younger days. Clothes were distributed to the household, with members of the same rank being clothed alike. Elizabeth's liveries exhibited considerable variety, with a medley of colours.

Elizabeth was a patron of the minor arts. Goldsmiths were regularly employed. In her private chapels she 'created an ambience of visual delights'.[76] She was a lover of jewellery. Her will includes a gold ring with a ruby for the Black Prince, and two gold rings for her friend, Marie de St Pol, Countess of Pembroke. One was set with a diamond, the other with a sapphire. In 1351-2 she purchased silk belts and gold chains, the former decorated with silver or enamel. One of the gold chains had pearls and diamonds in its design. Her beds had coverlets of fur and expensive cloth, while some of her own clothes were embroidered, including her peacock mantle and the shawl with parrots and cockerels which she left to her daughter. Her ecclesiastical vestments, many of which were bequeathed to institutions, featured both pearls and embroidery, the famous *opus anglicanum*, greatly valued throughout Christendom. She also built up a library. If her will is anything to go by, this centred upon biblical works and saints' lives, with books on canon law and theology.

Such a great lady had considerable patronage to dispense. In addition to goldsmiths and her various London suppliers, she gave her support to priests and scholars. She needed to help and advance her own officials. She held the advowson (that is, the right to nominate the priest) of a considerable number of churches in England, Wales and Ireland. A roll of the liveries of cloth and fur made in Elizabeth's household survives for 1343. It included not only the members of her household in the narrow sense but also her estate officials, relatives and members of her affinity. It begins with a list of fifteen knights, including her relatives Sir John Bardolf and Sir Thomas de Ferrers. Then there are 21 clerks, 93 esquires, 4 sergeants, 9 lesser clerks, 45 yeomen (*gentz de mester*), 51 garçons (*garceouns*) and 12 pages. Among her esquires are included various merchants who supplied her: Nicholas Theobald of Sudbury who supplied cloth and fur; Bartholomew Thomasyn, the London spicer; Roger Turtle of Bristol and Thomas Gotiller of Ipswich, both wine merchants; and Richard Felsted, her architect.[77]

It was traditional for the nobility, at all levels, to patronise religious houses. Elizabeth was no exception. She gave donations to the Prior and Convent of Ely, for example, to Walsingham Priory and to the Greyfriars in London. It was also customary to offer lavish support to religious houses that were family foundations. Thus the Augustinian Priory at Clare itself was substantially rebuilt through her patronage. It had been founded by her grandfather in 1248, and both her grandmother and her mother had been benefactors. It was also the site of her mother's tomb. Elizabeth was responsible for substantial building there, and her arms were included in the priory's stained glass.

She was responsible, moreover, for founding two new friaries. One was at Ballinrobe in Ireland and the other was, once again, at Walsingham in Norfolk. The Franciscan house at Walsingham was distinct from that of the Augustinians. In fact, the canons were opposed to the foundation of the new friary. They housed an important shrine to the Virgin Mary and they feared a loss of revenue to the Franciscans. Nevertheless, the lady proceeded to found the friary in 1347, apparently to provide a hostel for poor pilgrims on their way to visit Our Lady of Walsingham.[78] She was, moreover, particularly fond of the Franciscans.

Elizabeth de Burgh is most remembered, however, for her foundation of Clare College, Cambridge. This seems to have been entirely her own initiative, although she and Marie de St Pol, who founded Pembroke College, seem to have influenced each other. Clare took shape over a number of years.[79] The history of the college began in 1326 when the chancellor of the university founded University Hall. In 1336 Elizabeth granted an advowson to help support it. She decided, however, to take over the hall, and in 1346 she acquired royal licences to transfer two more advowsons and to allow Clare Hall, as it was now known, to acquire property to the value of £40 per year. In 1348 she acquired a papal licence to build a chapel, although this was not carried out until after her death. In 1359 she provided a set of statutes governing educational matters. In her will she left Clare Hall much of the furnishings of her own chapel, together with plate and £40 in cash.

Until late in her life, Elizabeth itinerated mainly between her residences at Clare in Suffolk, Great Bardfield in Essex, Anglesey in Cambridgeshire and Usk in Gwent. This was in keeping with aristocratic life. Transport was a problem, as much of the furnishings as well as the personnel of a noble household would travel from residence to residence. In terms of her own comfort the countess had two suspended carriages or 'chariots'. One was for her, the other for her ladies. Such carriages tended to be heavily decorated and well-furnished with cushions.[80]

Another form of display was domestic building. A new range was constructed at Usk Castle in her time, and improvements were made at Clare Castle and at her manor house at Bardfield. During the 1350s, however, she decided to build an entirely new residence, in London.[81] Her motives were probably two-fold. As we have seen she was gregarious, and a house in London would enable her to have more of the company of her friends. There were also religious motives. For some time she had been drawn to the Minoresses, an order of Franciscan nuns. Her friend, Marie de St Pol, the widow of Aymer de Valence, Earl of Pembroke, had founded a house of Minoresses at Denny in Cambridgeshire in 1342. The following year, having taken a vow of chastity, Elizabeth had received a papal indulgence allowing her to enter the precincts of the Minoresses with three ladies. This was later extended to 'four or five honest women and three honest and mature men'. She was now allowed to stay overnight, while her confessor was allowed to eat at table with the nuns. As Jennifer Ward puts it, 'Elizabeth wanted to participate in some way in the religious life of the Minoresses while at the same time enjoying a full social life'.[82] She then proceeded to build a very substantial house in the outer precincts of the Abbey of the Minoresses at Aldgate.

In her last years Elizabeth was found mostly at London, Clare and Bardfield. She continued to entertain lavishly her numerous guests. These included royalty, various earls and countesses, the Minoresses, the mayors and sheriffs of London and royal justices, in addition to her relatives and her own officials. Two of her children – William de Burgh, Earl of Ulster, and Isabella de Ferrers – were dead by this time, but she remained on good terms with her younger daughter, Elizabeth Bardolf, and her granddaughter, Elizabeth, Countess of Ulster.

Elizabeth de Burgh lived a life of display and conspicuous consumption. Her conventional piety did not run counter to this; indeed, in some respects it can be seen as a necessary component of aristocratic display. Much of what she did was conventional, such as the regular almsgiving from her table. The same was true of her death. Elizabeth died on 4 November 1360. Her will dictated a lavish funeral.

26. *Travelling in great style: a lady's carriage of the fourteenth century, from the Luttrell Psalter*

There were extensive bequests, although the Minoresses of Aldgate and Clare College were by far the greatest beneficiaries. She was buried in the church of the Minoresses. Her tomb was, no doubt, impressive, as it was used as a model by John Hastings, Earl of Pembroke, but sadly it has not survived.

Elizabeth de Burgh lived splendidly, but all this was predicated upon careful attention to her estates. She enjoyed an income of £2,500 to £3,000 a year. In addition to her Clare inheritance – the honour of Clare itself in eastern England, the lordship of Usk in Gwent, the Dorset lands centred upon Cranborne, and her third of the Clare lands in Ireland – she had her jointure from John de Burgh, her dower from Theobald de Verdon and the lands held jointly with Roger d'Amory. Needless to say, these estates required clear and effective control. They were grouped into bailiwicks, each with a steward and a receiver. The central financial office was the chamber and its principal officer was the clerk of the chamber.[83] Like most major landowners, Elizabeth relied heavily on her council, who collectively directed her affairs. A letter survives from 1343, for example, in which she wrote to her auditors ordering certain allowances to be made in the account of one of her bailiffs on the basis of information given before her and her council.[84] Councils were particularly important when it came to protecting estates in the courts. Elizabeth's councillors included men who had previously been in royal service. Among the clerks who were receiving her livery, that is to say those who were within her affinity, were several officials of the royal chancery and the exchequer, while the knights included no less a figure than Sir John Shardlow, justice of the Court of Common Pleas, who was also a neighbour and tenant of hers in Suffolk.

The difference between Elizabeth de Burgh and lesser ladies was one merely of degree. Petronilla de Nerford, the widow of an East Anglian knight, had three lawyers among her councillors in 1320.[85] They were Sir John Mutford and Sir John Bacon, both justices of the Court of Common Pleas, and John le Claver, a sergeant-at-law. All three were receiving fees and robes from her. Like that great lady Elizabeth de Burgh, Petronilla was also responsible for continuing the building programme of her predecessors. At Little Wenham, Suffolk, she and her husband, William de Nerford, completed the new manor house which she had inherited from Sir John de Vallibus in 1287. Little Wenham is a fortified manor house. It is unusual for its day, not least in being built of brick. According to Pevsner, 'it ranks with Stokesay and Acton Burnell of about the same years as one

27. Ladies were involved in domestic building, an important form of social display: Little Wenham, Suffolk, completed by Petronilla de Nerford and her husband

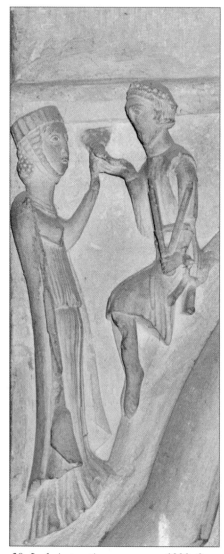

28. Lady instructing a mason, c. 1230, from the south choir aisle of Worcester Cathedral

of the *incunabula* of English domestic architecture'.[86] Its late thirteenth-century chapel boasts a carved figure on the roof boss thought to represent St Petronilla. Her cult was an extremely local one, more or less confined to East Anglia. She is depicted on screens in a number of churches. The Hospital at Bury St Edmunds was dedicated to her, as were a few churches and chapels. Pilgrims came to the Church of All Saints, Stanton, which possessed a statue of her, while among its relics the Abbey of Bury St Edmunds kept her skull, which was supposed to cure headaches. So Petronilla de Nerford, in addition to participating in the building of an architecturally significant manor house, seems also to have played a role in maintaining the cult of the female saint after whom she was named.[87]

A lady of the same station as Petronilla and of whose lifestyle we know something is Dame Alice de Bryene. Alice was the daughter of Sir Robert de Bures, lord of Acton in Suffolk. She married Guy de Bryene the younger, a Gloucestershire knight whose father had once been Admiral of the Fleet. Her husband died in 1386 and her father-in-law four years later. At some point she returned to Suffolk, succeeding her father in the manors of Acton and Bures in 1393. She lived until 1434. Her household account books, showing her daily expenditure, survive for the years 1411–12 and 1412–13.[88] From them we learn, once again, of her provisioning, of her quite lavish table, and of the steady stream of guests who came and went. There also survives a fragment of a letter book, belonging to the 1390s.[89] A total of eight letters, all of them in French, remain on a single leaf. The leaf is faded and torn, but a fair portion survives. Most of the letters are addressed to Alice herself and what is most striking about them is the respect and courtesy with which the lady was addressed.

One of the letters was probably written to her following the death of her father. The leaf is quite damaged at this point and the writer is therefore unknown. It may be from a relative and/or friend, but it could also be from one of her higher ranking advisers, perhaps one of the family's councillors. The letter is very conscious of her status, while at the same time offering advice. It begins: 'My very honoured and very sovereignly of right entire heart well-beloved lady (*treshonuree & tresoveraignement de droit entier coer biename dame*), I recommend me humbly to your very good nobility (*tresbonne noblesse*) as your subject (*suggit*) and servant readily prepared to do you service according to my power in honest manner.' After praying to the all-powerful God for good news of her estate and her health and for such increase in her honour as would be a joy and comfort to all her friends and servants to hear, the writer goes on to excuse himself to the very honoured lady (*treshonuree dame*) for not having come to her presence, the reasons for his absence (presuming the writer to be a he) being contained in other letters. If God pleases that he should still be alive and in good health, he promises to come after Easter next. His absence, he says, should not be put down to any lack of kindliness (*desnaturesse*) on his part, nor, by his faith (*par ma foi*), should she consider him to be unkind or disloyal (*disnaturel ne disloial*). He then proceeds to suggest that her household (*hostiel*) be put in good order; this advice appears to be couched in the form of a maxim, although the leaf is so damaged here that the meaning is by no means clear. It may well be that such advice was customary following a bereavement, and at the point at which a new master or mistress takes control.[90] The writer concludes with another matter of some practical importance. These are the arrangements for the property (*lenhe*[ritance]) which lately belonged to Sir (*monsieur*) W. de B, perhaps a member of the Bures family. 'I have informed RD', he says, who will 'tell you more plainly'.

Another letter seems to have been written by a supplier who has let the lady down. 'I recommend me', he says, 'to your ladyship (*seignuresse*) as much as I know how or am able to, desiring to hear and know . . . of your gracious estate, which may God through his mercy long hold in honour and ease'. He then excuses himself for his failure to supply a '*grant piece*'. The leaf is again badly damaged at this point, but it appears that he has been active on her behalf and that of '*monsieur*', and that he is about to depart for Scotland. In the meantime, she should have recourse to John Waltham, tailor of London, who will deliver to her whatever she wants. Again, she is *treshonuree dame* and *tresgraciouse dame*. He signs off, '*le vostre humble servant William Maldone*'. The reference to *monsieur* suggests that Alice's father is either still alive at this point, or that he has only recently died.

Two other letters are from her sons-in-law, John Devereux and Robert Lovell, married to her daughters Philippa and Elizabeth respectively. The former wrote to her from Calais, around Michaelmas 1396. John begins, 'Very honoured and very gracious lady, and my very reverent mother (*ma tresreverente Miere*), I recommend me to you', and continues 'desiring very gracious lady and mother to hear and know of your ease and the health of your body, which God through his mercy grant you in the manner that you know best how to direct, and beseeching your gracious blessing'. 'If it please you *ma treshonuree dame & Miere* to know of me at the making of these [letters],' he suggests, 'I am in good health (*en bon point*) thanks be to God.' It is a short, perhaps rather awkward letter. As regards the news in these parts, he says, great ordinance is being made at Calais against the coming of the King of France, but no one knows for certain whether he will come or not before the Kings of England and France transfer themselves to the marches of Calais. No one knows, he adds, whether he will come to St Omer or not. The event to which he is alluding seems to be the impending marriage of King Richard II and the young princess Isabel of France. Beyond this, however, John does not know what to write: 'Very honoured and very gracious lady and mother I do not know what else to write to you at present, except that the very powerful king of heaven grant you a long life and increase your honour to your entire heart's desire.' John's letter is full of respect, for sure, but one cannot avoid the sense that he is writing out of duty.[91]

Robert Lovell, on the other hand, was decidedly more florid and gushing. Like John he wrote to his mother-in-law from abroad; this time from Ireland, in 1397. He begins: 'My very honoured and with all my heart whole-heartedly well beloved lady and mother I recommend me to you as whole-heartedly as far as I know how and am most able, desiring sovereignly to hear and truly know good and joyous news of you and of your honourable estate.' 'My joy is renewed,' he says, 'when I hear good news of you,' and so on in the same spirit. 'And very honoured dame and mother,' he adds, ' because I am well certain that it would be very pleasing to you to hear of me and my estate, may it please you to know that at the departure of these [letters] I am healthy and happy, God to thank, thanking you (*vous esmerciant & remerciant*) in as much as I am able for the very great tenderness and love that you have had and ever have of my person and for the other innumerable kindnesses besides, which you of your very high gentility (*treshaulte gentillesse*) do me and show me without any desert on my part.' If he can do anything for her honour and pleasure in return, he says, then may it please her to command him to carry out her wishes and he will be ever ready to obey and accomplish them with all his small power (*a tout mon petit poair*), as he is very sovereignly held and bound. He concludes:

> My very honoured and with all my heart very whole-heartedly well beloved lady and mother may the blessed Trinity have you in his very holy keeping and grant you a good life and of long duration and good accomplishment of your honourable desires. Written at Trim in Ireland the third day of June.
> *Vostre humble filtz si vous plaist*
>
> Robert Lovell

There may have been genuine affection here, and Lady Alice may well have found this son-in-law charming. One wonders whether his speech was as smooth as his writing. His style was certainly different from John's. It may be noted in passing, however, that he actually gave her no news whatsoever, other than the fact that he was well. The important point is the respectful manner in which both men wrote to her. In broad terms, and when all allowances have been made for differences both in style and forcefulness, the terminology, the phraseology and even the content of these letters are heavily conventional. But this does not detract from the essential fact: whether you were friend, relative, adviser, son-in-law, merchant or servant, the lady was someone of whom you took serious account.

29. Ladies enjoyed hunting: here a lady is shooting a stag

Female landowners were barred from many of the public roles undertaken by their male counterparts. They could not sit in parliament, nor could they occupy posts such as sheriff, coroner or justice of the peace. Nevertheless they could participate in many aspects of noble life. Women were sometimes found hunting with their households. From time to time they, too, were fined for poaching deer in the king's forests. In 1280, for example, Matilda de Mortimer was pardoned with William and others of her household for taking one buck and one doe in Whittlewood Forest, while at the Pleas of the Forest of Pickering in 1334 it was presented that Lady Blanche de Wake and her men came into the forest on Monday 28 September last and took one young stag and two hinds and carried them away. At the Sherwood Forest Pleas in the same year, Lady Aleysia, wife of Stephen de Segrave, together with Thomas de Verdon and other unknown members of her household, was fined for entering an enclosure within the forest with greyhounds and poaching the deer.[92] According to the Scottish chronicler John of Fordun, it was while out hunting with her esquires and maidens in 1271 that Martha, daughter and heiress of the Earl of Carrick, encountered and forcibly detained her future husband, Robert Bruce of Annandale and Cleveland.[93]

Ladies also participated in that other preoccupation of later medieval landowners, litigation. It was an extremely litigious society and any lady who was in control of property would have needed to have more than a passing acquaintance with the land law. Dower, in particular, was 'women's business' and it brought them frequently to court. It was exceptional among the major civil pleas in requiring that a woman be the plaintiff, although if she were remarried she would have to be joined by her new husband. Dower, moreover,

30. Ladies dismembering a stag, from the Taymouth book of hours

with its many possible objections by the defendant, could involve quite complex litigation. Even though the law was becoming increasingly professionalised during the course of the thirteenth century, with many litigants employing attorneys to deal with the legal process as well as sergeants to speak on their behalf, this was by no means universally true and, in any case, plaintiffs needed to ensure that their arguments and instructions were being properly attended to.[94]

Ladies could also participate in direct action. Although they rarely took part in those raiding parties against property which were so characteristic of gentry feuding and which were often accompaniments to litigation, they could be present behind the scenes in their planning and instigation. In this capacity they sometimes perpetrated, or were accused of perpetrating, more serious crimes. A particularly intriguing case revolved around the lawyer Sir Edmund de Pashley of Sussex and his wives.[95] Sir Edmund made his will on 23 February 1327 and was dead by 27 March. His first wife, Maud de Kechenoure, had died in or by 1318, having borne him three sons, William, John and Edmund. On his death, however, two other women claimed to be his widow. One was named Joan; the other was Margaret de Basing, who also had three sons by him, together with one daughter. There can be no doubt that by the time of his death Sir Edmund had been living with Margaret for some time. Joan, however, claimed to be his lawful wife, and sued for her dower against Margaret de Basing. In support of her claim, Joan produced a petition. In this she not only stated that Sir Edmund had been instructed by his confessors to return to her, his lawful wife, but also that Margaret, knowing that he would never marry her, decided on a bold action to ensure that it would be her children who inherited and not Sir Edmund's sons by his first wife. First she poisoned Sir Edmund and then his eldest son, William. She then had his brother, the thirteen-year-old Edmund, and his page, done to death at Coulsdon in Sussex. Joan claimed that this was common knowledge in that county. Moreover, there is supporting evidence to back Joan's story. For one thing, her claim to have been dowered by Sir Edmund at the church door, at Mary Magdalene in Old Fish Street, London, was supported by the Bishop of London himself. Edmund de Pashley and his page were indeed murdered at Coulsdon on 13 March 1328. A year later a jury had named the assailants as two men acting on the instructions of Margaret de Basing. Three men sent to arrest her at Ticehurst were assaulted by a gang led by her sons. William, the eldest of Sir Edmund's sons, had in fact disappeared from the record around the same time as his father died. In the event, one of the named assailants and Margaret de Basing herself were eventually acquitted of the murder of the young Edmund. The facts, however, remain suspicious, as regards this crime at least. Sir Edmund, it will be recalled, had a third son, John, by his first wife. John, perhaps fearing for his own safety, made a pre-emptive strike against the property of Margaret and her sons after the death of his father, which resulted in a long-running feud between the two families. Despite his prompt action, John seems to have come off worst in this. Although he lived until 1366, he had long since come to terms and the main Pashley estates did indeed pass to Margaret de Basing's sons.

As has been said, the activities of a lady during marriage tended to be hidden from the records, masked under her husband's name.[96] This is true in documents of private as well as public provenance. Records emanating from estates and households will carry the husband's name, even if the wife was currently directing operations. It stands to reason that a woman could not have taken effective charge of her dower lands, or the lands that she had held jointly with her husband, unless she had had some prior experience. She was often left in sole charge through her husband's absence on business, at court, on military campaign, on pilgrimage or on crusade, for example. Sometimes this could land her with unusual difficulties, such as the raising of a ransom. It is specifically for this reason that the French writer Christine de Pisan advised that 'wives should be wise and sound administrators and manage their affairs well'.[97] She had a great deal of detailed instruction to give on their involvement in estate management. Closer to home, men would hardly have named their wives as executors so often in their wills unless they were confident that they could perform the requisite tasks. The difficulty lies in showing this directly, at least before Margaret Paston's letters bring it clearly into view. One useful nugget is the warrant of Katherine Neville, Duchess of York, which was sent to her husband's receiver-general, ordering a payment while her husband was in London for the coronation of King Henry VI. Katherine must have been used to taking charge. She married John Mowbray in 1412 and from 1417 to 1422 her husband was continually in France serving Henry V. Despite the surviving warrant, none of the three extant receiver-general's accounts for the duke makes any reference to Katherine's activities, even though they all refer to years during which the duke was partially or wholly absent.[98] With landed inheritances to preserve, marriage had to be a partnership, even if it was in many ways an unequal one. Rowena Archer is surely right to say that, 'A common interest in expanding and maintaining the property in their charge promoted a sense of common purpose in which both parties played complementary and overlapping roles.'[99]

It is significant that the *Rules* which the mid thirteenth-century Bishop of Lincoln, Robert Grosseteste, produced in French, on how to guard and govern lands and household, were addressed, in the first instance, to the Countess of Lincoln and that they assume that a lord or lady may equally be in control. Moreover, Robert's management is a wholly hands-on experience. The first rule, for example, teaches how lord or lady (*seingnur u dame*) shall know for each manor all its lands, rents, customs, usages, bond services, franchises, fees and tenements, while the third rule teaches how he or she should give clear instruction to the steward on how to conduct himself. Presumably so that there should be no doubt, this was to be done in the presence of some of his or her good friends (*ses bons amis*). The fourth rule teaches how the lord or lady should examine their estate to ensure that they can live throughout the year within their means. And so it goes on, moving into the details of estate management and household care. The ninth rule, for example, tells them what to say to both 'the high and the low' of the household to ensure that all their orders are obeyed.[100] A generation later Walter of Henley produced his *Husbandry*, a popular work, also in French, which was intended primarily for the aid of lesser landowners. There are thirty-five extant manuscripts. Most were owned by religious houses but one copy is found in a commonplace book belonging to an English lady during the mid-fourteenth century.[101]

Given the considerable administrative burden on ladies as well as lords, it is worth asking how they acquired the necessary skills. In all probability, most of the appropriate expertise was gleaned through example and the experience of living in the midst of an active household. They must generally have been able to read, at least to some degree. The literacy of ladies is, however, a difficult subject, once again through lack of direct evidence.[102] They were effectively barred from schools. Many of them would have received some formal instruction at home during their early years. With chaplains, private chambers and some books, most manor houses of any significance will have had the necessary facilities. As far as Latin is concerned, however, very few will have had the opportunity to become more than functionally literate. A knowledge of scripture will have been acquired by constant repetition and reading aloud from prayer books. For devotional tracts and other works of a deeper nature, those so inclined were mostly dependent upon being read to. There is good reason to believe, however, that ladies were often more at home with French.

Another work written specifically for a lady was the treatise on language produced by the Essex knight Walter de Bibbesworth.[103] He wrote it, he tells us, for 'ma dame Dyonise de Mountechensi'. Two ladies of that name are known, but given the period when Walter is known to have been active, the Denise de Montchesny in question is almost certainly the wife of Warin de Montchesny. She was widowed in 1255. Walter explains that he wrote his treatise so that Denise could teach her children the vocabulary of 'husbandry and management', which they would need when they became adult. Walter assumes that the lady already has basic French. His aim is to improve her French beyond the language she has picked up colloquially. It is quite clear from the treatise that the mother tongue of both Walter and Denise is English. They needed good French, however, because it was the language of *gentils hommes*. Unless one knew French one was 'thought of little account', as the chronicler Robert of Gloucester was to write a little later. It is also assumed by Walter, incidentally, that his readers have some knowledge of Latin, that is of the Latin primer, 'the book which teaches us clergie'. Whereas French was a language one learned through speech and polished through learning, Latin by contrast was a language that was entirely learned.

Walter's book for Denise de Montchesny reminds us that some medieval authorities stressed the mother's duty for the moral and primary education of their children, and that some mothers, at least, took this very seriously. The Psalter, or book of psalms, was often used as an alphabet book.[104] A Psalter which belonged to the Countess of Leicester around 1300 has a charming portrait of the Virgin as a small girl holding her own alphabet Psalter under her mother's ermine-lined mantle. The portrayal of St Anne teaching the Virgin to read becomes increasingly frequent, especially in books of hours, during the fourteenth century. Iconography has its own history, and it is always dangerous to interpret

31. Medieval authorities expected that ladies would teach their small children. A popular image was St Anne teaching the Virgin to read

art as a direct reflection of life; nevertheless the popularity of this image suggests that it does have some contemporary resonance.

Altogether, the ladies played a major role in sustaining and transmitting gentility.

CHAPTER 4

Visual Representation and Affective Relations

It is widely held that the visual representation of medieval women was predominantly religious or, at least, located within a religious context. Certainly, this is true of the eleventh to thirteenth centuries. Naturally they figure in the depiction of biblical narrative, while the image of the Virgin Mary was of increasing significance throughout this period. As daughters of Eve, women were portrayed as temptresses, as embodiments of sin. Even the devil himself could be pictured as a woman. But they were also portrayed as personifications of virtues as well as vices. On the walls of Henry III's Painted Chamber in Westminster Palace, for instance, eight virtues were depicted.[1] Queens and other great ladies are shown in manuscripts as donors and patrons. Overwhelmingly, however, women are portrayed through the clerical gaze. In the borders of manuscripts, for example, and on buildings and church furnishings such as corbels and misericords, women are satirised. This is true even of their virtues. False charity, for example, is shown by the image of a woman feeding nuts to a squirrel. In the Gorleston Psalter, of the early fourteenth century, faith is depicted as a woman praying to a monkey masquerading as a priest.[2]

Ladies' seals are, therefore, a precious source for the twelfth and thirteenth centuries as they emanate directly from the secular world. Of course, iconographically and perhaps to an extent in form too, they owe something to the Virgin Mary. But, as we have seen, they also reflect secular concerns, for example in the matter of fashion, where the long trailing manches or sleeves, popular since the middle of the eleventh century, finally went out of fashion towards the end of the twelfth. Equally precious to social historians are tomb effigies. Once again, these owe something to the Virgin, especially the Standing Virgin and Child.[3] However, there were also strong secular influences. The fact that tomb effigies portrayed their subjects as living rather than dead allowed for increasing realism. People were shown predominantly as young, although not invariably so. Theologically speaking, they ought to have been depicted aged 33, and in most cases this is consistent with the image.[4] Fashion-consciousness inevitably played a part, as did the depiction of family identity and association

32. The visual representation of women was heavily influenced by the Virgin Mary: Virgin and Child enthroned (c. 1160), Notre-Dame, Paris

through heraldry. So, too, did the standard conventions of female beauty. From the twelfth century onwards, the ideal of feminine beauty, as expressed predominantly by male writers, both rhetoricians and poets, remained remarkably consistent: golden hair, black eyebrows, white skin, high forehead, nose neither too short nor too long, lips small and slightly swelling, long neck, small, high breasts, narrow waist, and long arms with long thin milk-white fingers. Facially the idealised lady was of white and red hue, her teeth ivory, her eyes sparkling and usually grey.[5] This courtly image was all-pervasive and even came to influence the portrayal of the Virgin, though she was never, of course, quite like other women.[6] Later medieval poets, including Chaucer, deployed these conventions in subtle ways, but they did not substantially depart from them. Effigies were normally painted in bright colours, and the loss of the paint naturally blunts much of the impact. None the less, the stock physical features of the idealised portrait are often apparent.

33. *Women were often portrayed as the embodiment of sin: the devil himself is depicted as a woman in this psalter dating from c. 1270–80 (St John's College, Cambridge, Ms. K.26 fo. 231)*

The stone effigy of the lady appears rather late on the scene in England, especially when compared with her male counterpart. By the middle of the thirteenth century the knightly effigy was becoming increasingly common in the churches of southern and middle England. In contrast, a survey by H.A. Tummers lists only forty-four ladies belonging to the thirteenth century, of whom fewer than a handful can be dated securely to before 1280.[7] Less attention is sometimes paid to the effigies of ladies than to their male counterparts, except perhaps in the matter of costume. Yet what they lack in vigour, as compared to the military effigy in particular, they often make up for in serenity. Movement was depicted by the flow of the garments and

34. The stock features of female beauty are often depicted in monumental effigies. Note, for example, the long neck and narrow waist of Lady Joan Beauchamp, Worcester Cathedral

35. Late thirteenth-century lady from Wickhampton, Norfolk. Note the sleeved kirtle with surcoat above, as well as the veil and wimple denoting widowhood

the folds in the drapery. The mantle was sometimes tucked up between arm and body, and this too was designed to give a sense of movement. Hands could also be used expressively. Two of the finest female effigies of the thirteenth century are of members of the royal family, namely Lady Aveline de Forz (d. 1274), widow of Edmund Crouchback, Earl of Lancaster, and Queen Eleanor of Castile (d. 1290), widow of Edward I. Both are in Westminster Abbey, and both belong to the last decade of the century.[8] No doubt royal effigies set the fashion in England in terms of style. As in much thirteenth-century art, however, French influence was initially strong, even if the English effigy developed along its own trajectory. Among the features borrowed from

36. *Opulent lady from Gonalston, Nottinghamshire. Note the canopy, the veil with barbette and fillet circling her beautiful hair, and the cloak worn above her basic garments. She is holding a vessel for holy oil*

France were the double cushion and the attendant angels, items which became increasingly common during the fourteenth century. Another was the introduction of 'weepers', a representation of the funeral cortège, instead of rows of heraldic shields along the sides of the tombs.

The three main items of dress that were visible on a living lady were all depicted in effigy, although in only a minority of cases were all three discernible. The kirtle may be shown below a gown or surcoat, with perhaps a mantle or cloak over. Sometimes a girdle can be seen. The late thirteenth-century figure from Wickhampton in Norfolk, for example, shows only the basic garments: a close-fitting kirtle with sleeves and a sleeveless surcoat above. The lady is wearing a veil and wimple, no doubt to denote her widowhood. The wimple is a kerchief covering the neck, chin and sides of the head. It is fastened beneath the veil, a thin piece of cloth which is worn over the head and falls loosely to the shoulders. Standing on a dog, the symbol of faithfulness, the lady gives an impression of simple and unassuming piety. The figure at Gonalston, Nottinghamshire, by contrast, is altogether a more ornate affair. She lies between a floriated canopy, reminiscent of Queen Eleanor's at Westminster. In addition to her veil, she wears a fillet and barbette, respectively a circlet around the head and a band passing under the chin and pinned on top of the head.[9] Between fillet and veil her beautiful hair is shown to good effect. Her cloak adds to the sense of elegance and opulence. As an alternative to the praying attitude, seen for example at Wickhampton, this lady is holding an object which is most probably an *unguentarium*, a vessel for carrying holy oil. Other ladies are shown carrying a reliquary or a heart. Ladies are sometimes shown with jewellery. A sadly weathered lady at Darlington, for example, wears a large diamond-shaped brooch.[10]

Ladies may be depicted on funeral monuments, then, either in a pious manner or socially at ease, although that is not to say that the two are mutually exclusive. At Easington in County Durham there is a late thirteenth-century effigy in Frosterly marble, a rather striking local stone. On her kirtle the lady displays popinjays, the arms of several families in the north east. She is most probably Isabella Brus (d. by 1285), first wife of John Fitz Marmaduke of Horden.[11] Elegant and engaging, the effigy appears at first sight to be simple and unadorned. The lady wears a long mantle, elegantly draped. Her left hand holds a fold while her right lies across her waist with her mantle draped in multiple folds beneath her forearm. Her headdress is quite complex. She wears a fillet and barbette, with her hair in a crespine visible at the sides. She is also wearing a veil with, seemingly, a wimple beneath. Her head lies on a cushion. The overall effect is charming and graceful. She appears personally at rest. Moreover, she seems socially comfortable, with her husband's arms displayed proudly on her body.

Heraldry soon appeared on female effigies, as it had on seals, but it was never universal. The loss of paint makes it difficult to know, in many cases, how far and by what means ladies were able to be identified. The effigies are not, of course, in any sense individual portraits, although it seems likely that in some cases physical characteristics were taken account of. An unusual case is that of Edward III's queen, Philippa of Hainault, who is depicted in effigy at Westminster in a rather unflattering manner as stout and matronly. As the effigy was commissioned in her

37. This graceful and elegant lady from Easington, County Durham, is probably Isabella Brus, wife of Sir John Fitz Marmaduke of Horden. On her body she displays the popinjays from her husband's arms

lifetime, she probably chose to be represented in this way. It is, however, outside the mainstream of English effigies, being the work of a Brabantine sculptor from the court of the French king, Charles V.[12]

Perhaps in many cases ladies were identified by their setting. At Staindrop, County Durham, there are three fourteenth-century effigies of ladies, together with one of a small boy. They are all undoubtedly of members of the Neville family, but there is nothing visible to indicate the fact today. Staindrop appears to have been something of a female Neville mausoleum for much of the fourteenth century, with male members of the family preferring, it seems, to be buried elsewhere. The fine effigy of Robert de Neville, for example, 'the peacock of the north' who was killed fighting the Scots in 1319, is at Brancepeth, while Robert de Neville, his grandfather, was buried at Covenham Abbey. The separate burial place for female members of the family, whether due to accident or deliberate policy, seems to have been unusual. It did not survive the century, however, as the two high-quality alabaster double tombs of Ralph, 2nd lord Neville, and his wife Alice (d. 1374), and John, lord Neville (d. 1388), and his wife, Maud, in Durham Cathedral testify.

The earliest of the Staindrop ladies is stylistically similar to the Easington lady, with its voluminous mantle gathered in folds under the arms, and it may well have come from the same Durham workshop, although it is in sandstone. The Staindrop figures, however, are more ornate than the Easington lady, with carvings more in evidence. The second Staindrop figure, chronologically

38. Effigy of a Neville lady (probably Euphemia) from Staindrop, County Durham. Note the angels supporting her pillow, the drapes of her cloak and her buttoned sleeves

speaking, has, in addition to a canopy above the lady's head, an angel supporting a pillow on each side of her head and a dog with collar and bell on her left side near her feet. She has a lion at her feet. Her mantle lies in long graceful folds and her hands are clasped in prayer. The buttons of her tight-fitting kirtle are clearly visible. These were ornamental not practical. She wears a wimple, with a veil hanging over her shoulders and fastened by a jewelled fillet. She is thought to be Euphemia, the mother of Ralph, lord Neville, who built the south aisle of the church in about 1343.[13]

By this time, however, the stone effigy had a rival in a newer medium: the monumental brass. Full-figure brasses began in England with bishops and abbots during the 1280s and 1290s, but the second generation, which opened in about 1305, is dominated by lords and ladies.[14] Provincial workshops producing brasses of various kinds appeared at Lincoln, York, Newcastle and Shrewsbury but, as far as full-figure brasses are concerned, London dominated at the outset. Here, two early styles were significant: the Camoys style and its variant, the Setvans style. The Camoys style is named after one of its earliest surviving examples, the brass of Margaret de Camoys of Trotton, Sussex, who died *c.* 1311–12. The brasses in this style are so similar as to suggest a single workshop origin. The facial features, as described by Binski, are: eyebrows shown as being continuous with the bridge of the nose; eyes wide open and gentle of expression, with a clear distinction between iris and pupil giving 'a frank and noble gaze'.[15] The drapery also has characteristic fold-forms and the overall effect is sober and elegant. Many of the same features reappear on the brass to Joan de Cobham of Cobham, Kent. Although she seems to have died before 1298, the style is so similar to that of Margaret de Camoys as to suggest a date nearer hers. One notable difference is the canopy, which in Joan's case is based on the work of the court masons who were employed during the 1290s and were responsible for the tombs of Aveline de Forz and Queen Eleanor of Castile. What we see quite clearly here, then, is a downward dissemination of design features from royalty to nobility. Margaret de Camoys and Joan Cobham are thus the earliest surviving life-size figure brasses. It seems that at this early stage in the history of figure brasses certain families took the lead in expressing a preference over stone effigies. These included the Cobhams and the Setvans families. Joan de Cobham was, in fact, the daughter of Sir Robert Setvans of Kent. Sir William de Setvans of Chartham, Kent, has given his name to a short-lived style, probably of the 1320s, which appears to have been a variant on the Camoys, and would seem to have emanated, therefore, from the same workshop.[16]

The Setvans style was more expressive facially. Its influence can be seen as far afield as County Durham. In St Edmund's Church, Sedgefield, there is a fine brass of a lady, no doubt a widow, wearing the usual wimple and veil over a gown and flowing mantle. She is a tiny figure, only a few inches high, but of fine workmanship. Two heraldic brasses were once positioned on either side of her in the south transept and were probably associated with her. They are now on either side of her in a glass case on the wall of the nave. One of them carries arms that were almost certainly those of the Lisles of Sedgefield, a chevron between two ivy leaves slipped.[17] One would expect the arms on the lady's left to be her own

39. The 'little lady of Sedgefield': this tiny brass of a widow of the Lisle family is in the Setvans style. She was depicted with the arms of her husband and her father

family's and those on her right to be her husband's; the former indeed corresponds to the Lisle arms and it looks, therefore, as though 'the little lady of Sedgefield' belongs to the Lisle family. The arms to her right bear an equally rare charge. They are a gyronny of twelve, the tinctures being *or* and a now faded colour. No local family has been identified with these arms. They were borne in the fourteenth century by at least five families, the most prominent being the Bassingbournes who had interests in Hertfordshire and Cambridgeshire but also in Lincolnshire. It seems very probable that the little lady was commissioned from the Setvans workshop by her husband or his family and transported to the north-east.[18]

The producers of these brasses were the London Purbeck marblers who had played an important part in the dissemination of stone effigies. The market was at first similar, although the brasses were to reach a wider clientele. It is not surprising that many features should be common to both. Heraldry figured on brasses from the beginning. Margaret de Camoys' gown was festooned with shields, now lost, while Joan de Cobham displayed two shields on her slab, one on either side of her head and immediately below the canopy. The 'little lady of Sedgefield' had two shields inlaid into the transept, one on either side of her.

One of the fascinating features of the lady brasses is the development of headdresses. Of course the veil and wimple is often found, for quite obvious reasons, and in terms of sheer elegance it is hard to beat. Take, for example, Dame Alice de Bryene of Acton, Suffolk. Dame Alice was the great-granddaughter of Sir Robert de Bures whose fine brass is in Acton Church, Suffolk. She married the Gloucestershire knight, Guy de Bryene, who died young in 1386 leaving her with two daughters, Elizabeth and Philippa. She returned with them to Acton. In 1393 she succeeded as lady of the manor of Acton. She died on 14 January 1434 and is commemorated by the fine brass in the north chapel of Acton Church. The brass is simple and elegant. She is dressed as befitting a widow: a veil with ample folds on to her shoulders, a wimple and pleated barbe under her chin, a plain kirtle without a girdle and a full-length fur-lined mantle. In the folds at the foot of her mantle a tiny pet dog wearing an

40. Elegant simplicity: the widowed Alice de Bryene of Acton, Suffolk

ornamental collar reaches playfully up to her. Above the canopy two shields survive of the original four. They show, as one would expect, her husband's arms on the dexter: *or, three piles in point azure*; and on the sinister these are impaled with those of her father: *ermine, on a chief indented sable two lions rampant or*.

There can be no doubt, however, that to carry a fashionable headdress was a matter of status. Fourteenth-century headdresses were often of the crespine variety, characterised by two cauls or nets of stiff gold wire which tended to be semi-cylindrical in shape. Alternatively, they may be of the type of veiled headdresses known as nebulé zigzagged, or else the veil-less reticulated headdress where the net enclosing the hair bulges a little at the sides. It is in the fifteenth century, however, that the most extravagant headdresses are found, often following the fashion of the French court. There is, for example, the famous horned headdress, the chimney pot, the mitre, the butterfly, and the bourroulet – the horse-shoe headdress with large spots as Jane Keriell of Ash-next-Sandwich is depicted wearing. Some are unclassifiable, such as the headdress of Joan Peryent, of Digswell, Hertfordshire. Ladies depicted without headdresses tend to represent young maidens, although this is not necessarily true, as it suggests unmarried status rather than youth as such.

41. An elaborate horned headdress, depicted on a misericord in St Lawrence's Church, Ludlow. Note that she is bridled, the mark of a scold

42. The 'bourroulet' or horse-shoe headdress of Jane Keriell, from the Church of St Nicholas, Ash-next-Sandwich, Kent

From the late thirteenth century we begin to find effigies of lord and lady appearing together. Initially the effigies were entirely separate from one another but, as Tummers notes, they tended to be of similar conception and execution.[19] Increasingly, however, we find effigies constructed together out of a single block of stone, or in some instances oak. A joint effigy is, in a sense, a celebration of marriage, and one might think of its appearance as a natural development once female effigies had come into fashion. A lady would thus be associated with her lord in the parish (or greater church), just as she was associated with him in life. There were additional social reasons why this should have occurred. If the lady were an heiress, then the joint effigy celebrates the association of his line with hers. It makes a public

43. The strange, unclassifiable headdress of Joan Peryent, of Digswell, Hertfordshire. Note also the exquisite jewellery

statement similar to that made when the introduction of an effigy or effigies followed a temporary break in the lordship of a manor. But there may be an additional and more specific reason for the introduction of the joint effigy at this time. It is possible that the appearance of the legal device of jointure may be directly connected with its development. It was becoming increasingly common from the late thirteenth century for marriage contracts to contain a jointure, i.e. specific property from the husband's side which now became the joint property of the couple and their heirs. Should he predecease her she would hold the property for life, in addition to the one-third of his property which she was allowed as dower by law.[20] Moreover, it was not only by marriage contract that the jointure was introduced. Any man could convey part, but rarely all, of his lands to a third party during his marriage with a view to the third party re-enfeoffing himself and his wife jointly. In the event of his death, she would simply continue to hold this land rather than it passing directly to an heir. Is it a coincidence that the appearance of the joint effigy should follow hard upon the appearance of the jointure?

Whether the rise of the joint effigy can be explained in part by such considerations or not, it is not without wider significance that lord and lady are depicted side by side. This is an interesting contrast to the way in which they are sometimes depicted in stained glass in donors' portraits, where the lady stands behind the man, as though she were of less account,[21] not to mention the occasions where the lady is shown as supportive of the man's chivalric adventures. This is depicted most famously in manuscript in the Luttrell Psalter, *c.* 1345, where Sir Geoffrey de Luttrell's wife and daughter-in-law help him prepare for tournament or war. But it also occurs in glass. At Drayton Basset in Staffordshire, Ralph, Lord Basset, is depicted similarly in a state of preparedness, but this time on foot. His squire is holding his horse, while his wife is handing him his helm.[22] There is one further refinement, however, which is fascinating from the point of view of affective relations. This is the phenomenon of hand holding. Tantalisingly, it figures on one of the very earliest double effigies, even though

44. An early example of a hand-holding effigy: the Bassets of Winterbourne Basset, Wiltshire

comparatively speaking it is a rarity. The effigy, in low relief, is that of the Bassets of Winterbourne Basset in Wiltshire. It may be significant that the male figure is civilian not military, that is to say it may well have been thought inappropriate at first for martial figures to express affection. It is possible that the figure represents the justiciar, Sir Philip Basset, although the late thirteenth-century date makes this perhaps less likely. The figures are in an attitude of piety and rest, with their left arms held similarly across their chests. Several features suggest considerable intimacy – their closeness, for example, with their bodies not only touching but positively overlapping, a feature reinforced by their enclosure within a cinquefoil. Then there is the inclination of his head towards her, and the reduced distance indicated by the similarity and informality of their dress.

In order to comprehend this phenomenon it is necessary for us to examine noble marriage. As is often stressed, marriage for the medieval nobility was largely a matter of family strategy in which material concerns were uppermost.[23] Although children were not supposed to marry until puberty, that is at twelve years of age for girls and fourteen for boys, betrothal could take place from the age of seven onwards; moreover, the Church's rules were sometimes flouted and instances of both earlier betrothal and marriage are known. In practice, the fact that children, both male and female, were expected to accept marriage partners in line with the interests of the lineage tended to blunt the force of the Church's teaching, finally accepted as law in the time of Pope Alexander III (1159–81), that marriage rested purely upon consent. If a couple exchanged words in the present tense, i.e. 'I take you as my wife', and 'I take you as my husband', then this carried the full force of the sacrament. Alternatively, words of the future tense, 'I will take you as my husband/wife', followed by sexual intercourse had the same effect. It followed from this that a church ceremony was not strictly necessary for a valid marriage, and clandestine marriages, however undesirable, were as legitimate as public ones. Nevertheless, the Church preferred marriage to be a public affair, and the Fourth Lateran Council of 1215 made the system of the banns general throughout Christendom. The banns were to be read out on three occasions in church, with sufficient space between the readings so that anyone who knew of any cause why the marriage should not go ahead could come forward. Priests were forbidden to participate in any clandestine marriages. As part of the same spirit of rationalisation and universalisation, the same council reduced the prohibited degrees of consanguinity and affinity, within which couples could not marry, from seven to four. The Church could not, however, deny the validity of clandestine marriage, providing that both parties had freely consented and that there was no legal impediment.

There can be no doubt that the nobility largely conformed to these principles. Although clandestine marriages certainly did occur,[24] they were relatively rare. Well-regulated and public marriage dovetailed with strategically motivated family control. Gentle families as a whole practised social endogamy which helped to strengthen them individually and collectively, that is to say they tried to arrange their children's marriages within a circle of near equals, distant cousins and neighbours.[25] We sometimes learn how they conducted themselves in such matters from bishops' registers, although this is often in the context of doubt or

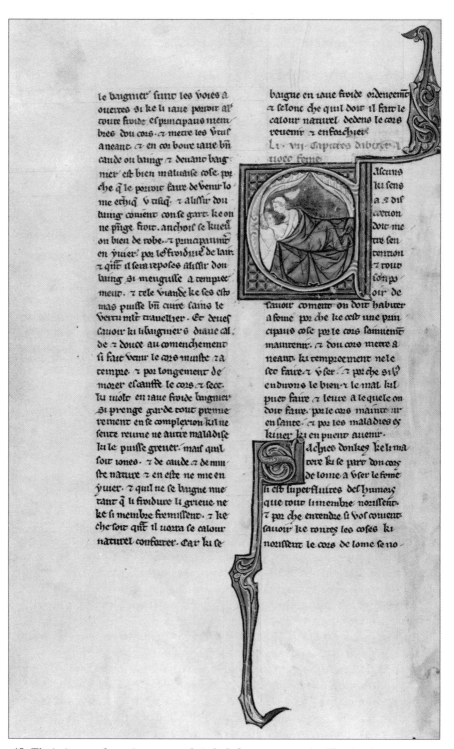

45. The intimacy of marriage: a couple in bed, from a manuscript illumination

disagreement. For example, the register of Bishop Godfrey Giffard of Worcester contains a memorandum under the year 1279 that on Sunday in the octave of Easter of that year, i.e. 9 April, in the porch of the queen's chamber at Woodstock, Sir Nicholas de Weston, knight, and his daughter, Amice, appeared with Sir Elias de Hanville, knight.[26] In the presence of witnesses, who included the bishop himself and the Earl of Warwick, Nicholas declared that he knew of no impediment to the marriage between Amice and Elias. The circumstances of the contract of marriage between them were then rehearsed. Amice said that on the journey from Northampton to Woodstock, the following words passed between them: 'I, Elias, accept thee, Amice, for my wife', and she answered: 'I, Amice, accept thee, Elias, for my husband'. After this, they exchanged pledges. The memorandum adds: 'And this was

46. The sacrament of marriage from the fifteenth-century font at Gresham, Norfolk. This is one of the best preserved of the fonts depicting the seven sacraments in England

done without compulsion but of their own accord, and there was no condition to the said contract.' Elias was then sworn, that is he took an oath, and he said that about the time of the feast of the Circumcision last, i.e. 1 January, outside a certain nunnery, they made a contract which they then repeated on the journey from Northampton to Woodstock. We can almost hear one of them saying to the other, 'Come on, we must make sure we say this in the right way.' Whether the families had agreed this in advance in this particular instance is not clear, but what is clear is that the marriage was now being made public.

The same register contains an entry which shows a marriage taking place in traditional fashion at the church door, although it was later disputed.[27] Before the bishop in the cathedral church at Worcester, early in November 1283, Thomas de Wychio, priest of the parish church of Hill Croome, deposed – that is to say he testified on oath – that on the feast of the Blessed Bartholomew the Apostle, four years before, i.e. 24 August 1279, Sir William de Montchesny and Amy, the widow of Sir John de Hull, were present at the door of his parish church with Nicholas de Hull, Thomas de Hull, clerk, Alice de Chester and others who were partly inside the church and partly out. The priest asked William: 'Oh, Sir William, do you wish to have the Lady Amy, widow of Sir John

47. The church porch, scene of marriage ceremonies: Church of St John the Baptist, Badingham, Suffolk

de Hull, knight, as your lawful wife?' William answered: 'I wish to have the Lady Amy as my lawful wife.' The reciprocal question was put to the lady and she answered in the same way. William then took the Lady Amy by the hand with these words: 'I, William, son of Warin de Montchesny, accept thee and I give thee my faith.' Again, the lady answered in the same manner. The priest then added, for circumstantial detail, that William had been dressed in a robe of black camlet and the Lady Amy in a robe of murrey colour, and that after they had contracted matrimony he solemnised their marriage in the church. He said that he celebrated the mass of the Holy Trinity, and that the service was solemnised in the morning before sunrise.[28] The priest further deposed that Sir William de Montchesny held the Lady Amy publicly as his wife until her death and that he buried her, as his wife, at the Franciscan friary in London, and that they had one child, Denise de Montchesny, born within wedlock. It was the legitimacy of this child, and hence of course her right to inherit, that was the issue here. Further depositions were made, to the same effect, by Nicholas de Hull, Thomas de Hull, who was clerk of the parish church, and Alice de Chester, who was in fact the chamberwoman of the late Lady Amy. The hearing ended with the bishop ruling that William and Amy were indeed lawfully married.

The nature of this dispute, a not uncommon one, helps to explain why it was so important to the nobility to deal publicly in such matters. There can be no doubt that they took great care, in general, about the legitimacy of their marriages. Consanguinity was a problem, especially as it covered not only biological kin, but kin by marriage and spiritual kin (i.e. godparents and their relatives). Not only were dispensations sought in advance over this issue, but after the fact as well, since people could enter into marriage within the prohibited degrees unwittingly. On 9 March 1290, for example, Bishop Godfrey Giffard examined the knights Sir William le Poer, Sir Robert de Bracy, Sir John de Thorndon, the Lady Petronilla de Tovy and the rector of the church of Piriton over the degree of consanguinity between Sir Walter de Beauchamp, knight, and the Lady Alice de Tovy, his wife. The bishop found that they were, indeed, within the fourth degree. However, as they were ignorant at the time they contracted the marriage that there was any impediment between them, he decreed that their marriage was lawful and their children legitimate.[29]

The predominance of arranged marriages, however, does not mean that marriages were necessarily loveless. In very many cases, no doubt, the girls were more than willing parties. An element of romantic love could sometimes enter into the situation. Elizabeth fitz Walter had apparently fallen in love with Reginald de Mohun – described as 'a very personable young man' – on the latter's chance visit to her parents' manor of Hull. He had stopped off on his way to do military service in Ireland, having been delayed at Fowey. She met and fell in love with him while he was hawking in the family's garden. Here, perhaps, family interests and personal inclination marched hand-in-hand; at least initially they did, for the marriage was to end unhappily. In 1333 Bishop Grandisson of Exeter appointed a commission, on the initiative of Elizabeth, to consider a divorce between her and Reginald.[30] Perhaps romantic attachment was always a dubious basis for marriage! More often, no doubt, affection developed after marriage. Although they should not always be taken at face value, wills sometimes contain indications of genuine marital love. William de Beauchamp, Earl of Warwick, for example, requested that his heart be buried wherever his wife should choose to lie.[31] A striking statement comes from a document known as a proof of age. This is where neighbouring landowners and others testify as to when a royal ward had been born, as evidence as to whether or not he had reached his legal majority. Their recollections are often by reference to personal details of their own. William de Quyntyn of Conyton, aged fifty-four, said that the heir in question had been born at about the time he had buried his wife, from which event he was 'almost mad with grief'.[32] A level of sentimental attachment within noble marriage was probably not at all uncommon. The manuals of instruction for secular clergy certainly taught so. In the early fourteenth century William of Pagula, for example, wrote that when a priest carried out the solemnisation of marriage he should instruct the man 'to put the ring on the fourth finger of his wife's hand. The ring, he explains, is a general sign of mutual love, while the ring is placed upon the fourth finger

48. Man and woman embrace, from an illuminated manuscript

because in that finger there is a vein which leads right up to the heart, 'and, likewise, the man and woman ought to be of one heart'.[33] Thomas of Chobham, writing in the early thirteenth century, says that: 'In contracting marriage a man gives a woman his body, and she hers; apart from the soul, nothing under the sky is more precious.' However, when the same writer proceeds to instruct husbands that they should correct their wives moderately and discreetly, and that a man's wife should be dearer to him than all his possessions, we have a timely reminder that the relationship is not an equal one.[34] The effigy at Winterbourne Basset hints at this too. In the midst of the depicted marital bliss, suggestions of male superiority remain: the fact that his hand is firmly over hers in an attitude of tender protection, her relative passivity, and the fact that his body is forward of hers.

49. A grief-stricken Edward I had elaborate crosses erected to mark the stages where his wife's coffin rested en route to Westminster in 1290: the Eleanor Cross at Waltham, Hertfordshire

50. *The hand-holding effigy of Ralph Greene, esquire, and Katherine his wife, at Lowick, Northamptonshire. Note the distance between the couple and the stiffness of the posture*

Curiously, as far as stone effigies are concerned, hand-holding seems to have been rather rare until a cluster appears in the late fourteenth and early fifteenth centuries.[35] Here the most famous examples are the effigy of Richard II and Anne of Bohemia, and that of Ralph Greene, esquire, and Katherine his wife, at Lowick, Northamptonshire. Ralph died in 1419. Despite the hand-holding, however, there is much less intimacy here than with the Winterbourne effigy. In fact, the figures are otherwise detached, front facing and a little stiff. The sense of distance is increased by his military dress and by his sheer bulk. Her headdress and his helm serve to distance them even further. Again, she is passive except possibly in extending her hand towards him. He has taken off his gauntlet in order to offer her the warmth as well as the protection of his hand. It may be argued that the effigy illustrates the sheer difficulty of depicting intimate details in this medium; his hand is held at an almost impossible angle. However, little effort is made to counteract the frontality of the figures.

Hand-holding is not the only way, of course, of depicting intimacy. An effigy at Inchmahome in Perthshire shows Walter Stewart, Earl of Menteith, and his Countess, Mary, in an embrace.[36] At Careby, Lincolnshire, a knight and his lady are depicted tucked up in bed together, presumably indicating that as they were in life, so they will remain together in death, eternally. The whole scene, moreover, is enclosed to reinforce this sense. They are not, however, attired for rest, but as in life. She is in veil and wimple and he in a mail coif. They are jointly, but at the same time separately, at prayer. When we examine them closely there is thus less intimacy than at first appears. Their lives are together but apart. His superiority is conveyed here by his size and forward posture, and by the prominence of his shield.[37]

Intimacy is a good deal easier to convey through the rival medium of brass. If there is a gap in the chronological record when it comes to hand-holding in stone effigies, this is remedied by the survival of mid- to late fourteenth-century brasses. The first to show a married couple[38] appears to be that of Sir John and Alyne de Creke at Westley Waterless in Cambridgeshire of around 1340–45. Looking at them closely one might perhaps detect a very slight turn towards one another facially, but essentially they are frontal and stiff. The brass is in the Seymour style. Just a few years later (*c.* 1347) we have a couple in the Hastings style. This is Sir John and Helene Wautone of Wimbish,

51. 'Together for eternity': at Careby, Lincolnshire, a knight and lady shown as though tucked up in bed

52. In this delightful brass the lady is turned towards her knight: Sir John and Lady Wautone of Wimbish, Essex

Essex. As the art historian Paul Binski puts it, 'The turning of the figures on their axis enabled the intimacy of marriage to be expressed.' True as this is, it is also the case that she is turned more fundamentally towards him, and in a rather reverential fashion, although it is perhaps not entirely clear how much of the reverence is for him and how much for God.

The earliest hand-holding brass seems to have been that of Richard and Margaret Torrington of Great Berkhampstead, Hertfordshire, in 1356,[39] while that of Sir Miles de Stapleton and his wife at Ingham, now lost, belonged to just a few years later (c. 1364). A particularly fine example is that of Sir John Harsick and his wife at Southacre, Norfolk, dating to around 1384. They are front-facing in stiff posture. As in the other cases, and with the stone effigies noticed earlier, her right hand is being held by his. She is clasped lightly and the overall effect is of an elegant but rather cold pose. In this the brass follows a general change in fashion, as the curvaceousness of the mid-century was replaced in the third quarter by a return to the gaunt, stiff frontality of the earlier brasses. There is more depth of feeling in the two fine brasses from Little Shelford, Cambridgeshire. The older, of Robert de Freville and his wife, Clarice, has the man holding his wife's whole hand firmly but warmly. Though they are front-facing there is, none the less, a strong sense of mutuality. In fact one can detect a slight sense of her body being turned towards his. The brass is of c. 1400 or just a

53. Robert de Freville holds his wife's hand warmly: brass of Robert and Clarice Freville, Little Shelford, Cambridgeshire

54. 'Deep hand-holding': Thomas and Margaret Freville, Little Shelford, Cambridgeshire

55. Sir John Harsick clasps his wife's hand lightly in this striking heraldic brass from Southacre, Norfolk

little before. The second Freville brass, of Sir Thomas and his wife, Margaret, is quite remarkable. They are turned towards one another, although she is perhaps turned more than he. His hand is again the dominant one, but they seem to be, as it were, deeply hand-holding, while the spread of her fingers makes her seem more animated and less passive in the situation. The difference between the two brasses is the more striking in that other features, such as the animated dogs and the male stance, remain very much the same.

One wonders if there is not perhaps a slight tension between the desire to portray mutual love on the one hand and the importance of conforming to the social dominance of the male on the other. One is reminded of the *Franklin's Tale*, where Chaucer has the chivalrous Arveragus making a pact with his wife, Dorigen, that they should put on an outward show for the world while sharing their lives on equal terms in practice. It was something of a morganatic marriage for she was of 'high kindred' as well as being 'the fairest under sun'. Having won her, Arveragus:

> Of his free wyl he swoor hire as a knyght
> That nevere in al his lyf he, day ne nyght,
> Ne sholde upon hym take no maistrie
> Agayn hire wyl, ne kithe (show) hire jalousie,
> But hire obeye, and folwe hir wyl in al,
> As any lovere to his lady shal,
> Save that the name of soveraynetee,
> That wolde he have for shame of his degree.

Dorigen responded in kind:

> She seyde, 'Sire, sith of youre gentillesse
> Ye profre me to have so large a reyne,
> Ne wolde nevere God bitwixe us tweyne,
> As in my gilt, were outher werre or stryf.
> Sire, I wol be youre humble trewe wyf;
> Have heer my trouthe, til that myn herte breste.'

Chaucer adds: 'Thus been they bothe in quiete and in reste.' (ll. 745–60)

In view of this, how exactly are we to interpret these fourteenth-century funeral monuments? Are they giving us access to a world of developing affective relationships, more domestic, more genuinely mutual than the relationships of twelfth- and thirteenth-century romances? Alternatively, are the conditions of social demand simply giving more scope to artists as they experimented in these media to display phenomena which had long existed? It would be a brave scholar indeed who would opt without hedging for the former. There is a third, perhaps rather cynical, possibility. This is that it became more fashionable to make a more outward show of affection, at least where social display via the plastic arts is concerned, but that this was an affectation overlying the continuance of a thoroughly and often brutally unequal relationship. Art, however, has a habit of re-impacting upon life, and if

56. Hand-holding without male dominance: Peter and Elizabeth Halle, of Herne, Kent

there were such a fashion it is at least arguable that it may have had some effect upon how lords and ladies might actually behave towards one another. While there may be something in this, it is salutary to remind ourselves of two facts. The first is that brasses and effigies which depict relationships are but a small proportion of the whole. The second is that mutual affection does not necessarily involve equality. In most, if not all, of the depictions discussed above male dominance is nevertheless present to a greater or lesser degree.

When all due caveats have been made, however, there is an argument for saying that the depiction, if not the exploration, of mutual affection within marriage became an increasingly strong feature as the fourteenth century progressed. It is an important theme in Chaucer. We have a royal tomb depicting hand-holding before the end of the century. Moreover, it is found elsewhere than on tombs, in the strict sense. A misericord at Norwich Cathedral shows a man and a woman holding hands in quite an intimate fashion. Judging by the associated heraldry, they appear to be Sir William Wingfield of Letheringham (d. 1378) and his wife, Margaret Boville.[40] Before leaving the brasses, moreover, it is worth noting that there are some in which the male dominance in hand-holding appears to be lost altogether. In these the hands are not so much clasped as held against one another. The brasses of Thomas, Baron Camoys (d. 1421) and his wife at Trotton, Sussex, and of Peter Halle, esquire, and Elizabeth his wife, at Herne, c. 1430, are of this type. It could conceivably be argued that this reflects artistic failure. One has only to examine the hands and faces to see that these are comparatively inferior productions. But it might equally be the case that the lack of male dominance is deliberate. The brass of Sir Edward Cerne (d. 1393) and his wife Elyne, at Draycott Cerne, Wiltshire, is possibly another example, but the positioning of the man's thumb perhaps retains just a hint of dominance. More striking than any of these is the brass of Sir John de la Pole and his wife Joan of Chrishall, Essex, c. 1370, where for once it is the lady whose hand is dominant. The hold is light but tender; undoubtedly she is unassertive, but that she is holding him is certain. Finally, we come to Sir Walter Mauntell (d. 1487) and his wife at Nether Heyford, Northamptonshire. The mutuality of this relationship is almost total. They are turned head and body towards one another and the hand-holding with the entire length of the hands seems to cement a mutual respect and affection. Again, the slight dominance of the thumb seems not to reverse the natural order of things but simply to negate the tendency for the man to dominate. Even his armour fails to overpower this sense of mutual respect. The very least that we can deduce from this evidence is that possibilities other than male dominance in marriage were conceivable. They seem to have been easier to imagine from the latter part of the fourteenth century. Nevertheless, strong mutual affection but within the framework of male dominance was imagined and depicted in effigy and brass long before this. If a more equal relationship was conceivable then arguably it is likely to have existed in reality.

One would dearly like to know more about how these images were inspired. Whose images are they? How much freedom did the designer have? How specific were the commissioners in terms of their requirements? Automatically one envisages a grieving relative or relatives commissioning a representation of

57. Just a hint of dominance? Sir Edward Cerne and Elyne his wife, of Draycott Cerne, Wiltshire

58. A lady holds her husband's hand: Sir John and Joan de la Pole, of Chrishall, Essex

59. Mutual respect and affection: Sir Walter Mauntell and his wife, at Nether Heyford, Northamptonshire

the deceased shortly after death. Often, no doubt, it happened just like this. But the reality was sometimes more complicated. A long time could elapse before an image was erected. In some cases its appearance had more to do with ancestry and claims of ancient possession of a manor than to the desire to honour the deceased. Matters of prestige were involved; the necessity of doing what was fitting and proper. Margaret Paston wrote to John Paston II, her son, 'Yt is a schame and a thyng that is myche spokyn of in thys contre that your fader's grave ston is not mad.'[41] On the other hand, we also know that the images could be ordered by persons themselves in their own lifetime.[42] Sometimes they figure in wills. On the whole, though, the amount of detail given on this issue in wills is severely limited. Isabel, Countess of Warwick, who died in December 1439, for example, arranged for her own effigy in her will.[43] Testators sometimes specified that tombs should contain images of themselves and their wives, but they rarely contained more.[44] Unusually explicit is the will of Sir Thomas Stathum of Morley, Derbyshire (1470). His body, he said, was to be buried in the south side of the chancel in the church of Morley at the altar of St Nicholas, under the low wall:

> and ther upon me leyde a stone of marble with iij ymages of laton oon ymage maade aftir me and th othir ij aftir both my wifis we all knelyng on our kneys with eche on of us a rolle in our handis unto ourr Lady saint Marye and to saint Christopher over our heedis with iiij scochons of myn armes and both my wifis armes quarterly to gedir . . .

Most interestingly, however, the extant brass seems to be based only loosely upon this specification. The figures, for example, are not kneeling, their hands are clasped in prayer, and the figure of St Anne is added to those of St Mary and St Christopher.[45]

More detail can be expected from contracts, but such documents are rare survivals for the late medieval period. The contract by which Richard II arranged for the metal components of his joint tomb with Queen Anne on 24 April 1395, while very detailed in some respects, specifies only that the images should be joined and that they should have their right hands holding.[46] One indenture surviving from the localities is that drawn up between Katherine, the widow of Ralph Greene of Lowick, esquire, and two male executors on the one hand and the two marblers of Chellaston, Derbyshire, on the other on 14 February 1419. The contract is for the construction of an alabaster tomb for herself and her husband, to be completed by Easter 1420 and at a cost of £20.[47] Many details are specified, including the eighteen angels around the base, the bear at her husband's feet, and the holding of hands: 'l'un des ditz ymages tenant l'autre per la main'. There can be little doubt that the lady was responsible for this. One is left wondering whether she and Ralph had ever discussed the matter in his lifetime. From Easter 1420 onwards she would have been able to gaze on herself and her husband in their state of eternal rest. A similar agreement was drawn up in 1515 between John Willoughby, esquire, and John Hippis, marbler of Lincoln. It specified:

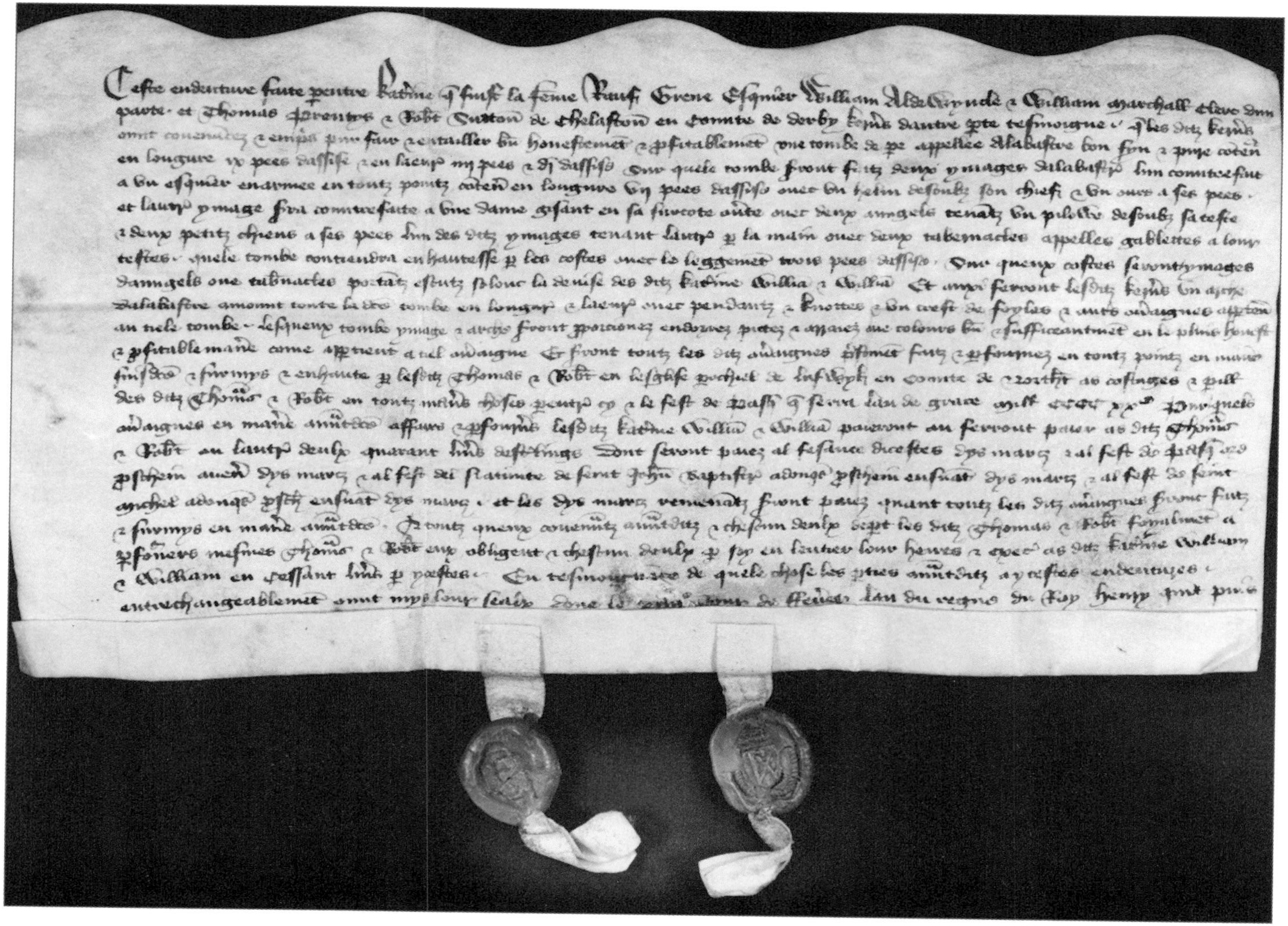

60. Katherine, widow of Ralph Greene, esquire, arranges for their hand-holding effigy to be erected in alabaster in their parish church at Lowick, Northamptonshire, 14 February 1419

That the said John Hippis shall make or cause to be made a Tumbe of the same stonne that my lorde Phitzhugh is of of vi fott in lenght and vij foote hight of the grounde to the upart part therof and in the backe stonne undur the vavyt [vault] to be made an ymage of a gentilman in his Coyt armye of copar and gylt and an othir ymage of a gentilwoman in hur mantill and Cyrcuyt of copar and gilt with an ymage of our lady over ther heddis with othir ymagis on of saynt John Baptiste and a othir of saynte Anne ethir of them a peticioner. And over yche of them a Scucion over ther heedis of ther armys with a scripture undur ther fett and by the sidis iiij Scucions of ther armys of Copar and gylt and this Tumb to be made aftur a patron drawne in parchment by the fest of saynt Anne . . .[48]

Two points are particularly interesting here. One is that the dimensions, at least, of the tomb were inspired by one that the commissioner had seen and approved of, which surely must often have been the case. John Hastings, Earl of Pembroke, who died in 1375, specified in his will that his tomb was to be as similar as possible to that of Lady Elizabeth de Burgh. The result must have been magnificent, for her will left £140 for the purpose.[49] Unfortunately, these tombs do not survive so that we cannot examine the likeness. It must often have been the case in the localities that people admired the tombs of their neighbours and sought to emulate them. The second feature of the Willoughby indenture which is of particular interest is the fact that a *patron*, i.e. a pattern or drawing of some sort, was supplied. However, this need not have been a detailed design. A manuscript in the British Library contains written instructions and crude drawings for a stained glass window commissioned by Thomas Froxmere between *c*. 1484 and 1488. They show Thomas and his wife as kneeling donors with their heraldic arms. It seems very likely that Thomas drew them himself.[50] Where monumental brasses are concerned, there can be no doubt that many customers must have chosen between standard patterns, often from pre-existing stock where only the inscriptions needed to be added. None the less, some of the trade in brasses, as in effigies, was clearly bespoke. There were surely times and places when a customer had some real say in the preferred design. One would dearly like to be able to see a woman's preference in a particular representation of hand-holding, not to mention a joint decision on this. One would give a lot, for instance, to know who inspired the comparatively slight but significant differences in the Freville brasses at Little Shelford. Did the Frevilles merely wish the second brass to be different, leaving the responsibility for the actual design modifications with the London workshop? Or did they themselves dictate them?

There are other ways of attempting to resurrect the sentiment expressed in the images presented by the tombs. Surviving letters, especially those of the fifteenth-century gentry, can be used to give us some insight. Margaret Paston's considerable correspondence to her husband, John Paston I, is remarkably consistent in the way that she addresses him. In the early years of their marriage she tends to open her letters with: 'My right reverent and worshipful husband, I recommend me to you', adding either 'with all my simple heart' or 'desiring heartily to hear of your welfare'. Later this settles down to 'Right worshipful husband, I recommend me to you', with or without 'desiring heartily to hear of your welfare'. This contrasts with his own (few) abrupt letters to her, which tend either to open simply, 'I recommend me to you' or to lack any address at all, on one occasion beginning 'I pray you see to the good governance of my household and guiding of other things touching my profit'.[51] Right worshipful seems to have been a generally employed form of address in a relationship demanding respect. John Paston III wrote to his elder brother as 'Right worshipful sir' and to his mother, Margaret herself, as 'Right worshipful mother'. However, when we examine the contents of Margaret's letters their relationship is immediately revealed as more complex. She generally manages him, in one way or another; occasionally she apologises, but sometimes she chides. To be sure, John Paston I was not the most attentive of husbands, and at times he could be quite tetchy. From time to time he asserted his role as master, at least verbally. But Margaret was no push-over. The dissonance between address and contents, encapsulating the distance between the public expectation and the private reality of relationships, makes Chaucer's pact between Dorigen and Arveragus at least feasible. As far as expressions of affection are concerned, Margaret and John are generally fairly restrained. Her concern for him is evident, not least from the way that she habitually signs off: 'The Holy Trinity have you in his keeping', and so on. Occasionally, we find affection from him too. After one of his rare visits to her, he wrote: 'Mine own dear sovereign lady, I recommend me to you and thank you of the great cheer that ye made me her', although the sentiment is rather blunted when he adds 'to my great cost and charge and labour'.[52] The letters of Margery Paston, née Brews, to her husband, John Paston III, convey a stronger mixture of respect and affection. In the famous valentines, written during their courtship, she writes: 'Right reverent and worshipful and my right well beloved Valentine'.[53] After marriage this becomes, 'Right reverent and worshipful Sir, in my most humble wise I recommend me to you'. On one occasion the mask slips when she addresses, 'Mine own sweet heart'. The visual depiction of affection within a convention of respect becomes believable when set against sentiments such as these.

Elizabeth Stonor is more tender still. Her addresses to her husband, William Stonor, are more variable than the Paston addresses. She, too, can use exaggeratedly respectful language: 'Right reverent and worshipful and entirely best beloved Cousin, I recommend me unto you on the lowliest wise that I best can or may'; but she can also write: 'Right entirely and best beloved husband I recommend me unto you in the most loving wise that I best can or may.'[54] A charming letter, dated 12 September 1476, which opens in the first way continues as follows:

And sir, as this day by your servant Thomas Mathew I received a letter from you, by which letter I understood that ye be somewhat amended and shall every day better and better than other by the grace of God. Also, gentle cousin, I understand that my brother and yours is sore sick of the poxes; wherefore I am right heavy and sorry of your being there, for the air of pox is

61. Intimate letter from Elizabeth Stonor to her husband, William, 12 September 1476

full contagious and namely to them that be nye of blood. Wherefore I would pray you, gentle Cousin, that ye would come hither, and if it would please you so to do etc. And if that it like you not so to do, Gentle Cousin, letteth me have hither some horses I pray you, and that I may come to you, for in good faith I can find it in my heart to put myself in jeopardy there as ye be, and shall do whilst my life endureth to the pleasure of God and yours. For in good faith I thought never so long sith I see you, for in truth I had well hoped that your horses should a been here as this night; and that I thought verily, and so pointed myself for to a be with you as the morrow at night with God's mercy, which should have been to me right a great comfort; for in faith I have not been merry at mine heart this sevennight day for divers matters . . .[55]

The letter is full of tender concern and betrays a level of intimacy and need hardly found in the better-known Pastons. A few months later she reminds him of an incident of which the full details are unfortunately lost: 'My own good husband I see well ye remember the putting at . . . out off the bed when you and I lay last together.'[56] Meanwhile, à propos of the frequent giving of tokens, she writes: 'Sir, I pray you send me no more rings with stones: for the ring you sent me by Hery Blakhall, the stone is fallen out by the way and lost; wherefore, I am sorry.'[57] She goes on to say, 'Good sir, let it not be long er I may see you; for truly me think right long syth I see you', as if to imply that tokens are all very well but what I long for is your self. There are no extant letters from William to her, and it may well be that he was more of a receiver than a giver of love.

In the case of his father, Thomas Stonor, and his wife Jane, it is the man who is the more effusive. Jane comes across as a somewhat blunt and perhaps short-tempered person, which is certainly how some people experienced her during her widowhood. More germane to the present subject is a letter written from Thomas to Jane on 8 October 1468: 'Mine own good Jane, as heartily as I can I recommend me to you . . .'. Having told her of the death of his mother and step-father and of several business matters, he continues: 'And Lemman (sweetheart), charge Wykys to get as much money as any be had; for I shall spend much money. And good sweet Lemman, be ye merry and of good comfort for to comfort me when I come. I can not come to you as soon as I would . . .'.[58] Hardly gushing and rather self-centred, perhaps, but nevertheless the language of love and intimacy is certainly present here. To be sure, these letters tend to reveal affection on one side of the marriage or the other; but it can hardly be doubted on the evidence they supply that Eileen Power was correct when she said that there must have been very many married friends in later medieval England.

Of course, the inspiration for these letters, most especially those of Margaret Paston, lies partly in the separation of lord and lady, in the absence of the lord from the manor. Many of the women's letters regret or complain of their husband's absence. This leads us to the question of how far they actually lived separate lives. The impression afforded by Margaret Paston is often reinforced by Christine de Pisan who, in *Le Livre des Trois Vertus* envisages the married lady being essentially responsible for household and estates while her husband is away at war, at court or wherever.[59] In recent years scholars working under feminist inspiration, especially literary scholars, have done much searching for entirely female social networks. In seeking essentially female audiences and, indeed, a specific female role in cultural production, these scholars have tended to exaggerate the separateness of the lady's life. It is certainly true that ladies were in touch with their female neighbours and kin and that these relationships could be invoked to good effect. There are also undoubtedly areas of life where men played little part. Childbirth is an obvious one, as is the ceremony of churching which followed.[60] It also seems clear that the lady shouldered much of the burden of educating very young children. In the religious life, too, there were some women for whom contact with men, other than those in orders, was undesirable. It is also true that men and women were generally segregated in church.[61] None the less, the effects of this can be exaggerated. The Pastons can be cited as evidence of the prolonged absence of the husband. However, there is every reason to suppose that in this, as in other matters, the Pastons were exceptional. Many men were absent from their estates in short bursts. Certainly, they expected their wives to shoulder the burden for them, as is the case with Thomas and Jane Stonor, for example. However, as Margaret Paston herself pointed out, too long an absence by the head of the household could be damaging in terms of the lord's interests, in dealing both with the tenants and with the locality. For this reason alone, many will have avoided it. As far as warfare is concerned, many men were away for single campaigns rather than for prolonged periods. Here there is a distinction to be made between the professional soldier, often unmarried and/or a younger son, and the established lord who played his part in national wars but not to the detriment of his other interests. Indeed, there is every reason to suppose that some military involvement was beneficial to his standing in the county when he returned. It may be true, of course, that London, with its many inns, came to be an increasing magnet for some lords. Even so, ladies, as we have seen, inhabited the same cultural world as the lords and, in the absence of their men, their lives continued to revolve around the household.

Lords and ladies, and for that matter their households, spent much time travelling and visiting other families. As we shall see, Sir Thomas Murdak of Edgecote was murdered while he was staying with not only his wife but also the greater part of his household at Stourton Castle.[62] Indeed, he was murdered by his entire *familia*. The household book of the Suffolk lady, Dame Alice de Bryene, for the year 1412–13, allows us to see the coming and going of her guests.[63] On many occasions, husbands and wives are found visiting Dame Alice together. On 20 October 1412, for instance, her household fed Sir John Howard with his wife and daughter, a maidservant, two esquires, two valets and three boys, William Clopton with his wife and one of his household, the wife of Thomas Pepyr with one of the household, a certain man from Sudbury, a man called Saltwell, who appears to have been a regular guest at the time, with two fellows, Richard Bonys with a fellow, and the maidservant of the manor. Altogether the pantry supplied 66 white and 8 black loaves, together with wine and ale, while the kitchen supplied a lamb, a swan, 4 conies, 5 partridges and 23 pigeons. In addition mutton and pork, milk and cream were purchased, while hay and two bushels of oats were provided for the guests' horses. Sir Andrew Boteler stayed on one occasion with his wife,

62. A gentle family dining with guests, from the Luttrell Psalter

maidservant and four of his household, and on another with his wife, maidservant, chaplain, esquire and two grooms. On 23 May 1413 Sir Richard Waldgrave stayed with his wife, his son, a maidservant, an esquire and six of his household, apparently for supper and extras, while two friars from Colchester with a clerk and Thomas Barbour stayed for one meal, and two other men were there all day.

This is not to say that husbands and wives were invariably found together as guests. Far from it. Sir Richard Waldgrave, for example, stayed on several occasions without his wife, but with members of his household. Ladies also stayed without their husbands. Among the female guests we find the wife of Robert Dynham, Margaret Sampson, Lady Waldgrave and Alice Boteler with members of their households. The most important point is that the Bryene dinner parties were often mixed, and that Dame Alice lived a very full social life. Some of her guests, like Sir Richard Waldgrave, were related to her by marriage, but many others were landowners and other personages from the locality. Whatever may have been true in some circles, including some elevated ones, Dame Alice de Bryene lived anything but a segregated life, and there is no reason to think this was true of a wife any more than of a widow. In truth, for the lord and lady of the manor life together and life apart were two facets of the same reality; although naturally some couples will have veered more towards one extreme than the other.

We should not be surprised, therefore, when we see them acting in concert. Legal documents show us formal relationships, as to a large extent do the visual arts. Once again, it is the fifteenth-century letters, however, which put the flesh on the bones. The element of partnership can be observed, for example, when they came to arranging marriages for their children. The Paston letters are a sure reminder that the ladies played a major part in marriage negotiations, even though the male head of the family had the more formal role. We see the respective roles clearly in the ultimately successful negotiations for the marriage between John Paston III and Margery Brews. On 11 June 1477 Margaret Paston wrote the following to Dame Elizabeth Brews:

> Madam, liketh you to understand that the chief cause of my writing to you at this season is this. I wot well it is not unremembered with you the large communication that divers times hath been had touching the marriage of my cousin Margery your daughter and my son John, of which I have been as glad, and now late-wardes as sorry, as ever I was for any marriage in mine life. And where or in whom the default of the breach is, I can have no perfect knowledge; but, madam, if it be in me or any of mine, I pray you assign a day when my cousin your husband and ye think to be at Norwich towards Salle, and I will come thither to you, and I think er ye and I depart that the default shall be know where it is, and also that, with your advise and help and mine together, we shall take some way that it shall not break; for if it did it were none honour to neither party, and in chief to them in whom the default is, considering that it is so far spoken.[64]

Thomas Brews, the father, appears elsewhere as the hard partner on the Brews side, and the conciliatory role of the women is clear enough. Margaret's letter is a skilled one, but its tone is predicated upon an assurance born of a practised and socially accepted role, a role which both women are effectively playing. But what is straightforward on the surface is often complicated beneath. An earlier letter from Margaret to Elizabeth contains this:

> But, madam, ye are a mother as well as I, where I pray take it non otherwise but well that I may not do by John Paston as ye will have me to do; for, madam, though I would he did well, I have to purvey for more of my childer then him, of which some be of that age that they can tell me well enough that I deal not evenly with them, to give John Paston so large and them so little.[65]

The letter seems to draw upon a peculiarly maternal sense of responsibility towards the children and upon a shared reaction to the exercise of that responsibility. However, the letter in question is one which John Paston III had devised for his mother to send as her own. Marriage negotiations, for the Pastons at least, were a hard-headed and manipulative business which might employ the full force of normative behaviour. Margaret Paston was a widow with adult children. Alongside her stood her eldest son, John Paston II, and his brother, John Paston III, seeking to get the best deal he could out of Thomas and Elizabeth Brews.

A glimpse of how husband and wife might work in tandem is provided by the Stonors. On 11 December 1476 Elizabeth Stonor wrote to William, her husband, as follows:

Furthermore, sir, pleaseth you it to wit that as on Friday last past I dined with my father and mother. And there was at dinner with them the friends [i.e. kin] of the child which was moved for one of my daughters at your last being here. And so after dinner they had their communication for the said matter, whereby I understood their dispositions how that they were disposed in the said matter. And truly it was nothing as it was spoken of at the beginning; wherefore I answered and said in this wise: that though she were my child, as she is, I could not answer that matter without you nor nought would do. How be it, I answered in your behalf: that I wist right well that ye would be right kind and loving father, if God fortuned that ye and they should deal.[66]

The child in question was a daughter by Elizabeth's previous marriage. However, her husband took formal responsibility. Although Elizabeth herself had conducted the major part of the negotiations, it was evidently invaluable to her that William should stay in the background holding a nay or a yea to the proposals. The separation of roles was more formal than real.

CHAPTER 5

Lady versus Lord: Antagonistic Relations

None of this, however, should encourage us to paint too roseate a portrait of medieval marriage. As has been said, those who sought to make a free marriage, had to 'resist both familial and feudal constraints'.[1] True, a modicum of protection was provided, both for widows and heiresses, in Magna Carta, but the extent to which this was a sudden step forward for women's rights has surely been exaggerated. Clause 6, for example, stipulated that heirs (including heiresses) should be given in marriage without disparagement and that before a marriage is contracted it should be made known to the heir's kin. It is clear, however, that some account was being taken of the question of disparagement before Magna Carta. Moreover, the other reference to the heir's kin was dropped from the reissues of the charter in 1216 and 1225. The real questions that arise are how much freedom of marriage actually existed for heiresses in the thirteenth century and beyond, and what were the consequences for the conduct of their lives?

The first point to make is that heirs and heiresses were not treated differently in law. The view that a female ward was penalised for refusing a suitable marriage or for marrying without licence, while a male ward could refuse without penalty, has been shown to be false. The plea rolls reveal hundreds of cases against males who married without the approval of their guardians, that is to say those who enjoyed the right of wardship and marriage. The legal action involved was known as 'forfeiture of marriage' and it was brought against both heirs and heiresses. The aim was to secure monetary compensation for lost rights. Many of the royal grants of wardship and marriage were purchased as speculative ventures, and they could be sold on for profit to a third party, for example. A guardian was not supposed to force an heir or heiress to marry; necessarily so, because marriage required consent to be valid. The Statute of Merton of 1236 stipulated that where an heir refused a reasonable marriage the guardian should be compensated by the value of the marriage. The great legal treatise known under the name of 'Bracton' tells us that this could be done either by the guardian holding on to the land until he had received the value, or by direct satisfaction being made to him. The Statute of Westminster of 1275 fixed the penalty for a ward marrying someone of his or her own choice while under age at twice the value of the marriage. The many forfeiture suits on the plea rolls were initiated by guardians seeking to realise the value of the marriages they had acquired. There are, however, many fewer cases against heiresses than against heirs. It may be that this is partly because the matter was more likely to be settled privately without action and partly because guardians simply retained the land as compensation. A case in 1278–9 shows an heiress and her husband suing for the return of her land from the guardian because he was retaining it despite the fact that they had paid for her marriage.

It is probable, then, that the canon law of free consent had some effect in encouraging alternative strategies. It is also true that heirs and heiresses could buy the right to marry according to their own wishes, although there are fewer requests from wards to arrange their own marriages in the thirteenth century than there had been in the twelfth. It could be argued that this is because the clause of Magna Carta relating to disparagement had taken effect and that a major cause of concern to families had largely been removed. Disparagement appears to figure only rarely in the records, although it does occur even in the fourteenth century. For instance, royal commissioners were appointed to ascertain whether Margaret, daughter of Sir Thomas Danyers, was being disparaged by her guardian. They were to inquire if the guardian in question 'has married or intends to marry her against her will, she being not of marriageable years, to an inept and insufficient person, which would be an offence to God and to the prejudice of the king and heir'. They were to examine her, both privately and in the presence of the guardian, John de Radeclyf, and of her 'friends', i.e. her kin, by which means they were to discover whether or not she was of marriageable years, whether she had indeed consented to the marriage, and 'whether the marriage be such as befits her estate'.[2]

The kin were another significant factor. The Crown sometimes allowed the marriages of heirs and heiresses arranged in their fathers' lifetime to be carried out after their deaths when their children became wards. Naturally, the kin were no guarantee that a marriage would be more to the liking of an heir or heiress. Most of the cases found in the records of the church courts where marriages have been annulled because of constraint involved not guardians but kin. Marriages that were arranged between children, by kin or guardians, could of course be repudiated when the couple reached the age of consent. One young man who repudiated an arranged marriage was John, son of Elias Giffard, whose father had found him a match in Auberée de Camvill. John was the famous John Giffard of Brimpsfield, a swashbuckling character who was very active during the baronial wars of 1264–5. His father, Sir Elias Giffard, died shortly before May 1248 when John was said to be sixteen years of age, or sixteen and more. He and his lands were therefore in the wardship of the Crown. According to one later witness, John avoided an arranged marriage by pointing out that he had married Auberée de Camville before his father's death. It is difficult to unravel the truth because this marriage was the subject of a dispute and of a royal inquiry late in 1259.[3] The witnesses were ostensibly recalling the events from memory; indeed, they were asked to say precisely how they remembered both the events and the dates in question. However, the fact that they were speaking on behalf of one party or the other undoubtedly coloured their testimony. What is undisputed, however, is that John repudiated Auberée at some stage or other.

As the documents are damaged we do not have all of the testimony. None the less, the gist of what was said on both sides is clear. One witness, Matthew of Brimpsfield, said that John was four years old when he was contracted with Auberée at Arrow in Warwickshire. She was aged four or five. He remembered the event because his father died in the same year, but he could not remember how long ago this was. He said that he had 'often heard John declaiming against the marriage and chiefly when he was of man's discretion and never saw them together after they were twelve or fourteen years old, nor did he [John] ever exhibit her in any of his manors'. Another juror, John of Rockhampton, said to have been examined at the instance of John Giffard's bailiffs of Rockhampton, said that John was twenty-six years old. He believed this to be the case because a neighbour of his had a son in the same year and he himself had lifted him from the sacred font. He said that he had often heard John declaiming against the marriage, and especially in the hall of Rockhampton in the presence of those who were lying around there. He reported John as saying that 'no one of the race of Le Longespey would adhere to any wife to whom he happened to be married in his boyhood'.[4] He did not know whether this was said in jest, however.

Another witness, John of Stonehouse, examined at the command of the bailiffs, agreed as to John's age and said that he had been four years and about seven months old at the time of the contract with Auberée but that he had never really married her. He, too, said that he had heard him declaim against the marriage. At this stage in the proceedings Auberée seems to have wept. The witness continued, saying that the girl had stayed at the Giffard manor of Rockhampton from the feast of Saints Simon and Jude (28 October) until the following Whitsun. When John came there and she questioned him – presumably asking him why he did not want to know her[5] – 'he answered nothing but afterwards avoided her presence'.

A variety of other witnesses confirmed the story. One said John was twenty-seven, another that he was twenty-eight. Perhaps the most reliable was John of Greenham Mill who said that John would be twenty-nine on St Walstan's day next (presumably the feast of St Wulfstan the bishop, on 19 January), which he knew because he had a child of his own who was born on the same day and would also be twenty-nine. If we take this date as the most reliable, it would appear that John was born on 19 January 1231. He was contracted to marry Auberée in 1235, perhaps during late August or early September. In October she was brought from her family residence at Arrow to the Giffard manor at Rockhampton, where she remained until the following Whitsun. If these dates are correct, John would have been seventeen on his father's death in 1248. This fits fairly closely with the inquisition post mortem following the death of Elias which gave John's age either as sixteen or sixteen or more. The dates in proofs of age are patently unreliable, and it is certainly possible that the correct dates are 1232 for John's birth and 1236 for the marriage contract, although it is unlikely that they are any later. The main point, however, is that these witnesses told a coherent and plausible story. It is highly likely that Auberée would have been supported in the Giffard household between betrothal and marriage. Such support was to figure in later marriage contracts. The experience must have been the more traumatic for a child if she was cold-shouldered when she arrived there. The implication of the story from the Giffard side is that she returned to her own family, perhaps at Whitsun 1236. The problem is that these witnesses were all tenants or neighbours of the Giffard manors of Stonehouse and Rockhampton. Witnesses from the other side told a different story.

Auberée was probably the granddaughter of Auberée de Marmion who had married William de Camville of Clifton, Staffordshire. The earlier Auberée had brought the manor of Arrow and other Warwickshire property to the Camvilles. The younger Auberée was not an heiress, but it was probably intended that she and John Giffard should have her grandmother's manor of Arrow.[6] The first witness on her side was Brother Richard, a canon of Studley. Brother Richard said that he had officiated at the marriage ceremony of John and Auberée on 20 August eighteen years ago, that is 1241. The marriage took place between the third and the ninth hour in the conventual church of Cook Hill (*Cochull Monialium*). The details of the ceremony indicate that it was properly conducted. The parties were first of all asked if they consented:

> after which the said John took the said Auberée from the hand of the witness [i.e. Brother Richard], saying 'I take thee to my lawful wife, to have and to hold all the days of my life'; and she answered 'I take thee, John, to my lawful husband, to have and to hold all the days of my life'; and so they mutually plighted their troth. Then, taking the blessed ring from the priest's hand, the said John espoused the said Auberée, saying: 'With this ring I thee wed and with my body and goods I thee honour.'

After mass had been solemnised, John took her back to the township of Arrow, from whence he had brought her, with 'a great company to feast with them'. Asked about carnal intercourse between them, Brother Richard said that John has a daughter by her, whom he supports as his own and who is now five years old. He also said that John had sought the king's writ to be allowed to raise an aid from his tenants for the marriage of his daughter. This would suggest that John was himself contemplating a childhood marriage for his own daughter. However, Brother Richard did not know how soon after the marriage carnal intercourse began. Asked how he could know or remember after such a lapse of time, Brother Richard replied, perhaps rather limply, that he knew that so much time had elapsed by the different places that he had lived before he became a canon regular, ten years ago. Asked about the ages of the couple, he said that he believed that John was eight. (In fact, if the events described took place in 1241, then John must have been at least ten, and probably eleven.) He did not remember the girl's age, but only that she was taller than her husband. As we shall see, it was in the interests of the Camville side to have the marriage take place later rather than sooner.

At this point, Brother Richard was asked whether he had come there to give evidence out of love for Auberée or out of hatred for the defendant. He replied, as one would expect, that he came because he knew the truth and for the safety of his soul. He said that he had not received nor would he receive any payment and that he was not connected by blood or affinity to the parties. Asked whether they stayed together as man and wife, he replied that as far as he knew from the reports of others they did so for more than five years, at Stonehouse, Rockhampton and

An early portrait in stained glass: Beatrix von Falkenburg, d. 1277, wife of Richard, Earl of Cornwall. Now in the Burrell Collection, Glasgow, the glass is thought to have been in the Franciscan Church, Oxford. (Burrell Collection, Glasgow Museums and Art Galleries, 45/2)

From marriage to annulment

(British Library Royal II D IX fos 288, 290v, 341, 269v, 282v, 334, 284)

Hand-fasting

The blessing

The feast

Litigation

Judgment

The wife disconsolate

Annulment

Carolle (round dance with music) in a garden, from a Flemish manuscript of the Romance of the Rose. *(British Library Harley Ms. 4425 fo. 14v)*

Visualisation was a significant aspect of later medieval devotion: Anne, Duchess of Bedford, at prayer before St Anne and her family, from the Bedford book of hours. (British Library Additional Ms. 18850 fo. 257v)

Lady receiving communion in her private chapel, from a Paris manuscript. Note the fashionable headdress. (British Library Additional Ms. 18192 fo. 196)

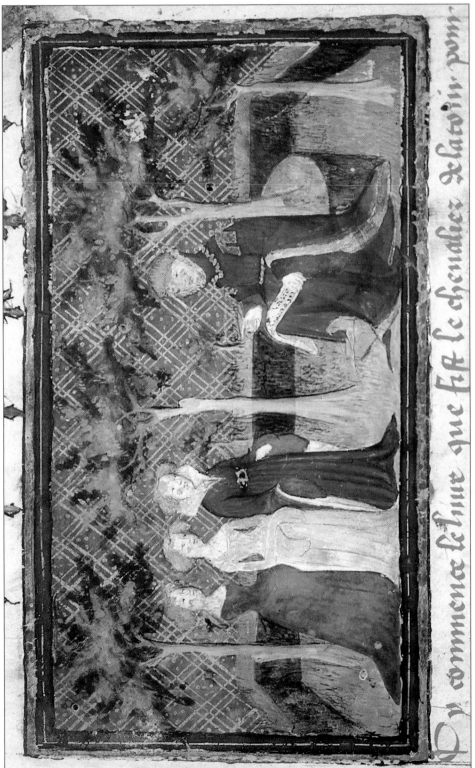

Geoffrey de la Tour Landry reading his book of advice to his daughters in the garden.
(British Library Royal Ms. 19C VII fo. 1)

The transmission of some prominent north-eastern arms:

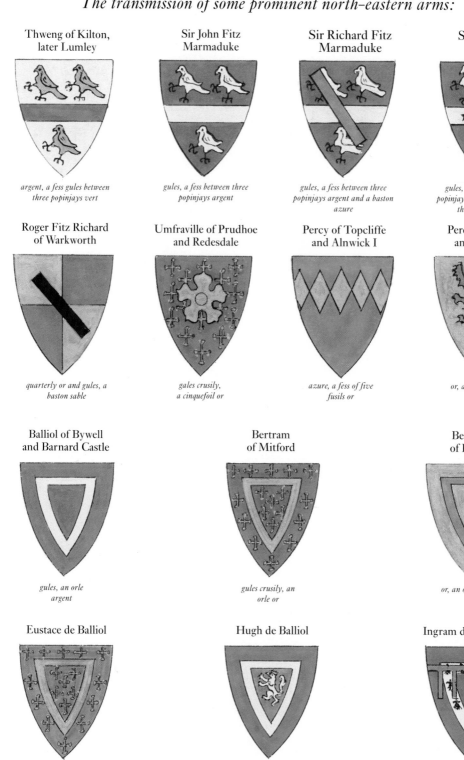

Thweng of Kilton, later Lumley

argent, a fess gules between three popinjays vert

Sir John Fitz Marmaduke

gules, a fess between three popinjays argent

Sir Richard Fitz Marmaduke

gules, a fess between three popinjays argent and a baston azure

Sir Robert de Lumley I

gules, a fess between three popinjays argent and in the fess three mullets sable

Roger Fitz Richard of Warkworth

quarterly or and gules, a baston sable

Umfraville of Prudhoe and Redesdale

gales crusily, a cinquefoil or

Percy of Topcliffe and Alnwick I

azure, a fess of five fusils or

Percy of Topcliffe and Alnwick II

or, a lion rampant azure

Balliol of Bywell and Barnard Castle

gules, an orle argent

Bertram of Mitford

gules crusily, an orle or

Bertram of Bothal

or, an orle azure

Eustace de Balliol

azure crusily, an orle or

Hugh de Balliol

gules, an orle argent, with an escutcheon azure, a lion rampant argent crowned or

Ingram de Umfraville

gules, an orle ermine, with a label of five points azure

other of John's manors. As to the clothes they were wearing at the time of the marriage, Brother Richard said that he remembered them both wearing green. He also affirmed that the local community regarded them as married. As to the time, place and cause of John's repudiating the woman, he said he knew nothing. It was Brother Richard who said that he had heard that John had avoided marriage as a royal ward on the grounds of his prior marriage with this girl.

The canon was obviously a very important witness. Other witnesses largely agreed with his testimony. Alice of Ragley agreed with Brother Richard, right down to the clothes the couple were wearing. She added that on the night after the marriage she saw them lying alone together and naked in one bed, which she believed they did more than a hundred times after. Moreover, she added, from then on John treated her as his lawful wife until last Michaelmas when he sent her back to her brother's house. She did not know the reason for this. She was present and saw all these things with all her fellow witnesses and many others.

Nicholas of Kingley also agreed with Brother Richard's testimony and added that Auberée was eight years old and more at the time of the marriage. Reynold of Ragley said that he was not present at the marriage but he 'often saw him treat her honourably as his wife, as he ought to do'. In other respects he agreed with Brother Richard's testimony and said that he could remember because at the time he was his father's attorney in the court of Auberée's father. Henry Ewerad said that he could remember the events because at about that time his wife bore him a daughter who is now eighteen. Robert Pretor said that the words used by John and Auberée when they had contracted to marry were as follows: John had said: 'Auberée, I thee wed and will have thee as my lawful wife as long as I live'. Auberée replied, 'And I thee, John, will have as my lawful husband as long as I live'. He said that he did not know how John had excused himself to the king, who had wanted to exercise his right to marry him during his wardship. Two others, Richard of Arrow and William of Arrow, also gave evidence. Richard, however, said that he knew nothing of the words of the contract. William said that he, too, knew nothing of the contract but only of the espousal. He remembered the events because he had a son born around the same time.

That is as far as the surviving documentation takes us. Auberée had produced considerable testimony in favour of a valid marriage. Once again, however, all but Brother Richard were of the immediate neighbourhood, if not the manor of Arrow, and can be expected to have been *parti pris*. Significantly, the document recording these testimonies ends with a memorandum that Nicholas of Kingley and all those who spoke after him, except Reynold, had lied when they said that Auberée was eight years old at the time of the contract. The implication is that she was actually under seven, in which case any marriage, or betrothal, between them would not be valid. It might well be that the two parties were describing two entirely separate events, a betrothal which took place at Arrow when the children were four and five years old, and a marriage ceremony which took place some time after. The validity of Auberée's marriage, and the legitimacy of her daughter, rested, however, on certain key issues. The Giffard case seems to have been that the marriage contract between the parties took place before they were seven years old, that John Giffard repudiated it well before the age of puberty (twelve for a girl and fourteen for a boy), and that they did not live together as man and wife, i.e. that they did not consummate the marriage. The Camville case was that they were legitimately married, that is to say they were of canonical age for betrothal, they contracted together with a correct form of words, and that they did indeed have sexual intercourse. On this reading, when John Giffard repudiated his wife he did so unlawfully. As so little of the testimony can be relied upon, it is very difficult to ascertain the true sequence of events. It seems plausible, however, that the couple did go through the ceremony at Cook Hill described by Brother Richard, possibly following an earlier betrothal at the manor of Arrow, but that they were still under age. It seems equally plausible that they lived together as lord and lady until he repudiated her, unjustly, at a much later date. Whatever, it seems unlikely that Auberée gained any satisfaction. John Giffard was to marry twice in future years. It may be significant that an Auberée de Camville was elected Abbess of Polesworth in north Warwickshire in 1277. Perhaps she was John Giffard's 'wife', or even his daughter.[7]

The important point is that a young man was able to thwart an arrangement made by his family, although he had to face considerable repercussions. Canon law put a great deal of emphasis upon free consent, but it would be naïve to conclude that free consent implied free choice, or that the equal position of male

63. A fashionable residence: the hall and north tower of Stokesay Castle, Shropshire, completed in the early fourteenth century

and female in law necessarily meant equal control over their own destinies. On the face of it, the fact that there are many fewer 'forfeiture of marriage' cases brought by guardians against heiresses than against heirs implies the opposite. In reality, people's freedom of action was determined by a complex mixture of rights, circumstances, and personality. And there can be no doubt that many high-born ladies had to fight hard to exercise any real control over their lives in the face of pressure from the crown, recipients of royal favour, and male relatives.

The histories of two thirteenth-century countesses of Warwick illustrate the point. The first is Philippa Basset,[8] the eldest of three daughters and co-heiresses of Thomas Basset, lord of Colynton and Whitford, Devon, and Headington, Oxfordshire. In 1205 Thomas purchased the wardship and marriage of Henry de Newburgh, Earl of Warwick, for 500 marks. Thomas duly married him to Philippa, who became his second wife. It was not an exalted marriage for a man of Henry's rank and it may well have been considered disparaging to him. But as a result, Philippa became a wealthy lady. When Henry died, on 10 October 1229, she was assigned a third of the Newburgh estate in dower. Meanwhile, she had inherited Headington, as her third share of her father's estate. On Henry's death she paid 100 marks to the king to be allowed to remain unmarried or to marry a man of her own choosing. By 4 November 1229, however, she had married the warlike Richard Siward, probably on the urging of her cousin, Gilbert Basset. In 1233 Richard, in company with Gilbert Basset and his brothers, rebelled. As a consequence, Philippa's lands, now controlled by Richard, became vulnerable. In January 1234 the Sheriff of Oxford was ordered 'to carry her houses at Headington to Beckley', where they were to provide the material for the rebuilding of the house belonging to Richard, Earl of Cornwall, which Richard Siward had fired. Meanwhile, however, she had been allowed to retain her dower lands and was given free passage to join her rebellious husband in the Marches. In 1242 their marriage was annulled. This may well have been because she had married under duress. Prior to the annulment, however, Philippa made an agreement with Richard for the equal sharing of their goods. But when it came to putting this agreement into operation they fell out, most particularly over the matter of Richard's debts. It was finally agreed, on 19 September 1242, that she would pay him £75 for his share of their goods minus the sum which he owed the merchants and which she would satisfy. She remained unmarried thereafter and died shortly before 29 November 1265. She seems to have regarded herself essentially as a Basset, despite her marriage to the Earl of Warwick. She was buried at Bicester Priory which had been founded by Gilbert Basset and endowed by members of the family, and she had herself given the canons 7s rent at Horton for a light to burn before the altar of St John the Baptist in their conventual church.[9] Her two marriages appear to have been determined by Basset family concerns.

More outrageous was the treatment of Countess Margery.[10] Thomas, Earl of Warwick, the son of Earl Henry, died in late June 1242. As he died childless, his heir was his sister Margery. Thomas and Margery were Henry's children by his first wife, Margaret d'Oilly. At the moment of Thomas's death, Margery was unmarried. However, that did not last long. By 22 August she was married to

John Marshal of Hingham, Norfolk, and on that day they were given seisin, that is possession, of her inheritance. In October, however, John died. The circumstances of this brief marriage are unclear. It may have been a pre-emptive strike on her part to control her own destiny; after all, she was one of the most eligible young ladies of her day. It may be relevant that the king had been away in Gascony since May. John Marshal does not appear to have made the journey there to perform homage and he was not styled Earl of Warwick. It seems unlikely that the marriage had royal approval. Be that as it may, Margery was now very much back on the marriage market. According to the provisions of Magna Carta (clause 8), a widow was not to be compelled to remarry as long as she wished to live without a husband, provided that she give security that she would not marry without royal consent, or the consent of her overlord if she did not hold of the Crown. The king determined that she should marry John du Plessis, a careerist in royal service. Once again, this was not a spectacular marriage in social terms for one as high-born as she and, for whatever reason, she decided to hold out against the marriage. On 25 December 1242 the king formally granted John du Plessis the marriage of Margery and the fine that she might make for marrying whom she wished if she could not be induced to marry him. She continued to hold out. On 26 March 1243 the king's patience broke. He sent a thunderous mandate to the Archbishop of York, the Bishop of Carlisle and William de Cantilupe.[11] The king had learned through experience, it read, that very many ladies of the realm had got themselves married obscurely (*indistincte*) to whomsoever they wished, without asking the king's permission and spurning the security which by law and ancient custom they ought to give that they will not marry without royal consent. Through this, both king and Crown were suffering injury and scandal. Because he wished to take tighter precautions in the future, so that further injury should not be generated for himself and his heirs through this kind of presumption and insolence, he was instructing them that, without delay and by the faith which they were bound to him, they were to take security from Margery, the sister of the late Earl of Warwick, one of the noblest women in the realm (*una de generosioribus mulieribus regni nostri*), and holder of a castle of enormous strength that was sited towards the Welsh Marches. As it was not expedient to the king that she should take any husband unless it were someone in whom he had complete confidence, they were to take Warwick Castle and whatever of her lands they chose into pledge, as security that she would not be united in matrimony with any man living without royal licence. If by any rash deed she should go against this, her castle and her lands so pledged would be forfeited for ever.

That there is anger in this is patent; but one also detects an element of weakness, petulance perhaps or spite. Nevertheless, Margery continued to hold out. In June she was named as solely responsible for the debts of the late earl, so she was clearly not yet married. By 14 September 1243, however, she had succumbed. On that day John was excused the £100 relief due to the king as the next tenant of the Warwick lands. But that was not the end of the story. It was not until April 1245 that John du Plessis was granted the earl's 'third penny', that is his share of the ancient royal revenue from the shire, and even then he was not styled earl. The most likely explanation for this was that Margery was suspected of having married someone else in secret, before submitting to the marriage with John. Had she done so, the king could not lawfully grant the earldom to John.

The next measure taken by the king was extraordinary. Should Margery die without heir of her body, the earldom would pass to Margery's aunt, Alice de Newburgh and her husband, William Mauduit. A group of royal councillors were instructed to arrange negotiations between John du Plessis on the one hand, and William Mauduit and Alice on the other, over the future of the earldom. Margery was not party to this. The resulting agreement, drawn up as a final concord in February 1247, stipulated that John would hold the lands for life together with the title Earl of Warwick. Formally speaking this was a purely private agreement, but the fact that only the king could grant the title betrays it as a political document. From August 1247 John du Plessis was styled earl. Although Margery was referred to as the wife of John du Plessis in the negotiations, the implication is that John did not expect to have children by her. Though formally married to him, she presumably continued to withhold sexual relations. On 18 October 1250 it was entered on the Chancery Rolls that Margery, Countess of Warwick, had bound herself by charter that if she should be lawfully convicted of having contracted matrimony with anyone before John du Plessis, Earl of Warwick, took her to wife, her lands would be forfeited to the king for ever. The king granted that if they were to be divorced on those grounds then John would hold the lands for life, after which they would pass to the king and his heirs.[12] The likelihood that Margery did in fact have a secret husband seems very strong. Poor, defiant Margery died on 3 June 1253. For a further ten years after her death, the lands of the Earldom of Warwick were held by a man whom she did not want and who very probably had no title at all to them. Even the land that came from Margery's mother, the barony of Hook Norton, was diverted from Margery's nearest heirs to Hugh du Plessis, John's son by his first wife.

Such ladies were victims, though not passive ones, of the intense pressure that the Crown could bring to bear. They are, therefore, in a special category. For any lady who was unhappily married, however, the consequences were potentially very serious. The husband simply had so many advantages in law. On marriage, a woman came under the husband's rod, as the lawyers put it, a phrase meaning essentially 'under his authority', but one with unmistakable physical overtones. It was not only legal treatises but practical lawyers who were insistent upon this. At the end of the thirteenth century chief justice Mettingham referred to 'primacy and mastery at the table and everywhere else'. Moreover, it was not only her person which the man controlled but also her property. Another lawyer put this crisply in 1299: a wife, he said, 'can have no property except in her dress'.[13] Any money or movable goods that she possessed became entirely her husband's. Strictly speaking, under common law, a married woman had no right to make a will since she had no goods of her own. However, the church courts encouraged the making of wills, and husbands frequently gave permission for their wives to do so. From the middle of the fourteenth century onwards this began to change and by the mid-fifteenth century such wills became rare.[14] With regard to a wife's own lands, there were certain complications but very little real restraint. The husband could sell or lease the land without reference to her. Only after his death

64. Wife beating, from a manuscript of the Romance of the Rose

could she cancel this, by legal action, on the grounds that she had not been consulted and that she could not gainsay her husband during his lifetime.[15] He could not go to court over his wife's lands, however, without her. In short, as Paul Brand puts it, 'the husband's power over his wife's property was power without enforceable responsibility'.[16]

What, then, was an unhappily married woman to do? In certain circumstances her marriage could be annulled. (On marriage, marriage litigation and annulment see Colour Plates.) There was no divorce in the modern sense of the term. The word *divorcium* had two meanings.[17] It could refer to annulment proper, divorce from the chains of marriage (*divorcium a vinculo*), or it could refer to a judicial separation, divorce from bed and board (*divorcium a mensa et thoro*). There were six major reasons for granting an annulment. One was the existence of a prior contract. The second was consanguinity and affinity. The Fourth Lateran Council of 1215 had reduced the number of prohibited degrees from seven to four, but this still left a couple unable to marry sinlessly if they had a great-great-grandparent in common. Even this was far from being the whole of the prohibition. Marriage was forbidden between spiritual kin and kin by marriage. The former covered the immediate family of those who had sponsored a person at baptism or confirmation. The latter, affinity, barred a person from marriage with the blood relatives of someone with whom they had had sexual intercourse. The third cause was impotence. The procedure adopted in English church courts to secure proof of this matter was for a group of 'honest women' to seek to sexually arouse the reputedly impotent man. Cases from both York and Canterbury are quite explicit in showing that this could involve a really thorough testing! The fourth cause was force and fear. Here the courts exercised considerable discretion. The duress had to be real, involving either imminent physical harm or loss of inheritance. There could be no annulment, however, if the couple had enjoyed normal relations afterwards. The fifth cause was the impediment of crime. This required not only adultery and an awareness of the existing marriage by both parties, but also either plotting the death of the other spouse or a promise of marriage during that spouse's life. The sixth major cause was marriage under age. A marriage contracted with a child below the age of seven was invalid. As we have seen, a child married between seven and puberty had the option of ratifying it on reaching puberty.

As an expert on the subject has written, 'The most striking fact about divorce litigation in medieval England is how little of it there was.'[18] In the surviving records of the church courts suits for *divorcium* were far outnumbered by those for the enforcement of marriage contracts. One of the problems arising from clandestine marriages was that proof was inevitably difficult should the partners disagree as to what had transpired. It is not altogether surprising, therefore, that the most common cause of marriage litigation before the ecclesiastical courts was enforcement of marriage contract. It may well be that some people who were married under age repudiated the contracts without any court action and that many who regarded their marriages as invalid simply divorced themselves.[19] After all, the courts largely considered cases on the basis of an action brought by an interested party. However, it does not appear from the records that annulment

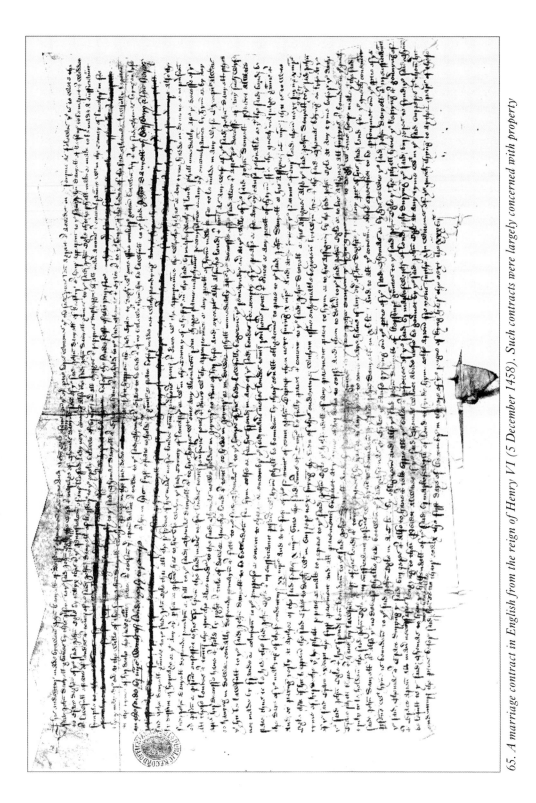

65. A marriage contract in English from the reign of Henry VI (5 December 1458). Such contracts were largely concerned with property

was easy to achieve, even in cases of consanguinity. The church generally preferred to preserve marriages. So where did this leave the lady? It is well known that in general the nobility were treated more leniently than other sectors of the population. They were more able to secure dispensations to marry kin, for example, and they seem fairly readily to have acquired pardons after the fact for marrying within the prohibited degrees. Annulment, however, is a different matter. They were able to secure annulments on the grounds of consanguinity and affinity, and it is also observable that men sometimes remarried in the expectation of acquiring a dispensation. How common this was, however, especially among the gentry, is unclear.

Couples can sometimes be seen making their own arrangements, as did Richard Siward and Philippa Basset, for example, when she made an agreement with him for the equal sharing of their goods prior to the annulment of their marriage. It must have been difficult for a woman to secure an annulment unilaterally, however, even if her case came within one of the accepted causes. Another possibility, however, was judicial separation. Church courts could grant this on three grounds: adultery, heresy and cruelty. Almost all the known separation cases in England were in fact brought for cruelty. On the whole, though, it seems that the courts tried to keep couples together wherever possible, and strongly disapproved of mutual pacts of separation. Moreover, the church seems not to have been concerned with the physical support of the parties, which was a matter for the civil courts. This must have held many ladies back from the brink. At this point they were largely reliant on their kin. There are examples of a woman being rescued from a husband who was maltreating her, but this was probably quite rare.[20]

One way out for a married lady was to find a lover and arrange her own abduction. This phenomenon caused so much concern in the thirteenth century that it eventually resulted in legislation. Clause 34 of the Statute of Westminster II, in 1285, provided that a wife who was living with her adulterer and who remained unreconciled with her husband at the time of his death should lose all right to her dower.[21] There can be no doubt that this provision gave rise to a new legal action, that of trespass for ravishment. This had appeared before the end of the thirteenth century. It was an action brought by a man to deal with the elopement and abduction of his wife. The action was for ravishment rather than rape, i.e. for abduction rather than for forcible coitus. The action was a popular one and it has been described as fulfilling a need. But it was decidedly male-centred. It implied that a wife was a form of property. Frequently a man sued for the abduction of his wife and for the carrying off of his chattels, that is to say for the jewellery and the clothing she took with her. Interestingly, in the courts it was occasionally countered by the view that a husband's boorish behaviour justified his wife's leaving him.[22] What the Crown courts could not do was order the return of the wife. For this a man's only recourse was to the church courts where he could sue for the enforcement of a marriage contract.[23] Perhaps they rarely did so.

There is no doubt that the new rule on dower carried some bite. In 1302 William Paynel and his wife, Margaret, petitioned the king for her dower as the widow of her first husband, John de Camoys. The king's advocate pointed out

66. *Jealous husband, from a manuscript of the* Romance of the Rose

that Margaret had in fact eloped with William and committed adultery with him. She was, therefore, barred from her dower by statute. The response from William and Margaret was extraordinary. They produced a charter whereby John de Camoys had formally granted his wife to William. They also produced certificates from the Archbishop of Canterbury and from the Bishop of Chester showing how they had been charged with adultery in the ecclesiastical courts and had cleared themselves. However, the king's court would have none of it:

> William and Margaret can not deny that Margaret in the life-time of her husband John went off and abode with William, altogether relinquishing her husband John, as plainly appears because she never in the life-time of her husband raised any objection, and raises none now, neither in her own person or by another in any manner whatsoever, but by way of making plain her original and spontaneous intention and continuing the affection which in her husband's life-time she conceived for the said William, she has since John's death allowed herself to be married to the said William; and . . . William and Margaret say and show nothing to prove that the said John in his life-time ever received her back as reconciled. . . .

Needless to say, they failed to get her dower.[24]

Despite the male counter-attacks through statute, elopement clearly remained a possible escape route for women unhappily married. The statute of 1285 offered some legal redress but it did not curb the abduction, or in legal parlance the ravishment, of daughters and wives. Naturally, widows and heiresses remained particular prizes. It is not always clear whether abductions were voluntary or not. Maud, widow of William Longespée, notified the king that Sir John Giffard had abducted her from her manor of Canford, Dorset, against her will and taken her to his castle at Brimpsfield. John appeared before the king, maintained that this was not against her will, and offered a fine of 300 marks for the marriage which had been contracted between them. The fine was due, in this scenario, for having married without licence. On 10 March 1271 the king ruled that if she were not happy with this, John should stand trial for his actions.[25] Given that she was too unwell to appear, commissioners were sent to inquire and report back. In the event the marriage stood.

An example of an abducted heiress is Joan de Langley.[26] Joan was the great-granddaughter of Sir John de Langley, a knight with considerable property in Gloucestershire and Warwickshire. John died in 1326 aged about 67. Two of his sons died in his lifetime, a third was a priest, and a fourth, Geoffrey, survived him by only a year. Geoffrey's widow, Mary, married Sir William de Careswell. The surviving son, Thomas, arranged a jointure of the Langley estates so that they passed to Mary and William for life, with succession afterwards to Geoffrey, the young son of Geoffrey de Langley, and his issue, and failing them to Sir William de Careswell's own heirs. Mary died in September 1333, but Careswell lived for another twenty-five years, keeping Geoffrey de Langley the younger from his inheritance. In the event, Geoffrey predeceased Careswell, but left a daughter, Joan. In order to maintain his position, William acquired her marriage and wardship. He married her to John de Charlton, who had secured possession of her inheritance, on William's death, by 3 May 1359. Two years later, Sir John de Charlton complained that Joan had been ravished and abducted by John de Trillowe, John de Langley (a distant cousin) and others. In the autumn of 1363 the parties came to terms. Charlton was bought off with a sum of 200 marks and £20 annual rent from one of the Langley manors. In the transactions, Joan appears as the wife not of Charlton but of Trillowe. It is possible that her marriage to Charlton had been annulled, but it could equally be that Joan had contracted an earlier, perhaps clandestine, marriage with Trillowe. Whichever is the case, Joan seems to have been a pawn in several men's ambitions. In fact, the struggle over her inheritance continued after her untimely death in October 1368. Trillowe now claimed to hold by 'the courtesy of England', as was customary if he had a child by her. Five other claimants were waiting in the wings to fight over poor Joan's inheritance.

A particularly interesting abduction case comes from 1382 when Sir Thomas West and his wife Alice petitioned the king's uncle, the Duke of Lancaster, for redress for the ravishment of their daughter. It is interesting for two reasons. It shows in detail how an abduction might be arranged, and it led to further legislation:

> Thomas West and Alice his wife humbly pray, that whereas Nicholas Clifton was lately with the retinue of the said Thomas on the last voyage to France and Brittany [1380]; and then the said Nicholas was familiar with the said Thomas for some time, until the Sunday after the feast of the translation of Saint Thomas last past [12 July 1382], on which day he came to the said Alice at her manor of Testwood in the county of Southampton, to ride with the said Alice to a certain place; and upon this the aforesaid Alice, with her son Thomas and her daughter Eleanor and others of their meinie, went towards this same place, by abetment and counsel of the said Nicholas, the said Alice having faith in him; and the said Nicholas led the said Alice to a great wood in the New Forest, where the said Nicholas, who was armed, had several other men at arms and archers by his ordinance and arrangement, in ambush with the intention of ravishing the said Eleanor; and he went and approached the said ambush, taking them with him, and they made assault upon the said Alice and Eleanor and their meinie with drawn swords, bows and arrows drawn back to the ear, and ravished the said Eleanor, with most evil affray to the said Alice and her company, who thought that the great and treacherous insurrection had been renewed [i.e. the Peasants' Revolt of 1381]; from which affray the said Alice has taken such illness that it is like to be the cause of her death; for which they pray remedy. [27]

Sir Thomas West also obtained a commission for the arrest of Nicholas Clifton and his accomplices. The horse and effects that were taken with Eleanor were valued at £45. Clifton had to secure a pardon. The events as related in the petition, however, should not be taken entirely at face value. Undoubtedly, the amount of violence or at least threat of violence was exaggerated in order to secure a commission. What we have here is a classic case of abduction. As a result of this case, or so Thomas West himself believed, the Statute of Rapes was passed at the parliament of 1382. This effectively disinherited a woman who afterwards consented to her ravishment. Henceforth, it was not only dower that was affected but jointure and any inheritance. The Commons sought the remedy, according to the official Parliament Rolls, because 'divers malefactors from day to day ravish women, ladies, damsels and daughters of the gentle of the realm'. Hot on the heels of the legislation, Thomas and Alice West petitioned again, this time that the statute should be back-dated to cover the case of Eleanor and Nicholas. They obviously feared that the couple had either married or would soon do so. Thomas and Alice wished to avoid having Nicholas as a son-in-law at all costs. The respective social positions of West and Clifton add some poignancy to the situation. Nicholas Clifton was but the younger son of a knight, landless and something of an adventurer. Military retinues such as that of Thomas West were often staffed by this type of man. West, on the other hand, was a successful son of a successful father, whose family was destined for the peerage. True, Eleanor was not his heir; in fact, he was to be succeeded by his son, Thomas. But she may have been his only other child and Nicholas Clifton was patently not the sort of man with whom he wanted a matrimonial alliance. It seems very likely that Nicholas and Eleanor were previously contracted in some way and it is interesting to observe the stealth Nicholas had to employ in order to secure her abduction. Whether Thomas was ever reconciled with them is unclear. He died in 1386. When Alice West died in 1395, however, she left money and goods to Nicholas and Eleanor and to their son, yet another Thomas; evidently she had ultimately been won round.[28] Of course, ravishment continued notwithstanding the statutes.

The most extreme measure a woman could take was, of course, murder. One lady who was accused of killing her husband was Juliana, widow of Thomas Murdak, lord of Compton in Warwick- shire and Edgecote in Northamptonshire. The Murdaks were long established in both counties. Thomas succeeded his brother, John Murdak, some time after 1298.[29] By then he was already married to Juliana, one of the daughters, and ultimately co-heiresses, of Sir Philip de Gayton of Gayton, Northamptonshire. Their son, another John, was seventeen

67. This fifteenth-century gatehouse is all that remains of the medieval castle of Stourton, Staffordshire, where Thomas Murdak was murdered on 11 April 1316

years old when his father was murdered.[30] Thomas Murdak and Juliana had thus been married for some considerable time before their marriage came to an abrupt end.

The murder took place on the Monday of Easter week, that is 11 April 1316, seemingly after nightfall, at Stourton Castle in Kinver Forest. The details of his murder and some of the events surrounding it can be reconstructed from the evidence which came into the royal courts, in a typically piecemeal fashion, over the next thirteen years.[31] After the murder, his body, headless and cut into quarters, was dumped at his manor at Edgecote, presumably in the expectation that a coroner's inquest would conclude that he had been killed locally. How long a time elapsed before any action was taken is unclear. The first that is heard directly in the records was during the Easter term at the Court of King's Bench in 1318 when the Sheriff of Warwickshire was ordered to arrest John, son of William Murdak, for failing to follow through his appeal against Juliana, Alice le Chaumberere and Adam le Someter for the death of his relative. John seems to have been Thomas Murdak's nephew and was probably his nearest adult kinsman, in which case he was the most suitable person to bring the ancient action of appeal, most probably in the county court. His failure to follow his action through left him liable to pay a fine, which was why the case appears before the royal court. The failure to prosecute did not necessarily mean the end of a case, however, for it could be continued in the king's name (or 'at the king's suit' to use the technical term). This is precisely what happened here, with disastrous consequences for Juliana. At the Michaelmas term 1318 the Warwickshire sheriff informed the court that he had conducted the formal process leading to outlawry. The defendants had been 'exacted', that is to say they had been summoned to the county court on four successive occasions and on their failure to appear the man had been outlawed and the women waived, the female equivalent of outlawry. In terms of the murder itself, however, what is immediately interesting is that the names of Juliana's co-defendants indicate that they were her servants. Adam le Someter was a form of groom (a sumpter being a pack-horse) while Alice was clearly what we might call an upstairs maid. The obvious suggestion is that it was a domestic crime. The names might also indicate that Juliana was at large with only a skeletal household.

The indication of a domestic crime is borne out by a second appeal. This was made by an approver, Robert Ruggele of Yelvertoft, who turned king's evidence. An approver sought to save himself from the gallows by undertaking to secure the conviction of his associates.[32] Robert made his appeal before the Northampton-shire coroner on Friday 30 September 1317. He named six other persons who were involved in the crime in addition to Juliana and himself. He also gave further details of the crime. The first blow was struck by William, son of Richard de Bodekisham, who was the victim's dispenser. He hit Thomas Murdak on the head with a staff as he lay in bed. When Thomas tried to rise he was stabbed by Robert the Chaplain with a *bidewe*, which was presumably some form of dagger, 'up to the hilt'. Robert was the victim's seneschal or steward, the man who looked after the financial affairs of his household. The fatal blow seems to have been struck by Roger the Chamberlain who cut Thomas open above the navel. Roger is described as Juliana's chamberlain, so that he too was an important member of the household. In short, the actual perpetrators of the killing were the knight's own principal household servants. The crime was aided (technically abetted) by William Shene, the cook, another of the knight's servants, and by Adam the Palfreyman who is most likely the man referred to earlier as Adam le Someter. Alice le Chaumberere is not mentioned, suggesting perhaps that her chief significance was her closeness to Juliana.

What we have then is a domestic crime but a domestic crime in a medieval sense. We are reminded of the nature of medieval private life, a life led surrounded by servants. The entire household seems to have been involved in the crime. Further names arise when the story is related by the jurors of Wardon Hundred when they appeared before the king's travelling justices, the justices in eyre, at Northampton in 1329–30. In addition to the others we now find Robert the Sumpter (*sometarius*); John, son of Juliana, chaplain; Adam Boffard; William le Taillour and three women, Matilda de Hastang, Mabel de Blayworth of Edgecote and Mabel, wife of Hugh the clerk of Edgecote. These last seem to give us the ladies of the household. The name Hastang, that of a major gentry family in Warwickshire and elsewhere, reminds us that the children of one gentry family could often be brought up in the household of another. Mabel de Blayworth had property of her own, so that she was not an entirely insignificant figure. Whether the additional men were all members of the Murdak household is unclear. Adam Boffard could be identical with the Adam le Someter alias Adam the Palfreyman we have encountered earlier. The approver had called him Adam the palfreyman of John de Vaux, the constable of Stourton Castle, where of course the murder took place, and Robert the Sumpter is similarly described as the constable's palfreyman here. This is a complication which we shall need to turn to again later. If Juliana plotted the murder of her husband she seems to have had his whole household, or virtually his whole household, with her, together with some of their host's.

Had Juliana incited their household against her husband? Or had his servants their own reasons to hate their lord? Were they simply manipulated by her? Some insight into Juliana's personality is perhaps afforded by the responses of two of the sheriffs towards her. The Sheriff of Warwickshire had rescinded his outlawry or waiving of Juliana, having been informed that his colleague in Staffordshire had her in custody. This turned out to be untrue; in fact, she had left the county. The Sheriff of Staffordshire had, therefore, made a false return. Either he had been incompetent or he had connived at her escape. Whichever is true, he had bought her some time. That she could persuade men to look favourably upon her is doubly suggested by the actions of another sheriff in a similar situation. This time it was a sheriff of Warwickshire who was at fault. After some further delay we find that this sheriff was ordered to bring the procedure of exaction and outlawry against her again or, if she appeared in his county court, to produce her at the King's Bench at the Hilary term 1320. His failure to make any return to this was followed by a repeat order to bring her at the next return day, 8 July. At this point he said that she had indeed appeared at the fifth county court, on 23 June, and that he had arrested her and detained her in prison. However, she was so ill and weak that he could not produce her without fear of her dying. She was pregnant, he maintained, and there was danger both to her and her offspring. However, it was shown to the court – it is not clear by whom – that she was in good health and quite capable of appearing in court. Furthermore, it was stated that the sheriff had taken her to his manor at Shilton, just across the county border in Leicestershire, where 'she wandered at her will out of prison'. Moreover, it was explicitly stated that the sheriff had 'falsely and maliciously made the said return in favour of the said Juliana and to retard the execution of the king's order'. He was therefore ordered to produce her on 4 October during the Michaelmas term. Like his predecessor in Staffordshire, he was now to answer for his false return. Had he felt sorry for her and the state she was in? Or had he been captivated by her? Not surprisingly, however, he now produced her in court and she was committed to the Marshalsea prison.

The remainder of Juliana's story is easily told. She was brought to court and questioned with regard to her late husband's death. Since she denied the charge a jury was summoned for 20 January 1321. A jury of twenty-four is indicated of whom twelve were to be knights 'girt with the sword'. They reached their verdict on Friday 23 January 1321. On oath they said that Juliana had feloniously and insidiously (*seductive*) killed Thomas who was formerly her husband. The word *comburenda* – she is to be burned – is written in the margin of the roll. The sentence was deemed appropriate because Juliana's crime was one defined as 'petty treason', analogous to the murder of a master by his servant or an abbot by one of his monks.[33] This barbaric punishment, although considered to be ancient, may have been adopted largely in consequence of its becoming the standard punishment for lapsed heretics in the twelfth century.[34] A particularly interesting instance of its use was in the Isle of Wight following the murder of a minor landowner, Simon of Atherfield, by his wife Amice on 21 March 1211. For several years local people venerated him as a saint and the Bishop of Winchester collected the oblations from his tomb.[35] In romance, burning figures as appropriate for a married lady found guilty of adultery. According to the prose *Tristan* it arose initially through advice given to Apollo by Gloriande, Queen of Leonois, and was consequently adopted throughout Britain and Gaul.[36] Whether Juliana Murdak was actually burned is unclear. The records of the royal chancery suggest, rather, that she was hanged.[37] If so this is likely to have been as a result of her status more than anything else. The number of instances of burning in both the thirteenth and fourteenth centuries suggests that people were not usually squeamish about it.

The murder of Thomas Murdak was clearly a premeditated crime. But by whom was it planned? So far discussion has concentrated solely upon Juliana and the Murdak household. There is, however, a further dimension to this crime. How the Murdak household came to be at Stourton Castle is unclear. It was common, of course, for noble households to receive guests. Households were itinerant and must quite often have stayed with others. Stourton was held with the keepership of Kinver Forest, an office in the gift of the king. It had been given by Edward II to John de Vaux in the fourth year of his reign. John was, therefore, the host of the Murdak household and almost certainly in residence there at the time of the murder. Although John, son of William Murdak, had appealed Juliana

68. *Record of the trial of Juliana Murdak, convicted of the murder of her husband in January 1321. Note the abbreviated word* comburenda *– 'she is to be burned' – in the bottom left-hand margin*

and the two servants for the killing, an inquisition before the Staffordshire keepers of the peace named Juliana, Robert de Yelvertoft, Roger who was Juliana's chamberlain, William son of Richard, the esquire of Sir Thomas Murdak, and Matilda de Hastang, with the assent and procurement of Sir John de Vaux, Elias his brother and Robert the chaplain of the said Thomas. Robert de Yelvertoft was none other than Robert Ruggele of Yelvertoft who turned approver in September 1317. The story he told, which gives us the details of the crime and implicates Thomas's household in the actual murder, also identifies Sir John de Vaux as the prime mover. He was commanded and sent by Sir John, he said, to commit the felony. Juliana he accused of abetting the crime rather than being the principal instigator. This, at least, was according to the account as it was reported in the Court of King's Bench at Michaelmas term 1320. By this time the approver had died. The summary account on the Eyre Roll of 1329/30 puts it slightly differently. John he accused of counsel, precept and mandate, Juliana of counsel and precept, the three principal servants of the actual crime and the two others of abetting the crime. In other words it seems that John and Juliana planned the crime while John himself sent Robert Ruggele to see that it was carried out.

John de Vaux was found in the City of London and delivered to the custody of the Constable of the Tower. Brought into court he claimed benefit of clergy, or in other words that as a cleric he should escape the jurisdiction of the royal court and be tried before ecclesiastical judges. He claimed then that he should not have to answer the charge without the presence of the ordinary, the ecclesiastical official who, in theory at least, would determine his status. This was not yet a matter only of ascertaining literacy, as it became later, but also of examining the man's tonsure and his letters of ordination. There was, however, one common bar to benefit of clergy for men in lower orders (i.e. below subdeacon), which is undoubtedly what John de Vaux was claiming to be, and that was bigamy. The definition of bigamy, however, covered not only a clerk who was twice married but also a clerk who had married a widow.[38] It was duly objected that John was indeed a bigamist, having married Juliana at Lichfield on Thursday 15 April 1316, i.e. three days after the murder of Thomas Murdak, and had kept her as his wife until the present time. The sheriff was ordered to produce a jury of twenty-four of whom twelve were to be knights 'girt with the sword' on 20 January 1321 to decide this issue. This was the same day as Juliana was convicted; the jurors may well have been the same. The jury confirmed that he was a bigamist, having married Juliana on the day mentioned. As regards the felony itself, a second jury was summoned for the Easter term. The verdict of the named jury was finally delivered, over three years later, on 25 June 1324. They found that John was not guilty of the said death, nor of sending or procuring or abetting it. He was therefore acquitted.

Can we trust in this verdict, the verdict of a group of male landowners? Of course, we cannot know the evidence which they had before them. However, the circumstances are very much against John de Vaux. Admittedly, the evidence of the approver is suspect in that it was in his interests to offer as much additional information as possible and to incriminate others. The effect of widening involvement in the crime would also have been to have taken some of the heat off Juliana. After all, others had responded to her in the same way. On the other hand, the circumstantial detail offered by the approver seems impressive. Moreover, the original indictment before the keepers had named John de Vaux among the guilty parties. The murder was committed at his home. Some of the dead man's household seem to have joined his household afterwards. According to the 1329/30 record the perpetrators included Roger the chamberlain of John de Vaux, elsewhere referred to as belonging to the Murdak household, while the approver tells us that William Shene, servant of Thomas Murdak, had become John's cook. Of course, it could be argued that these men simply joined the new household with Juliana. However, it does look as though his own servants were also involved, i.e. Robert the Sumpterman who sounds suspiciously like the approver, and Adam Kyng, John's groom (*palfridarius*). That these men were lowly servants involved in transportation, as it were, might suggest that John de Vaux was not present at the castle that evening and that he was either expected or had recently left. It is just conceivable that John was not party to the crime, but it is difficult to believe it. What we can say for certain is that the murder was committed by the dead man's household together with servants of John de Vaux in the latter's home. Did he believe that Thomas had been killed at Edgecote? Could all of this have been perpetrated without his awareness or suspicion? He certainly married the widow in undue haste. If he were not a party to the crime, then John de Vaux must have been extremely naïve.

The very least that can be said is that the jury gave John the benefit of the doubt. The jury which convicted Juliana was also, of course, all male. Of all the defendants in the case, of whom there were at least fifteen, she was the only one to suffer the penalty. Everything seems to indicate a serious disparity in the way Juliana and John were treated, perhaps signifying a difference in the way their crimes were perceived by a (male) locality.[39] It leads one to suspect that an element in her conviction was the suspicion of sexual immorality. It is here that the formal exclusion of women from public life, and the underlying patriarchal attitude it reflects, has practical consequences.

One wonders how Juliana was perceived at Gayton. In the north chapel of Gayton Church there are three effigies. The first of these, an early fourteenth-century knight, is undoubtedly Juliana's father, Sir Philip de Gayton. The second is a lady, thought to be Scholastica, Juliana's sister and co-heir, who married Geoffrey de Meux. Above this effigy and resting upon corbels is a third effigy, that of a small child. It was discovered in 1830 built into the exterior wall at the east end of the chapel, and facing inwards. It was rescued from there and placed in its present position. The following words are inscribed in the stone: 'Here lies entombed Mabel daughter of Thomas de . . . (*Hic jacet in tumba Mabila filia Thome de . . .*).' The last word is worn away. It has been suggested that it read Murdak, that the stone had been defaced, and that here we have the child that Juliana was carrying during her imprisonment.[40] Sadly, this seems unlikely. There seems insufficient room for the missing word to have been Murdak. Moreover, neither of the mutilated coats of arms at the head of the effigy corresponds to the Murdak arms.[41] On the other hand, one of them does correspond to arms borne by a member of the Gayton family, Sir John de Gayton of Rutland.[42] It seems then that the dead child was indeed a Gayton, but not a Murdak.

69. Wooden effigy of Sir Philip de Gayton, father of Juliana

It should not be assumed that an accusation of petty treason would invariably result in the execution of the dead man's wife. A remarkably similar case occurred in Lincolnshire in 1375. Here the widow was eventually acquitted. Sir William Cantilupe was murdered at his home in Scotton, while lying in his bed at night.[43] The twelve persons indicted included his wife, Maud, Agatha her maid, Sir William's steward and Richard Gyse, his esquire. The killers had bathed the body after the murder and carried it in a sack for 4 miles. They then dressed it in rich garments, together with sword belt and spurs. Another local landowner, Sir Ralph Paynel, was accused of harbouring the four principal suspects at his manor in Caythorpe. The case proceeded rather differently from the Murdak one, however. Maud herself 'appealed' her fellow suspects of the crime, as an innocent widow would have been expected to do. When the Court of King's Bench visited Lincolnshire in the autumn of 1375, she withdrew her appeal. Maud and the steward were then tried and found innocent. No one was brought to book. The case against Maud seems less clear-cut than that against Juliana. Another major difference between this and the Murdak case, however, was the lack of sexual innuendo. Although Maud did indeed marry again, it was not for a few years and not to Sir Ralph Paynel. The context of Ralph's involvement would appear to have been the familiar one of gentry feuding. It seems highly likely that Juliana Murdak was a sexually bewitching woman, and this may well have influenced opinion against her. One is reminded of the attitude of contemporary judges towards rape.

70. *Effigies of Scholastica, sister of Juliana, and the child, Mabel de Gayton, once thought to have been the daughter of Juliana*

Glanvill's treatise on the laws and customs of England, written 1187–9, tells us that in his day the appropriate penalty for rape, as for other 'felonies' was execution.[44] The treatise known under the name of 'Bracton', written a half-century later, indicates that the official penalty had by then softened, and clearly bemoans the fact.[45] The rape of a woman (*raptus mulieris*) is forbidden by both human and divine law. The defilers of virginity and chastity are akin to murderers, he argues, since those conditions cannot be restored, while virgins and widows, like nuns, are dedicated to God and their defilement is effectively a crime against Him. Moreover, there is no other way that this infamy can be contained. He applauds the ancient laws of the Romans, the Franks and the English, where not only the perpetrator and his abettors, but also any animal that was with him – his horse, his greyhound or his hawk – suffered severe penalties. In those days even if a woman had been a whore before, she was not a whore then because in crying out against the evil deed she had refused her consent. In Bracton's time the rape of a virgin was punished by the loss of eyes and testicles: the eyes because it was they which had given the man the sight of the maiden's beauty and his testicles because it was they that had excited his lust. Lesser punishments were considered more appropriate for the rape of others – married women, respectable widows, nuns, acknowledged concubines, even prostitutes – for they were all under the king's peace; unfortunately, Bracton does not tell us what these punishments were.

The standard procedure in such cases, established by Glanvill's day, was for the wronged woman to bring an action of appeal against her attacker. An appeal brought by a woman was procedurally different from one brought by a man. As a woman could not offer battle, as long as she made no technical errors in her appeal, the accused had either to go to the ordeal or offer a fine for a special inquest. After the abolition of the ordeal following the Fourth Lateran Council of 1215, the appeal, if it went through to its conclusion, would automatically come before a jury. Some legal historians have expected to find accusations of rape being brought maliciously, and have maintained this even against the run of existing evidence. Thus, for example, C.A.F. Meekings in his study of the Wiltshire Crown Pleas of 1249 wrote: 'The procedural advantages which a woman possessed in an appeal of rape caused the justices to look keenly at most such appeals, especially against accessories. It was frequently found that such appeals had been instigated by enemies of the appellee, who made use of the women as a tool in order to defame and embarrass a prominent neighbour. It is a little remarkable that our roll has no example of this sort.'[46] This view has been reiterated despite the fact that relatively few examples have actually been found. In his introduction to the 1235 Surrey Eyre, Meekings added: 'A woman thus possessed a great procedural advantage. This presented a strong temptation to cunning men. If they were at odds with a neighbour they might persuade a woman, say the daughter of one of their tenants, to bring an appeal against him and thereby, if all went successfully, at least seriously embarrass him, at best ruin him . . . about half the surviving eyre rolls show the justices discovering at least one example of it in appeals of rape.'[47] Moreover, the fact that this was a regular exception which a man might invoke against the validity of a case means that it could be used by a defendant, though guilty, to cast serious doubt upon his guilt. Even so, the incidence is not particularly high.[48]

The dearth of such cases is not, in fact, surprising. Seeking justice against a rapist must have been an arduous and deeply unpleasant experience, just as it is today. Bracton's treatise describes the entire procedure. The raped woman had to raise the hue and cry, go immediately to the neighbouring townships and there show to men of good repute the injury that had been done to her, the blood and blood-stained clothing, and her torn garments. She had then to go to the reeve of the hundred in which the crime had been committed, to the king's sergeant, to the coroners and to the sheriff. After that, she had to make her appeal at the next county court. She could go straight to the royal justices, but they would direct her to sue at the county. Her appeal would then be enrolled by the coroners, exactly as she made it. To be valid it had to cover a number of specified facts, such as where she was at the time the alleged offence was committed, where she was going to and coming from. When her appeal finally came before the judges she had to restate it in exactly the same words as she had used in the county court. Her oral appeal was followed by the reading of the coroners' rolls. If the accounts varied, her appeal would fail. Bracton explains that the reading from the roll should not come first precisely because the appellor, in this as in any other case, could then phrase the appeal accordingly.

If the accounts tallied the accused could then seek to invalidate the appeal by raising one of the various exceptions to it. He may object on a technicality. He may argue that he did not deprive her of her maidenhood because she is still a virgin. In this case she has to be examined by four law-abiding women to ascertain whether or not she was defiled. Even if they found in the affirmative this did not of course prove the individual's guilt; this issue had still to go before a jury. The accused may also say that he had had the woman as his concubine and lover (*amica*) before the time mentioned in the appeal, which fact if true would seem to invalidate any action for rape. Or he may say that he had defiled her with her consent, or that she has appealed him out of hatred of another woman who is now his concubine or wife and at the instigation of one of her kinsmen. He may object, moreover, that he was out of the realm or in a place from which he could not have committed the act at the time mentioned. Or he could claim that there was an omission in her appeal, in that she says no more than that he lay with her, not that he had taken her maidenhood. There are many other possible exceptions, says Bracton, but he cannot at present call them to mind.

Such was the procedure in the appeal of the rape of a virgin. Other appeals of rape must have been similar in most respects, although their incidence is relatively rare. In fact, the number of rape cases on the plea rolls of Bracton's day is not particularly large. Indeed, it is perhaps surprising that women were prepared to bring the cases at all. The conviction rate was extremely low, and the penalties laid down by Glanvill and Bracton were rarely, if ever, exacted. In many cases the parties reached an agreement. Often we are not told the nature of the agreement but occasionally it is specified as marriage. It is a fairly safe bet that this was the substance of the agreement in the majority of cases. When a woman withdrew her appeal, however, the court could still proceed to find a man guilty. In such a case he was fined.[49] The fines on the Pipe Rolls from Glanvill's day and after suggest that in reality this had long been the worst a convicted rapist could normally expect. There is every reason to suppose that many of Glanvill's male contemporaries regarded rape less seriously. In his handbook for churchmen, *Gemma Ecclesiastica*, Gerald of Wales gives a striking example of male virtue. A vagrant, who considers himself to be a sinner, tells a virtuous man of his one good deed. While pillaging a convent, he listened to the pleas of a young nun and refrained from raping her. Both the virtuous man and Gerald himself applauded the deed. 'Consider too,' he adds, 'how convenient it would have been to have lustful carnal intercourse with all these women at hand.'[50]

It seems certain that marriage is the key to understanding many of the rape cases that actually came before the courts. The judges often explicitly permitted the marriage of the parties or, occasionally, ordered it. According to Bracton a man may avoid the full penalty of the law if the defiled woman claims him as her

71. Man and woman fighting, perhaps attempted rape: a fourteenth-century misericord from Ely Cathedral

husband. But it must always be her choice, never the other way around: 'Otherwise a serf or common man could perpetually dishonour a noble woman of good family (*mulierem nobilem et generosam*) by a single act of defilement and then marry her to the disgrace of her lineage (*in opprobrium generis sui*).' Glanvill presumably had the same problem in mind when he said that the families should always be consulted before an appeal of rape could be concorded by marriage.[51] It is likely, then, that many if not most appeals of rape were intended to enforce marriage. Often a woman would have had her family behind her as it would be hard for her in practice to act alone. This helps to explain why Bracton's account runs together as one malicious accusation by a woman and instigation by a kinsman. A kinsman might act presumably to vindicate a woman's and hence the family's honour, in circumstances where this had been put in doubt.[52]

Another scenario was also possible. Appeals concorded by marriage may amount to a 'public declaration of a sexual relationship . . . adopted as a means of coercing parents and families into consent to a match of which they had previously disapproved'.[53] In such a case a woman was, once again, not acting alone but, this time, with her collusive lover in the background. All in all, there was almost certainly little relationship between appeals of rape in the records and the actual incidence of rape in society. Most rape then, as now, will have gone unrecorded. High-born girls must have been less often the victims of casual rape than their contemporaries, in any case, because they spent little time on their own. The household afforded some protection. As we have seen, the would-be lover or seducer with some access to the household was a different matter.

The spate of legislation in parliament that characterised the first half of the reign of Edward I profoundly affected the law on rape. Clause 13 of the Statute of Westminster I in 1275 prohibited the taking of a damsel who was under-age, with or without her consent, or of a dame, a damsel who was over-age or any other woman without her consent. It also provided that if no one sued within forty days then the Crown would do so, the penalty upon conviction being two years' imprisonment together with ransom at the king's will; in effect, a fine. Following the statute the justices became more reluctant than ever to allow women's appeals to go through to judgment. In fact, the exceptions they allowed defendants to make were increasingly trivial.[54] Equally significant, however, is the statute's inclusion of matrons as well as maidens, for in practice the courts appear to have been reluctant to allow appeals other than by virgins.[55] Clause 34 of the Statute of Westminster II of 1285 made rape a capital offence, even where consent was given afterwards. This was also the clause which denied dower to the adulterous and unreconciled wife. The prescription of the death penalty was a dead letter from the start. The most significant features of the statute were the dower clause and the discounting of the woman's wishes. Despite the fact that she was the victim, the wishes of others were allowed to override hers; the opportunity of choosing marriage was taken from her. The result of the statute was paradoxical. While it gave rise to an action for ravishment for men, the appeal of rape dwindled into insignificance, with conviction even rarer. In the words of J.B. Post: 'By interpretation and extension, therefore, the Statutes of Westminster turned the law of rape into a law of elopement and abduction, which inhibited the purpose of the woman herself – whether outrage at a sexual assault or the desire to further or avenge a consenting relationship – and fostered the interests of those who wanted material recompense for the material disparagement wrought by self-willed womenfolk and suitors.'[56]

Most conflict between ladies and lords in medieval England was in one way or another over property. The matter of dower, for example, engendered endless litigation. Dower was in essence a wife's right to life tenancy of a share of her husband's lands after his death.[57] In origin it applied only to the land with which a husband voluntarily endowed her upon their marriage at the church door. It was limited to a third, in the interests of the heirs and of the lord, the value of whose wardship would be greatly reduced if she had more. It was customary, however, for a widow to be entitled to a third, even without her husband's express endowment. By the time of Glanvill's treatise of 1187–9 a writ of dower was in existence (the writ *unde nihil habet*), which allowed a widow to sue for her dower which was being wrongfully withheld.[58]

Magna Carta contains important provisions on dower. Clause 7 provides that:

After her husband's death, a widow shall have her marriage portion and her inheritance at once and without any hindrance; nor shall she pay anything for her dower, her marriage portion or her inheritance which she and her husband held on the day of his death; and she may stay in her husband's house for forty days after his death, within which period her dower shall be assigned to her.

Freedom from payment was of vital importance, for without it the provision of Clause 8, that no woman shall be compelled to remarry, would have lost its force.[59] Only if she were financially secure could a woman afford not to take a husband. On the whole, the evidence suggests that the Crown honoured the freedom from payment, even though it was excluded from the reissues of Magna Carta in 1217 and 1225. Clause 7, however, was extended in the reissues. If the couple's home had been a castle, a suitable house was to be found for her. She was to have the right of taking provisions from the woods, known as estovers. Moreover the wording of the main provision was changed to make it more explicit: 'Let there be assigned to her for her dower a third part of all the land of her husband which was his in his life, unless she was endowed of less at the church door.'

It is unlikely that any change in custom was actually intended, the rule being that she should have a third of all the land that he had had at the time of their marriage. During the course of the thirteenth century the courts came to interpret this differently. By the time of the legal treatise written by Britton in the time of Edward I, and very probably before, it had become the rule that the widow was entitled to a third of any property which her husband had held at any time during their marriage, even if he had subsequently parted with it, an interpretation that was clearly more favourable to the widow. The common law became in fact the champion of dower. There can be no doubt that women's position did change in this respect, as a reaction against the behaviour of King John and the other Angevin kings. The Statute of Merton of 1236 legislated against women having their dower lands taken from them and provided for damages for the period between the husband's death and the recovery of possession. It was aimed at lords as well as heirs. Later in the century the Statute of Westminster I of 1275 extended the usage of the writ of dower, while the Statute of Westminster II of 1285 offered protection against collusive action designed to deprive a woman of her dower.

But legal principle was not social reality. The very fact that legislation was necessary suggests that many women found it difficult to obtain their dower. Of course there were very many who had little or no difficulty and many heirs who complied swiftly and with good grace. But the plea rolls show that there were literally thousands who were not so fortunate. As has been said, 'Magna Carta's miscellaneous array of alterations and amendments to the rules on dower meant, for the most part, improvement of widows' legal position during the first third of the thirteenth century. And at the same time disgruntled sons and stepsons, brothers-in-law, and lords continued to devise ways to redress the balance: by simple inaction, by negotiation, by collusive suit, by violence if necessary. When they did, another recruit would be added to the army of doweresses whose complaints march across the plea rolls.'[60]

This is not to say that the problems were all encountered on one side. A writ was available for an heir who found that the widow's share had come to more than one-third; he could sue for 'admeasurement' to bring it down to size. The Statute of Gloucester of 1278 gave the heir a writ of right if the widow attempted to grant away her land beyond her lifetime. Chicanery aside, however, the main problem was simply that the interests of heir and widow were diametrically opposed.

The aggravation caused by the existence of dowagers, from the heir's point of view, can be illustrated by reference to the Earldom of Warwick.[61] The resources directly deployed by the earls of Warwick were much depleted in the thirteenth century due to the longevity of their widows and it has been argued, effectively, that this severely limited their capacity to take an active part in national affairs. The twelfth-century earls had already experienced this problem. In the thirteenth century it became acute. Philippa Basset, who was widowed in 1229, lived until 1265, surviving Earl Henry by thirty-six years. During this time she, and her second husband, held one-third of the entire Newburgh estate. Countess Ela Longespée, who was widowed in 1242, lived until 1298, surviving Earl Thomas by no less than fifty-six years. She then held a third of all the lands that had passed to Earl Thomas on his father's death. She therefore held less than Countess Philippa, but it was still a substantial portion of the Warwick estates. Ela was a rich widow, and she became even richer when she outlived her second husband, the justiciar Philip Basset. From 1242 moreover, until the death of Margery de Newburgh in 1253, there were three ladies operating under the title of Countess of Warwick.

It was not simply one earl and his wife who suffered a depletion of resources for each generation of dowager. Countess Philippa outlived not only Earl Henry but also Earl Thomas, his sister Margery and her 'husband' John du Plessis. Countess Ela outlived not only her husband, Earl Thomas, but also Margery and John du Plessis, and the next earl, William Mauduit, who died in 1268. In fact, she very nearly outlived his successor, William de Beauchamp, as well, predeceasing him by only a few months. The situation for these earls must have been the more galling when the dowagers in question were not their own mothers. It has been argued that Earl Thomas was 'paralysed' by the loss of so much of his property to Countess Philippa, who was in fact his step-mother. She held many of the earldom's chief assets: Brailes, Claverdon and the forest of Sutton in Warwickshire, Chedworth in Gloucestershire and East Knoyle in Wiltshire. Moreover, her second husband, Richard Siward, was not exactly savoury. It is hardly surprising to find that Earl Thomas was engaged in a series of lawsuits against them during the 1230s.[62]

Earl William de Beauchamp was rather better off, despite the longevity of Countess Ela, in that he brought his own Beauchamp resources to the earldom in 1268. However, these too were encumbered by dower. Angaret, his grandfather's second wife, held her dower until her death in 1280. It is perhaps not too surprising that he had to be coerced into assigning her full dower to his aunt, the widowed Countess Alice Mauduit, in 1268.[63] The most galling to him was probably Countess Ela, given that the relationship between them was so distant. Although William was eventually able to negotiate with Ela Longespée for the recovery of some of her dower lands, it is probably true to say that the resource problems continued to cast a shadow over the earl's involvement in national affairs.

Historians looking particularly from the vantage point of national politics are rather inclined to see matters from the point of view of the male heir. It is not necessary to do so, however, to see that the situation was likely to cause consternation and conflict. Looked at from the dowager's point of view we find that she often found resistance to her claims from her late husband's heir. Again, the situation must have been more difficult if the male heir were not her son or grandson. Another person who often stood in the way of the widow was the man who had received custody of the heir and his lands in wardship. For example, Thomas Basset of Headington secured the wardship and marriage of the fourteen-year-old Earl Henry II de Newburgh, and married him to one of his daughters, Philippa. Alice de Harcourt, widow of Earl Waleran, had to fight for her dower in the courts, not against her step-son, but against Thomas Basset, 'who expected to get the maximum return for his outlay on the wardship'.[64]

Such problems were by no means confined to great lords and ladies. The same factors applied right across the spectrum. Indeed, they could create very considerable difficulties for lords with only one estate, as they could for ladies whose dower came from limited resources. In the last analysis their gentle status rested upon those resources. Conflict was endemic. A good example from the early thirteenth century is that of the Mancetters of north Warwickshire. With only a single estate at Mancetter, Hugh de Mancetter had to contend with his estate supporting his widowed mother, Emma, now married to Gilbert Croc. At the eyre of 1221, the visitation of the king's travelling justices, Gilbert was accused of entering the manor house with accomplices and stealing 5s of the money that the miller was accounting to the lord. At the 1232 eyre Hugh complained of the waste that they had been making in the land they were holding as dower, namely that they had pulled down seven houses, up-rooted two gardens and stolen twenty oaks from the wood. The parties were now concorded, with Gilbert and Emma agreeing to desist. They were clearly squabbling over limited resources. The situation was doubly difficult for Hugh as he was currently trying to improve his estate.[65] A situation of this type could cause serious difficulties for a family with a single manor.

The development of new legal devices in the later thirteenth and fourteenth centuries allowed even more land to pass into widows' hands. Jointure was property which the husband and wife held together, so that it stayed automatically with the survivor when one of them died. It could come about through a marriage contract, through joint purchase or through enfeoffment. A landowner could convey land to one or more persons who then reconveyed it to him and his wife jointly, often with remainder, that is succession after the deaths of the landowner and his wife, to one or more named heirs. The wife was thus secured a life interest, and the lord could decide on his own ultimate heir. There was now less chance of the land passing to an overlord in wardship. During the fourteenth and fifteenth centuries most marriage contracts contained a jointure, the share of the husband's lands involved depending upon negotiation and the comparative social status of his wife. Jointure, moreover, did not affect a widow's entitlement to dower; on the contrary, the law protected her in her entitlement to both.[66] The jointure was a step along the way towards a more complex procedure known as enfeoffment to use. By this a man would grant some of his lands to a group of friends, relatives or retainers with instructions to hold them to his use while he lived and to dispose of them after his death according to his stipulations.

The use involved a legal fiction. While the group, known technically as feoffees, became the legal owners of the land, in practice the original grantor retained the land and its profits until he died. The device was widely in use by the mid-fourteenth century. By these means a man could provide for his wife and for his children, arrange for the payment of his debts, and keep his lands out of the hands of his overlord.

In fact, lords were doing more than making provision for their wives. They were acknowledging the significance of partnership and exhibiting considerable trust in the future discretion of their wives. Noble widows of the later Middle Ages could find themselves in an extremely advantageous position. In addition to her own inheritance, if she had one, she enjoyed dower and jointure, with no responsibility for maintaining her husband's heir. Successive marriages resulted in some very powerful ladies indeed.[67] Elizabeth de Burgh, lady of Clare, is one of the best-known examples, largely because she left so many records behind her. She was born in 1295, the youngest of the three co-heiresses of Gilbert de Clare, whose death at the Battle of Bannockburn in 1314 brought his male line to an end. She married three times, bearing one child to each of her husbands, John de Burgh, who was the eldest son of the Earl of Ulster, Theobald de Verdon, and Roger d'Amory. Roger died in rebellion in 1322. Elizabeth lived until 1360, managing an estate which in the 1320s produced an estimated income of £3,000 per annum. Her only son was murdered young, leaving her granddaughter, Elizabeth, Countess of Ulster, as his sole heiress. She carried her inheritance to Lionel, Duke of Clarence, one of the sons of Edward III.

The most notorious dowager is perhaps Katherine Neville, daughter of Ralph, 1st Earl of Westmorland. Her father betrothed her to John Mowbray, Duke of Norfolk, and they were married in the chapel at Raby Castle early in 1412, by the Abbot of Jervaulx. Mowbray appears to have received very little of the dowry that came with her. 'It was a cruel irony indeed', writes Rowena Archer, 'given the extent to which Katherine was to milk the Mowbray estates on her husband's death.' Norfolk died in 1432, whereupon the lady acquired a life interest in his estates. By the 1440s she had married beneath herself, in the person of Thomas Strangeways, a servant in the Norfolk household. After him she married Viscount Beaumont. Then came the marriage that raised eyebrows. In her sixties, she married the teenage John Woodville. One contemporary chronicler referred to this as *maritagium diabolicum*. Even then, she survived him by fourteen years, finally dying in 1483.

Needless to say, what the late K.B. McFarlane referred to as the 'new and disproportionate weight of widows' in late medieval society[68] caused financial problems for male members of their families in particular, and led to more examples of relative political obscurity, reminiscent of the thirteenth-century earls of Warwick. The Mowbrays were a case in point; another was the Cliffords. Between 1314 and 1436 the Cliffords were never free of such problems. One of the dowagers was Euphemia, daughter of Ralph Neville, who was a Clifford widow for forty-eight years. Between 1391 and 1393 there were three widows being provided for from the Clifford estates. One of the ironies of this situation was that these ladies, so far from being disparaged, were now in a position to disparage themselves, simply by exercising their freedom of choice. What is perhaps most surprising is that men seemed to have accepted 'the problem' of noble dowagers with resignation. The situation was more complicated, however, than simply male versus female interests. Men wanted the best for their wives and their daughters, or perhaps one should say for their families through the marriage contracts demanded for their daughters. And many men had an enhanced lifestyle through marriage to dowagers.

At the same time, however, there does appear to have been a shift away from inheritance by daughters during the later medieval period. A recent study in the history of the law of real property from the late thirteenth century to the eighteenth century has argued that its driving principle was increasing discrimination against the 'heiress at law'.[69] That a relatively small amount of land passed to heiresses at law during the early modern period can be shown statistically. It appears that between 1540 and 1780 only 5 per cent of inheritances went to daughters and only 8 per cent went to heiresses at all, if collateral females are included. This is well below the level that would apply if biological factors and the common law rules of inheritance were allowed to run their course. 'Putting down the heiress at law', it is argued, 'would be a not inappropriate subtitle for the landowners' legal history.'[70]

The trend against the heiress is deemed to have begun in the late thirteenth century with the entail or 'estate tail'. The rise of the entail is best seen in the context of conditional gifts and their protection. The most significant conditional gift that a landowner might make was to his son and his son's wife to provide for their issue. Before the clause of the Statute of Westminster II in 1285 which dealt with such gifts (*de donis conditionalibus*) the common law interpreted them in such a way that once the couple had a child together they could dispose of the land as they wished. If they were to part with the land, however, the original grantor's intention was frustrated and the family suffered a loss of property to little effect. This interpretation was probably holding back the growth of marriage contracts involving money portion and jointure, because the bride's father would be handing over his money in the expectation that his grandchildren would inherit at least a portion of his son-in-law's lands.[71] Although the poor drafting of this statute caused confusion for a time, it came to restrain alienation of the land by the grantees and to offer protection to the issue of the marriage as long as that issue continued.[72] The potential brake on the development of marriage contracts was removed. However, the entail had other consequences, one of which was the development of tail male. Given that the land in question would revert to the grantor and his heirs in default of issue, he could also nominate successive heirs and their issue who would succeed to the land in turn. Enfeoffment to use, for example, generally included such provision. It was thus open to landowners to exclude females from the succession for as long as possible. There can be little doubt that landowners saw descent to heiresses as the end of their line, and a prospect to be avoided. Historians have tended to sympathise with this position.

However, one should be wary of seeing the beginnings of a male conspiracy against the heiress in the later thirteenth and early fourteenth centuries. Admittedly, it would be possible to argue for a deterioration in the treatment of women before the law in this period. The abysmal conviction rate in cases of rape and the development of ravishment as a trespass could certainly be cited. So, too, could the changing attitude of the church courts towards wives' wills from the middle of the century. One is also reminded of the differential treatment of Juliana Murdak and John de Vaux when it came to husband murder. However, there is no statistical evidence available on how the entail was used in this period. How prevalent was tail male? A broader study of jointure, entail and family strategy during the period from around 1275 to, say, 1350 would be required before a strong argument could be made. Meanwhile, the idea of male landowners collectively conspiring against a common law that protected women has to be treated with some caution. After all, the common law did not fall from the skies; it was itself made very largely by men, through the complex interaction of Crown, lawyers and social pressures. Admittedly, existing law could always be circumvented through new devices. The jointure and the enfeoffment to use have long been recognised, for example, as means of avoiding the feudal incidents of wardship and marriage. On the whole though, it is more convincing to see entail as an element in the history of family strategy which included provision for daughters as well as sons, protection of daughters and of family interest, and an increasing partnership between husbands and wives. If this was detrimental to the heiress at law, it was more to do with the underlying patriarchal attitudes and assumptions of medieval society than to a conscious reaction against an improvement in women's position under the law.

CHAPTER 6

Literature, Gender and Ideology

In her *Doctrine for the Lady of the Renaissance*, published as long ago as 1953, Ruth Kelso trawled the myriad treatises of the fifteenth to seventeenth centuries in search of a portrait of the Renaissance lady. She concluded that 'there was no such thing as the lady so far as theory went, no formulated ideal for the lady as such, distinguished from the gentleman or from any other woman. That many books of a theoretical sort were written for and about the lady the list appended to this volume furnishes ample evidence, but . . . the contents, it is scarcely an exaggeration to affirm, apply to the whole sex rather than any favoured section of it. The lady, shall we venture to say, turns out to be merely a wife.'[1]

A lady, in other words, is defined by her status, derived from her parentage and sustained through her husband. What was true of the sixteenth and seventeenth centuries was equally true of the Middle Ages, as Ruth Kelso herself indicates: 'The concept of the term lady is vaguer therefore than the concept of gentleman. One gains the impression of a type emerging with the middle ages and continuing unchanged through the renaissance. The wife of a knight was a lady, and so was the wife of a renaissance gentleman. The gentleman differed considerably from the knight, but their wives would not have found much to wonder at in each other, once they got below such matters as dress and table manners. At best the ideal quality of the term lady never had the serious import of gentleman.'[2] That she is substantially right is indicated by Andrew the Chaplain in his *De arte honeste amandi* (the so-called *Art of Courtly Love*), written, most probably at the court of the Countess Marie of Champagne, during the latter part of the twelfth century: 'a noblewoman is one descended from a vavasor [knight] or a lord, or is the wife of one of these, while a woman of the higher nobility is descended from great lords. The same rules apply to men, except that a man married to a woman of higher or lower rank than himself does not change his rank. A married woman changes her status to match that of her husband, but a man can never change his nobility by marriage.'[3]

But since the lady indisputably existed in reality, if not in theory, Ruth Kelso proceeds to seek her in the perfect woman derived from the early modern treatises. The portrait, unsurprisingly, is essentially a Christian one: 'These, then, were the moral and intellectual qualities praised in women: chastity – supported by modesty, humility, constancy, temperance, and piety – humanity, courtesy, courage, justice, prudence, and learning. Add beauty and the image of womanly perfection appears.'[4]

Mutatis mutandis, a similar list would be very easy to construct for the medieval period, if not from the notion of the perfect woman then, at least, negatively, from the depiction of female vices. One substantial difference in the Renaissance period is the new emphasis upon education for girls.[5] The difficulty is to move beyond such normative portraits to how lords actually perceived ladies and to how the ladies perceived themselves. And, how far did the values contained in these portraits actually impact upon gentle lives?

One means of approaching these questions, arguably, is through the advice which the knight Geoffrey de la Tour Landry gave to his daughters. His book, the *Livre du Chevalier de la Tour*, was written in 1371–2 by a French noble, lord of Latourlandry in the canton of Chemillé, Maine-et-Loire.[6] Always supposing that his prologue is to be taken entirely at face value, it was written as a book of advice for his daughters. He was helped in his task, he tells us, by two priests and two clerks of his household. Three daughters are known – Marie, who married Gilles Clerembault, and Jeanne and Anne, both married to sons of Louis, Vicomte of Rochechouart, counsellor and chamberlain to Charles V. He also had at least two sons for whom he wrote an anterior work which is no longer extant. Active in the Hundred Years' War, Geoffrey is found fighting against the English from 1346. From 1378 to 1383 he is mentioned several times with the rank of *chevalier banneret*. His work was known in England; indeed, two copies are extant in the British Library. Significantly, it was translated into English in the middle of the fifteenth century and published by Caxton, in a rather literal translation from a different manuscript, in 1484.

Geoffrey's main source was a collection of *exempla*, taken from the Bible and other sources, called the *Miroir des bonnes femmes* or *Miroir aux Preudes femmes*, a work which appears to date from before 1300. Other sources include a thirteenth-century poem called the *Vie des Peres*, female saints' lives and secular tales adapted from popular *fabliaux*. Several stories are taken directly from sermons. Much of the work deals with examples of 'bad' and 'good' women and it has been observed that his good women appear even more virtuous and his bad women more wicked – and more severely punished – than those in the *Miroir*, his main source. However, Geoffrey also drew from his own experience and the work as a whole has an immediacy and urgency of its own.

In addition to his teaching 'of moral evil and of good' and of right Christian behaviour, Geoffrey is much concerned with comportment and it is this which gives his work a secular and, one might say, gentle flavour. For example, he explains how women should behave courteously and meekly:[7]

> After, daughters, ye must be meek and courteous, for there is none so great a virtue to get the grace of God and the love of all people; for humility and courtesy overcometh all proud hearts that be fell (wild) as a sparrowhawk. Be he never so ramageus (untamed) ye may overcome him with goodly and

And hir name was Charitee

O pylgrymes in goodly wyse,
Sche dyde moste treuely the servyse.
With chere benygne and glad vysage,
Sche brought hem to ther herbergage.

72. Charity in operation: a lady of the manor offers hospitality to pilgrims

courteous demeaning; ye may make him come from the tree to your hand. And if ye fare rudely and be cruel with him, he will flee his way and never come at you. And since that courtesy and softness may overcome a wild bird that hath no reason, needs it ought to refrain felons (fierce) proud heart of man and woman. And humility is the first entry and way of friendship and worldly love and that overcometh great hearts, and assuageth ire and wrath of all persons.

He goes on to say that he has himself known many ladies and gentle women who have received much love from great and small for their courtesy and humility:

And therefore I rede (counsel) you be courteous and humble to great and small, and to do courtesy and reverence and speak to them fair, and to be meek in answer to the poor, and they will praise you and bear forth of you good word and good fame more than will the great that ye make courtesy to. For to great ye make courtesy of right, the which is due to them, but the courtesy that is made to poor gentlemen, or to other of less degree, it cometh of free and gentle, courteous and humble heart. And the small people that the courtesy and humbleness is done to holdeth them worshipped thereby, and wherever they cometh they praiseth and speaketh good of him that doth them reverence and courtesy.

Not long ago, he tells them, he was in a company of knights and ladies when a great lady took off her hood and bowed to a tailor. And one of the knights said: 'Madame, ye have done off your hood to a tailor.' And she said that she was 'gladder that she had done it off to him than to a lord. And they all saw her meekness and wisdom, and held her wise.'

The knight has more to say on actual deportment: 'Afterwards, in saying your prayers at mass or in other place, be not like the crane or tortoise that turneth their heads and faces backward and looketh over their shoulder and ever staring with the head like a vane'.[8] Hold your head firm, he says, as the beast which is called a *lymer* (bloodhound) that looks ever in front of him without turning his head hither and thither:

73. Devil inciting two women to gossip when they should be at prayer: fourteenth-century misericord from Ely Cathedral

'And, therefore, be firm and looketh forth right afore you plainly, and if ye lust to look aside turneth your body and visage together, and so your countenance be most firm and sure; for they that looketh back and are oft staring with the head are oft scorned and mocked.'

There can be no doubt that women of breeding were expected to be recognised as such through their speech and their demeanour. Thomas Hoccleve, Chaucer's younger contemporary, expresses this clearly in *The Emperor Jeruslaus's Wife*:[9]

> But this lady un-to a Nonnerie
> That was but there fast by hir drow,
> Wher the ladyes of her conpaignie
> Were ful glad, and of her genterie
> Receyued hire al thogh that no notice
> They had of hire estat of Emperice.

The same had been true back in the late twelfth century, or so, at least, Andrew the Chaplain tells us in *De arte honeste amandi*.[10]

The knight of La Tour Landry, however, goes on to give his daughters examples of what he means. In doing so, he takes us well beyond the matter of bodily carriage. There were four knights, he says, that wished to marry for worship, without coveting lands or goods. They were looking for kings' daughters, women of noble birth, and 'of good name' and of 'firm behaving', who were 'well mannered and conditioned'; their wives must be seen to have what women ought to have [sic] and to be likely to bear children. One of the knights was the King of England, who had heard that the King of Denmark had three fair daughters. He therefore sent certain knights and ladies from among the most sufficient of his realm to see which of the daughters would be the most suitable for him. And so the daughters were arrayed and brought before them:

> And them seemed that the oldest was the fairest but she had not the most sure manner in her beholding but oft looked here and there and turned oft her head on her shoulders and had her sight ventillous (shifting) like a vane. The second daughter had much talking and spake oft tofore she understood that which was said to her. The third was not the fairest of them, but she was most agreeable and maintained her manner more sure and sadly (seriously) and spake but little and that was well demurely, and her regard (aspect) and sight was more firm and humble than that of the other two.[11]

The ambassadors duly took their advice back to the King of England. Needless to say, the king's choice was a foregone conclusion, but not before the matter had been debated by his council. It was put to him that it was 'more worship' to marry the eldest. The king chose the youngest: 'For there is no beauty nor nobleness that is peer to good manners'.

The knight offered a second example, drawn it would appear from his own personal history. His friends were suggesting a particular marriage for him:

> and my father brought me to see her that I should have, and there we had great cheer, and my father set me in language with her that I should have knowledge of her speech and language. And so we fell in words of prisoners, and I said: 'Damsel, it were better to fall to be your prisoner than to many other, for I trow your prison should not be so hard to me as it should be and [=if] I were take with English men.' And she answered, 'I have seen some [= someone] not long since that I would were my prisoner.' And I asked if she would put him in evil prison, and she said nay, she would keep him as she would her own body; and I said he was happy that might come into so noble a prison. What shall I say? She loved me well enough, and had a quick eye, and a light, and there was many words. And so, at the last she was right familiar with me, for she prayed me two or three times that I should not abide long but that I should come and see her however it were; of the which I had had marvel seeing that I was never acquainted with her, nor had spoken nor seen her before that time.

He later told his father that, although she was both good and fair: 'I would not of her, for she was so pert and so light of manners that caused me to be discouraged from her, of which I have thanked God since divers times.' As he had already admitted that 'she knew well that folk were about to marry us together', it is difficult not to feel that the knight was more than a little hard on her. After all, he had opened the familiarity. He adds cryptically that less than a half-year later 'she was blamed', although he did not know whether this was justly or unjustly. 'And after', he adds, rather unfeelingly, 'she died.'

Reputation was all-important and reputation could so easily be lost. It is partly this that lies behind Geoffrey's advice not to become involved in chiding or brawling with brainless folk.[12] He counsels: 'It is great folly to every woman to chide or else to answer unto them that be of such ungodly conditions, full of noise and strife, and cruel, wilful and hasty.' On one occasion, finding a gentle woman involved in just such an argument with a man, Geoffrey had intervened:

'Madamoiselle! I pray you that ye answer not unto this fool, that is of such condition rather to speak evil than well.' But she would not do by my counsel, but chidde with him and answered worse than she had do before, saying unto the man that he was not worthy. And he answered her that he was better worthy a man than she for a woman. And so much the words and the noise increased between them both till at the last the man said unto her he knew such one that had her at his commandment both day and night when that he would, so that there was much foul speech between them, and before much people, and the woman defamed for her hautyuete (haughtiness) and her folly and chiding. And therefore her shame and disclaunder (slander) was shewed openly there before the people that had no knowing thereof before. . . . it is a mischaunt (wrong) thing for any gentle woman either to strive or to chide in any manner, as I shall shew you example by the property of some beasts, as ye may see by the cur dogs; of their nature they growl and bark evermore, but gentle greyhounds do not so. And so ought it to be of gentle men and gentle women.

It is a message which Geoffrey was fond of conveying. On another occasion he relates the story of a gentle knight's daughter playing at table – one would like to know the nature of the game – with a gentle man, who is described as 'riotous' and 'comberous' (quarrelsome). She accused him of misplay, an argument arose between them and she lost the game through her chiding. Geoffrey, once again, counselled her to leave the matter but she continued to argue with him, 'and the words rose so till he said if she were wise and good she would not come to men's chambers by night darkling without candle nor to coll (embrace) nor kiss men in their beds alone, as she did'. To her protestations that he lied, he replied that so and so had seen her do it. The result was the same as before: 'And sum said it had be better for her to hold her peace and have said no word, and that she had beat herself with her own staff; that is to say, by her tongue and her speech.'[13]

As far as outward behaviour is concerned, the thrust of what Geoffrey is saying is supported by Chaucer in his portrait of the prioress, Madame Eglentyne. As has long been recognised, the essence of Chaucer's satire is that the prioress behaves exactly like a secular lady.[14] When all due allowances have been made, in terms of literary convention and courtly ideals, his portrayal takes us close, arguably, to how contemporary ladies might have behaved. We should not forget that nuns were overwhelmingly drawn from the upper strata of society. Some nunneries were highly aristocratic; many others drew on the gentry and upper sector of urban society. Nunneries were often closely linked to the gentry of their locality.[15] Madame Eglentyne was so concerned with how she appeared that part of her was outside of her body, watching herself. Our concern is not with the propriety of her behaviour as a nun, but with what she saw.

74. Playing backgammon, from the Luttrell Psalter

Chaucer tells us, first of all, of her demeanour: Of her smiling she was 'ful symple and coy', i.e. quiet. Her greatest oath was but by 'Seynte Loy', that is to say hardly an oath at all. Her deportment, too, was excellent:

> And sikerly she was of greet desport,
> And ful plesaunt, and amyable of port,
> And peyned hire to countrefete (imitate) cheere
> Of court, and to been estatlich of manere,
> And to ben holden digne (deserving) of reverence.
>
> (*General Prologue*, ll. 137–41)

She is dignified, but with more than a suggestion perhaps of haughtiness, two behavioural characteristics which are often close to one another in practice; in other words, she was conscious of herself as a lady. Very striking is the emphasis Chaucer places upon her table manners:

> At mete wel ytaught was she with alle;
> She leet no morsel from hir lippes falle,
> Ne wete hir fyngres in hir sauce depe;
> Wel koude she carie a morsel and wel kepe,
> That no drope ne fille up-on hire brest.
> In curteisie was set ful muchel hir lest.
> Hir over-lippe wyped she so clene
> That in hir coppe was no ferthyng sene
> Of grece, whan she dronken hadde hir draughte.
>
> (*General Prologue*, ll. 127–35)

Significantly, it is in the context of table manners that Chaucer employs the term courtesy. She sings divine service 'entuned in hir nose ful semely' and she speaks insular French, apparently 'ful faire and fetisly' (i.e. elegantly). The traditional satire against the 'Anglo-Norman' dialect must have had added force in the dying days of regularly spoken French in England. Like many secular ladies, the prioress keeps hounds, which she pampers with roasted flesh, milk and wastel-bread. She is conscious of her dress.

Her wimple is pleated and her cloak elegant. She wears jewellery: a coral bracelet, green beads, and a gold brooch on her cloak with the motto 'Amor vincit omnia' ('love conquers all'). Although she was physically quite large, she looked like, and endeavoured to look like, a heroine from romance. And finally Chaucer points to the sensibility of the lady: 'Al was conscience and tendre herte.' In all probability, softness of heart was generally expected of the lady as opposed to the gentle man. Taken to excess, especially self-conscious excess, sensitivity can dissolve into sentimentality, and it may be that when Chaucer smiles at the prioress, 'so charitable and so pitous' that she weeps if she encounters a mouse caught in a trap, he is pointing up the shallowness of refined manners *per se*.

In short, Madame Eglentyne looks like a lady and, one might say, behaves in a ladylike fashion. It is little wonder that the host, when he calls upon her to tell her tale, treats her courteously and calls her Lady Prioress:

75. *'All was conscience and tendre herte':*
Chaucer's Prioress (from the Ellesmere
manuscript)

and with that worde he sayde,
As curteisly as it had been a mayde,
'My lady Prioresse, by youre leve,
So that I wiste I sholde yow nat greve,
I wolde demen that ye tellen sholde
A tale next, if so were that ye wolde.'

(*Shipman's Tale*, ll. 445–50)

Between them, Chaucer and Geoffrey de la Tour Landry probably take us quite close to the behavioural traits of the medieval lady. The knight is not solely concerned with aristocratic manners, however. Having reinforced his message about unwise words causing 'disworship' and shame, he moves opportunely to how a woman should treat her husband:

And as well every woman ought to be ware in answering her husband before people, for many causes, as for to hold her peace and be still she shall have worship and be held wise of all that know and see her. And if she answer unto his displesaunce (displeasure) there shall come unto her harm and disworship, as it is said before.[16]

Geoffrey has a great deal to say to his daughters about the relationship between husband and wife, the great thrust of which is to underline female subservience. Sometimes this involves relating the dire consequences that resulted in past times, biblical and classical, from women's wilfulness and disobedience; for example, when a lady left her husband through her wrath. Other examples, however, are nearer to home, and sometimes involve direct sanctions:[17]

I would ye knew another example upon the woman that would not eat at the bidding of her husband. There was a lady that would not come eat with her husband when he was at meat, for no thing that he could say nor command her. And he saw that. And when he had eaten he sent for his swine-herd, and made fetch the kitchen cloth that his dishes were wiped with and spread it on a bord (table) and set meat theron, and made the swine-herd sit down there at. And then he called his lady, his wife, and said her: 'Since ye will not eat in my company with me, ye shall sit down and eat here with the swine-herd, for there shall none other man hold you company at your meat.' And whether she were wrath or glad, he made her sit down. And she wept and made much sorrow that her husband would chastise her so, to make her be served in so ungoodly wise. And therefore, all women ought to eat with him in his presence rather than with any other.

Caxton's text adds that realising her lord was mocking her she refrained her proud heart and knew her folly.[18] Disobedience could spill over into domestic violence. Geoffrey finds this especially justifiable when a lady publicly reproves her lord:[19]

Also, a woman ought not to strive with her husband, nor give him no displeasaunce nor answer her husband after strangers, as did once a woman that did answer her husband afore strangers like a rampe (ill-mannered woman) with great villainous words, dispraising him and setting him at nought, of the which he was oft ashamed and bad her hold her peace for shame, but the more fair words he spake the worse she did. And he that was angry of her governance, smote her with his fist down to the earth. And then with his foot he struck her in the visage and broke her nose, and all her life after she had her nose crooked, the which shent (ruined) and disfigured her visage after, that she might not for shame show her visage, it was so foul blemished. And this she had for her evil and great language that she was wont to say to her husband. And therefore the wife ought to suffer and let the husband have the words, and to be master, for that is her worship. For it is shame to hear strife between them, and especially before folk.

As an example of domestic obedience Geoffrey tells the story of a merchant's wife who obeyed her husband in all things. Three merchants were riding home from a fair, conversing as they went. The subject of obedient wives was raised and each claimed his own wife to be the most obedient. They then decided on a wager to test the issue. Each of them would command his wife to leap into a basin that they would set before her. They swore that none of them would let his wife know of the wager, but that each would say: 'looketh, wife, that I command be done'. At the first merchant's home the basin was duly set before the wife and she was commanded to leap in. Not unnaturally, she asked why. The merchant replied, 'for it is my luste (wish), and I will ye do it.' 'By God', quoth she, 'I will first wete whereto ye will have me leap into the basin.' She would not do so for anything the merchant said. He therefore gave her two or three great strokes with his fist. They then moved on to the second merchant's house, where he commanded the same. When she in turn refused, he took his staff and beat her. They then went to the third merchant's house where they found the meal already prepared. The merchant whispered to one of his fellows, 'after dinner I will assay my wife, and bid her leap into the basin'. When they were at dinner he said to his wife, 'whatever I bid, look it be done, how ever it be'. Although she loved and 'dread him', and she heard his words, she did not understand their meaning. For dinner they had rare eggs, but there was no salt on the table. Whereupon, the husband said: 'wife, sele sus table'. She understood him to mean 'seyle sus table', i.e. 'leap on the borde'. Frightened to disobey him, she did just that, scattering meat and drink and breaking the glasses. 'What', said the good man, 'then can ye none other play, wife?' 'Be ye wode (mad), sir,' she said, 'I have do your bidding as ye bade me to my power, notwithstanding it is your harm and mine; but I had lever ye had harm and I both than I disobeyed your bidding. For ye said, "seyle sus table".' 'Nay,' he replied, 'I said, "sele sus table", that is to say, "salt on the borde".' 'By my troth', she said, 'I understood that ye bade me leap on the borde.' They then fell to laughing. The other two merchants said that there was now no need for him to command her to leap into the basin, for she had obeyed enough. They agreed that he had won the wager. After this, the wife was greatly praised for her obedience to her husband, 'and she was not beat as were the other two wives that would not do their husbands' commandment'.

The knight goes on to say that poor men chastise their wives with fear and strokes but that gentle women should be chastised with courtesy.[20] However, it sounds rather hollow after what has gone before. In any case, Geoffrey seems impervious to the humiliation suffered by the merchant's wife. The extent of wife-beating in later medieval society is unknown, and unknowable, but it was sanctioned by both common and canon law. Admittedly, both systems of law held that this should not be done immoderately, but that can hardly have given much comfort or have had much practical effect. One could argue that the ironic portrayal of a wife beating her husband, so common on misericords, would lose some of its force if this were not a true inversion of reality.[21] However, violence was only one element in domestic lore. Having counselled his daughters that a woman should not publicly reprove her husband, the knight does, however, admit that it can be otherwise when they are alone: 'But I say not but when they be alone, but she may tell him with goodly words and counsel him to amend if he do amiss.' It is a theme to which he returns. Of the good Queen Esther and her wrathful husband, he writes: 'But many times when she saw him by himself, and that he was out of his ire, with her fair and humble speech she could so well behave herself unto him in goodly wise that she showed him all his fault.'[22]

All of this, of course, is seen through male eyes. Through biblical example in particular, Geoffrey de la Tour Landry warns that women should not divulge their husbands' secrets and that they should exhort their husbands to serve God with great devotion. The latter was something of which the Church had long made considerable use. In his *Manual for Confessors*, written around 1215, Thomas of Chobham enjoined priests to instruct wives to use their intimacy with their husbands to influence and correct their behaviour:[23]

> In imposing penance, it should always be enjoined upon women to be preachers to their husbands, because no priest is able to soften the heart of a man the way his wife can. For this reason, the sin of man is often imputed to his wife if, through her negligence, he is not corrected. Even in the bedroom, in the midst of their embraces, a wife should speak alluringly to her husband, and if he is hard and unmerciful, and an oppressor of the poor, she should invite him to be merciful; if he is a plunderer, she should denounce plundering; if he is avaricious, she should arouse generosity in him, and she should secretly give alms from their common property, supplying the alms that he omits.

This role of preacher to her husband differs markedly from the role Thomas of Chobham, and other clerical writers, assigned to the husband in relation to the wife:

> And in turn, the confessor should persuade the husband to manage his wife with decent demands, and to exhibit the respect owed as to part of his own body. And if she is foolish, he should rebuke her moderately and decently,

and if there is need, he should restrain her. For he should employ greater
diligence in guarding his wife than in guarding any earthly possessions,
because nothing should be dearer to him than his wife.

In other words, as Sharon Farmer says, 'just as saintly preachers served as
conduits of divine grace in the public sphere, pious wives could serve as
conduits of divine grace in the private sphere'.[24] Moreover, there is no doubt
that churchmen acted upon this, not least in dealing with the powerful. One
prominent example is Earl Simon de Montfort. Adam Marsh, the Franciscan
reformer, communicated directly with both Simon and Eleanor, his wife, in the
latter case seeking directly to influence him through her. Naturally, the
likelihood of success with this tactic depended upon the individual relationship
and also upon the extent to which the views and values of wife and husband
coincided. Simon and Eleanor were both strong characters, but the history of
their marriage, in so far as it is exposed to view, suggests that they pursued
their shared self-interests collectively and vigorously.[25] And one should not
forget the intercessionary role of queens, acting as a conduit for royal
patronage. This had become powerfully institutionalised by the thirteenth and
fourteenth centuries. Although it underlined the expected submissiveness of
the royal wife, it also allowed for the king and queen acting in consort, and on
the latter's initiative. One favoured time for the receipt of petitions was royal
childbirth with the queen interceding on behalf of petitioners from the
childbed itself.[26]

What effect the churchmen had in general is, of course, unknowable, but the
fact that they were utilising a well-known phenomenon suggests the strong
possibility, and therefore the actuality, of considerable intimacy within marriage,
and points to other possibilities within relationships than the one which Geoffrey
de la Tour Landry highlights and applauds. Much depended upon personality
and strength of character. It is hard to doubt that some women will have been the
dominant partners.

If, in general, Geoffrey's book is written from the accepted male standpoint,
backed by the full ideological weight of traditional authorities, it is hard to doubt
that on certain matters he is much closer to the views of clerical moralists than to
the standards of secular society. One of these matters is dress. And here, again, if
we interrogate his text other possibilities emerge. A particular target was ladies'
headdresses, and it was a subject which Geoffrey returned to again and again. He
repeats the gist of a bishop's sermon on the subject of ladies and gentle women
who were 'marvellously arrayed' in divers and quaint manners and had high
horns[27]:

he said that the women that were so horned were like to be horned snails and
harts and unicorns. . . . And he said that they were like the harts that bare
down their heads in the small wood; for when they come to church and holy
water be cast on them, they bow down the head. 'I doubt', said the bishop,
'that the devil sit not between their horns and that he make them bow down
for fear of holy water.'

76. 'I doubt that the devil sat not between their horns': misericord from Minster-in-Thanet, Kent, showing woman with horned headdress with devil above

The sins most involved are, of course, pride and lechery, the latter also engendered by the short gowns that showed their breeches which men were inclined to wear. With these and the horned headdresses, men and women mocked God. Those who were most blameworthy, however, were those who introduced the new fashions. He adds, most interestingly, that 'all good women ought to be afeared to take any such array till it were taken in all the country, and that they may no longer flee it for worldly shame'. Clearly new fashions spread through peer pressure. For Geoffrey, speaking via the bishop, it was the ladies who were most to blame, for when one sees 'a lewd woman have a new guise', she goes crying to her husband, 'Why may not I have such array as well as she? Am I not as well born as she?' This she does whether her husband can afford it or not. And so, the bishop says, 'but she have it, her husband shall never be in peace with her'. And then, of course, she parades it so that other ladies react in the same way. Geoffrey would no doubt have preferred people to behave in the way that they did at a feast when, according to the bishop's sermon, a lady appeared so strangely attired that the company ran towards her and stared at her as though she were a wild beast. Her headdress was full of long pins so that it looked like a gibbet. She was duly scorned by the entire assembly of lords and ladies who said that she had a gallows on her head.

On another occasion, Geoffrey recalls a debate between a baroness who lived in Gascony and a French lord. She informed him that she had recently come from

Britain and that his wife was not arrayed according to the latest fashion, principally that her hoods, tails and sleeves were not furred enough. The knight answered:

> since she is not arrayed on your guise, and that ye think her array and her fur too little and that ye blame me for it, forsooth ye shall have no more cause to blame me, for I will make array her as nobly as any of you all and as quaintly; for ye have but half of your hoods and coats furred with ermine and miniver, and I will do better to her, for I will fur her gowns, colours, sleeves and coats, the hair outward; thus she shall be better purfiled (trimmed) and furred than other ladies and gentle women.

What he will not do, however, is to array her immodestly like the English women with their great purfiles and slit coats. The central message here from Geoffrey is that his daughters should eschew new fashions coming from abroad, and stick to the raiment of their own country.[28] Ultimately, it is the husband who is the arbiter of fashion.

All of this is part of Geoffrey's railing against immodesty and pride. Other targets are women who keep a surfeit of gowns, those who washed their hair in wine and other things 'for to make the hair of colour otherwise than God made it', and those who 'popped' (painted), blanched and plucked their faces, for this was one of the sins most displeasing to God. One lady is pictured enduring a thousand years in purgatory with, among other things, hot burning needles through her brows for just such activity.[29]

77. Young lady at her toilet, from the Luttrell Psalter

But what the knight of La Tour Landry has revealed is the role gentle men played in the spread of fashions. It was a matter of aristocratic pride that one's ladies should be dressed both richly, one might say extravagantly, and à la mode. A good example of this, as we have seen, is provided by the buttterfly headdresses of Long Melford.[30] One irony, given the popularity of Geoffrey's text in fifteenth-century England, is that the traffic in new fashions was, in reality, from Paris to England and not the other way around.

Before leaving Geoffrey de la Tour Landry we should make reference to the debate between the knight and his wife over whether ladies and damsels should love paramours in certain circumstances.[31] The debate is, of course, an artificial one, but it is not just a matter of falling in behind literary convention. The knight deliberately allows himself to speak for the men the girls are likely to encounter. The arguments he uses are the traditional ones, stressing love as the bringer of honour as well as pleasure, in addition to stirring men to the exercise of valour. The granting of love, he says, is alms to make a good knight. The lady de la Tour Landry is able to counsel her daughters not to believe their father in this instance. She warns them, in effect, against the ways of men, and in particular against the easy words employed for their sport by deceivers and beguilers of ladies and damsels. In other words, the girls should avoid receiving the language of love. It leaves them open not only to carnal temptation itself but to back-biting and defamation. In the course of the debate, she throws back at her husband the story of how he visited a lady with the prospect of marriage in mind only to reject her because of her forward behaviour. In this way, the daughters could lose their own marriages.

The tendency of women to police each other within patriarchal value systems is something which receives insufficient attention. It has a strong presence within medieval culture. The Paston letters provide two famous examples of cruelty exercised by mothers towards their daughters, who were unwilling to obey or to conform to family expectations. Agnes Paston beat her young daughter, Elizabeth, regularly, as well as shutting her away from all company around the time that the family wished her to marry the fifty-year-old and rather disfigured Stephen Scrope. It became so bad, a relative reported, that her head had been broken in two or three places. Margaret Paston tried all means to dissuade her own daughter, Margery, from her marriage with the family's bailiff, Richard Calle, and effectively ostracised her thereafter when she failed to comply.[32] In the twelfth century the life of the recluse Christina of Markyate tells how her parents refused to accept her vow of chastity and pushed her into marriage. When she would not consummate the marriage, her mother beat her and tore out her hair. She also had recourse to various old women who were purveyors of love potions and charms.[33] One of the most revealing features of these episodes is the way in which the older women acted in consort not only with relatives, neighbours and friends, but also with ecclesiastical authorities. Margery Paston was examined and cajoled by the local bishop. In the case of Christina of Markyate a visiting bishop, Ranulf Flambard, is reported to have attempted to seduce her as a means of breaking down her resistance.

We can be sure that the language of love was much used, and that its use was much influenced by romance. For many literary scholars romance has a particular association with women, both as patrons and as audience. On the face of it, there is a reasonable case for this. After all, romance is about love and the expression of human feeling. The great twelfth-century romancier, Chrétien de Troyes, tells us himself that his romance of Lancelot, *Le Chevalier de la Charette*, was commissioned by Countess Marie de Champagne. In his *Yvain* he pictures the sixteen-year-old daughter of a knight reading a romance to her parents in their garden. Similarly, in *Troilus and Criseyde* Chaucer has Pandarus encountering Criseyde in a private room where she is engaged in a group reading of the *Siege of Thebes* with her ladies:

> [Pandarus] fond two othere ladys sete, and she,
> Withinne a paved parlour, and they thre
> Herdun a mayden reden hem the geste
> Of the siege of Thebes, while hem leste.
>
> (Bk 2, ll. 81–4)

Moreover, Chaucer has his Nun's Priest say:

> This storie is also trewe, I undertake,
> As is the book of Launcelot de Lake,
> That wommen holde in ful greet reverence.
> (*Nun's Priest's Tale*, ll. 3211–13)

Chaucer, however, clearly regarded romance as an outmoded and rather inferior genre, and his comment should not be taken at face value.[34] Romance had low credibility in his eyes and the suggestion is of female gullibility rather than a single-sex audience for romance. It is certainly true that ladies figure among the owners of romances in fourteenth- and fifteenth-century England, from queens, like the hapless Isabella, wife and widow of Edward II, down, but the evidence of wills points unequivocally to a mixed audience and shared interest.[35] Elizabeth la Zouche, for example, owned a *Lancelot* and a *Tristrem* which she left to her husband in 1380. Sir Richard Roos, thought to have been the translator of Chartier's *La Belle Dame sans Merci*, left a manuscript (British Library Royal MS 14E.III) containing the *Quest of the Holy Grail* and the *Mort Artu* to his niece, Alyanor Hawte, sometime damsel to Queen Margaret of Anjou, in 1482. In surveying the evidence Carol Meale writes: 'This is not to say that the taste for Arthurian romance, and the story of Lancelot in particular, was an exclusively female one – men bequeathed Arthurian texts to their daughters, sisters and wives, and women left them to their sons and husbands, as well as their daughters.'[36]

Arguably, feminist literary historians sometimes make too much of occasional evidence of female ownership in their search for a separate and distinctive female role within, and contribution to, medieval literary culture. The name Anne Hampton occurs in the sole surviving copy of the translations of the *Holy Grail* and *Merlin* made by the London skinner, Henry Lovelich, and the same hand that records this name also glossed passages highlighting the ancestors of Lancelot.

But it is also the case that among the owners of the manuscript in the fifteenth century was John Crok, brother of St Bartholomew's Hospital, who annotated it to the effect that Henry Lovelich had translated the works at the instance of Harry Barton, fellow skinner and twice mayor of London. There are also marginal annotations by John Crok's friend, the London stationer and book-lender, John Shirley. The so-called 'Findern' manuscript of south Derbyshire, which contains a copy of *Sir Degrevant*, has many names in its margins. Most of them are female and most of them are connected in terms of family or propinquity. But even if this manuscript was 'assembled as a women's book', as has been suggested, this does not prove that its readers were exclusively female, any more than male names would suggest an exclusively male audience.[37]

The Paston evidence points in the same direction.[38] That the Paston men read romances is certain from John Paston II's inventory of books and from the letters which show a two-way traffic in their books between the George Inn in Lombard Street, London, where they lodged, and their estates in Norfolk. John's sister, Anne, possessed a copy of the *Siege of Thebes* which figured in this traffic. In June 1472 John Paston III recommended to his elder brother that he become acquainted with the Earl of Arran, who was also lodged at the George. He added: 'He hath a book of my syster Annys of the Sege of Thebes. When he hathe doon wyth it he promysed to delyver it yow.' The inventory contains evidence for the lending of books. One was John Paston's copy of *Troilus* which Sir William Brandon had lent to Dame Wingfield.

These matters are important because where one reads, and with whom one reads, often has a bearing on how one reads (or, of course, listens). Reading among the laity was largely a household activity, a group activity conducted in private chambers or solars as opposed to the public arena of the hall.[39] The difference between entertainment in the chamber and the hall is graphically presented in the alliterative *Parlement of the Three Ages*:

> And than with damesels dere to dawnsen in thaire chambirs;
> Riche Romance to rede and reken the sothe
> Of kempes and of conquerours, of kynges full noblee,
> How tha[y] wirchipe and welthe wanne in thair lyues;
> With renkes in ryotte to reuelle in haulle.   [knights]
> With coundythes and carolles and compaynyes sere.   [part-songs]
> (ll. 249–54)

The range of material that the members of a lay household might encounter in this way is shown by Digby 86, a manuscript produced in south-west Worcestershire during the years 1282 and 1283.[40] It belonged successively to two minor landowning families, the Grimhills and the Underhills. It was almost certainly produced for Richard de Grimhill and passed to his daughter and co-heiress, Amice, and her husband, Simon de Underhill. It belongs therefore to the cultural world of the gentry of the late thirteenth and early fourteenth centuries. It is a trilingual manuscript. Roughly half of its items are in French, a quarter each in English and Latin. They include a wide variety of works, both religious and secular, in verse and in prose: doctrinal treatises, a calendar of saints, prayers, medical recipes, spells, veterinary precepts, proverbs, notes on the interpretation of dreams and prognostications, saints' legends, moral and didactic verse, satire, lyrics and romances. Among the French works are found items of moral instruction as well as scurrilous pieces like *La Vie d'un Vallet Amerous*. Among the English pieces are several which are unique to this manuscript, including *The Fox and the Wolf* and *Dame Sirith*, the earliest English fabliau. There is also *The Thrush and the Nightingale* and the extraordinary poem called *The Names of a Hare*, which, as John Frankis says, 'gives an unparalleled insight into medieval rural superstition'. The mixture of literary works and matters of more practical use suggests that the manuscript had a dual function: it gave guidance and it provided entertainment. That this entertainment was intended to be social rather than private and individual is shown especially by the Anglo-Norman poem called *Ragemon le Bon*. This was a parlour-game, in which fortunes were told by the drawing of lots. Despite jokes about women and cuckoldry, it was clearly meant for mixed company, as the last ten or twelve stanzas are addressed specifically to women. In short Digby 86 was intended for use by a gentle household. It may have been written by a member of the Grimhill family. But it could equally have been put together by a cleric; if so the most likely contender would be a private chaplain in the manorial household.

The contents of Digby 86 are a reminder that romances are often found in manuscripts in company with saints' lives and, indeed, as is often remarked, the two have many features in common, especially where romances produced in England, with their obvious didactic quality, are concerned. Digby 86 also reminds one of the later medieval 'household' books, some of which probably come from an urban setting and tend to be dubbed 'mercantile' or 'bourgeois'. These have romances, saints' lives, works of spiritual improvement and items of practical value. Probably the best known of these is Ashmole 61 which also contains a number of courtesy texts.[41] It has been suggested that these tended to belong to women as educators of small children and household managers.[42] It is an interesting idea, but there is no actual evidence to support it. Once again, it argues for too strong a separation of lives and functions. The point is that young women encountered romances, and similar works, with other material that was normative, within a family setting. It will be recalled that the maiden in Chrétien's *Yvain* was reading to her parents. It was in these circumstances in particular that romances and saints' lives helped to 'constitute social identities through powerful appeals to the imagination'.[43]

Before looking in more detail at the content of romance, it is worth stopping to examine an area where the search for female circles has borne more fruit; that is within religious culture. Felicity Riddy has argued recently that *The Canterbury Tales* gives us access to the sub-culture of the closed female communities, as represented by the the prioress and the second nun, relating the Marian miracle of the chorister killed by Jews and the story of St Cecilia respectively.[44] A fourteenth-century analogue of the *Prioress's Tale* occurs in the Vernon manuscript, a manuscript contemporary with *The Canterbury Tales* and which, it has been suggested, was written for a community of nuns or, possibly, for a household of devout gentlewomen.[45] It now contains nine, but originally there were forty-one, miracles of the Virgin, preceded by prayers to her and followed by the northern homily cycle. The book also contains a strikingly large number of works written specifically for women readers by Aelred of Rievaulx, Richard Rolle and Walter Hilton, as well as the *Abbey of the Holy Ghost*, which instructs the reader how to build a nunnery in the heart, and the *Ancrene Riwle*, written for a group of female recluses. It also contains other texts known to have been read by devout women, such as Bishop Grosseteste's *Château d'Amour*, as well as the romances *Joseph of Arimathea* and the *King of Tars*.

One of the features of convent life, which was regularly criticised by bishops in their episcopal visitations to nunneries from the thirteenth century onwards, was the way that religious communities were allowed to fragment into separate *familie* or households.[46] Recent archaeological evidence suggests that in some cases such *familie* actually lived in separate buildings.[47] According to Riddy, 'Some of these *familie* may well have formed reading communities, their members teaching one another, sharing books and discussing them together.'[48] Particularly interesting is the fact that Prioress Margaret Sylemon left to Nuneaton Priory a book containing the *Château d'Amour* which was owned by herself and her pupils (*et discipulas suas*). Margaret was prioress from 1367 to 1386 and the pupils were presumably novices or younger nuns. The manuscript survives as McLean 123, and it bears the name of another female owner, Alicia de Scheynton, followed by a note saying that after her it passed to the convent. Wills of lay women also contain bequests of books to convents, perhaps encouraged by their relative poverty as religious houses. It may be true that the literary culture of nuns and devout gentlewomen overlapped and that a network existed among them for the acquisition of texts.[49]

Other forms of association existed, however, entirely within lay society. One was spiritual kinship. Interestingly, Dame Matilda Bowes, a widow, left her god-daughter, another Matilda, daughter of Lord Hilton, a gospel book in French in 1420. Spiritual kinship could provide women with social networks that crossed the generational boundaries, extending both motherhood and sisterhood. There was also association during widowhood. Many devout widows decided to devote the remainder of their lives to contemplation, living in chastity and probably eschewing remarriage. Some of them formalised their situation by making a vow and came to be known, in consequence, as vowesses. The vow was made before a bishop prior to mass. The woman in question would place her written vow at the bishop's feet and read from it (or, if she were illiterate, her reading would be led by the bishop). She then marked the document with a cross and gave it to the bishop for safe-keeping.[50] The woman's clothes were blessed and asperged, followed by her ring with which she was then invested.[51] How many noble women in these circumstances joined reading circles it is impossible to know. But pious all-female reading circles do seem to have existed. Henry VII's mother, Lady Margaret Beaufort, Countess of Richmond, commissioned Wynkyn de Worde to print Hilton's *Scale of Perfection* in 1494 and she and her daughter-in-law, Elizabeth of York, jointly presented a copy of it to Mary Roos, one of Elizabeth's ladies. This 'aristocratic trio', linked in this way, constituted a small reading community who supported one another in their prayers.[52] A generation earlier, the household ordinances of Cecily, Duchess of York, Edward IV's mother, who was widowed in 1460 in her mid-forties, show that during dinner she would listen to readings. During supper the duchess would repeat to the others present what she had heard earlier in the day and after supper would relax with her gentlewomen.[53] In Felicity Riddy's view these women formed a reading community of precisely the same kind as that which, seventy or eighty years before, probably commissioned the Vernon Manuscript.

However, one must be careful. These were very high-ranking ladies indeed, and they may have been far from typical even in widowhood. There is no reason why after-dinner readings should not have involved mixed audiences, even for widows. There is no suggestion that Dame Alice de Bryene, for example, shut herself off from normal social intercourse. Indeed, as we have seen, all the indications are that she did not.[54] Moreover, one hardly needed to belong to an exclusively female network to own devotional works. Many ladies possessed books of hours. Saying their hours was a devotion urged on young women, not least by Geoffrey de la Tour Landry in his advice to his daughters. It was a strong feature of later medieval piety. Many books of hours must, in effect, have belonged to households rather than to individuals, especially where they were de luxe manuscripts for show rather than for use. Of course, show and use are not mutually exclusive categories. The French poet Eustace Deschamps, in satirising female desire for books of hours, emphasised their need to be seen in church with expensive examples:

> A book of hours, too, must be mine,
> Where subtle workmanship will shine,
> Of gold and azure, rich and smart,
> Arranged and painted with great art,
> Covered with fine brocade of gold;
> And there must be, so as to hold
> The pages closed, two golden clasps.[55]

The idea behind books of hours was that they should be read eight times a day at the canonical hours. They could be read in private, at home or in chapels, or they could be taken into church where they could be used to follow along with the priest as mass was being said. They were certainly owned by men as well as women, but there are grounds for associating them particularly with women. A study of 1,000 owners of books in wills shows that of the 53 owners who were women as many as 30 owned books of hours. Only 28 of the male owners had books of hours, i.e. almost as many in absolute terms but proportionally far less.[56] They tended to be bequeathed by the women to daughters or to daughters-in-law. One manuscript carried an inscription indicating that it was a gift by Elizabeth Hull, Abbess of Malling, to her godchild, Margaret Neville. Some books of hours contain owner-portraits. While this is true of socially elevated male as well as female owners, the books of hours clearly had particular resonance for women. Most owner-portraits are found at the beginning of the Little Office of the Blessed Virgin Mary or failing that before the prayers that were specifically addressed to the Virgin. The sense of personal devotion is heightened where the portrait either contains or is paralleled by a depiction of the Virgin herself. In these instances the Holy Mother is being actively visualised by the worshipper in a manner much encouraged by later medieval devotional literature. [See colour plates] The emotional response to the Virgin as mother is obviously more appropriate to the female than to the male reader. It is hardly surprising, therefore, that books of hours were commissioned for women on the occasion of their marriages, and often by their future husbands. One should not be over-cynical as to motive. It is none the less true that contemplation of the Virgin, and indeed of the portraits of female saints who are also found depicted in the books of hours, emphasises certain 'exemplary' aspects of female behaviour: humility, purity, devotion, submissiveness and servility.

In short, it would be quite wrong to envisage female piety as entirely divorced from that of their male kin. Take the case of the so-called Lollard knights, whose religious sympathies worried late fourteenth-century chroniclers. Sir John Clanvowe, the author of *The Two Ways*, was actually accused of heresy. The will of his relative, perhaps his daughter-in-law, Lady Peryne Clanvowe, reveals the same traits as his. There is the same disdain for the body and the same distaste for worldly pomp. There is also, however, an emphasis upon charity and good works, and she was probably more orthodox than heretic. She left a book in English called *The Pore Caitif*, a somewhat suspect work, to Elizabeth Joye, one of her executors, but she also left a mass book to her brother. What was orthodox and

78. A devout widow? A lady sits at a knight's feet (the Norton effigy, Cleveland). Note the open book and the simple attire

what was heterodox was often unclear and the Lollard 'sympathisers' were not homogeneous in their views. What is important, however, is that male and female members of the gentry inhabited the same moral and intellectual climate and were touched by the same traits in contemporary piety.[57] Theirs was a religiosity very much in tandem across gender. Even vowesses, however, were not wholly shut off from the male world, in that their dead husbands were ever present in their minds and their activities. It may well be this situation which is represented in the fine early fourtenth-century effigy of a knight at Norton, in Cleveland, where a lady sits above the knight's feet on his right side. She has an open book in front of her, but she is looking towards him, in dutiful if not reverential fashion. It could be that she represents a member of a religious order, but her singularity strongly suggests the representation of a devout widow, who will now devote the remainder of her life to contemplation, living in chastity and probably eschewing remarriage.

The image of an all-female world of religious piety must be tempered in another direction too. It has been shown convincingly that many later medieval devotional texts, written by cloistered men for a female readership, promote spiritual friendship betwen the sexes, in a 'discourse of familiarity'.[58] Not only do these texts tend to foster what was called 'reasonable affection', as distinct from the carnal type, but they talk in terms of love between spiritual brothers and sisters and point to circles of chaste male and female friends. Although elements of misogyny frequently surface, there is less of an obsession with celibacy and with the special female proclivity to sins of the flesh. There is more than a suggestion, in fact, of spiritual equality. Such writings are addressed in the first instance to nuns by cloistered men, and they appear to have been modelled ultimately upon a tradition of correspondence between male members of the regular clergy. There seems little doubt, moreover, that relationships of this kind did actually develop between male and female religious, transcending the text as it were, and notwithstanding the fact that such associations were officially frowned upon by the Church.[59] But even though the formal address to cloistered nuns tends to remain, these texts were also copied for specific laywomen. There is no doubt that they achieved wide circulation. From the texts the women derived not only spiritual instruction but also 'an ideology of mixed-sex spiritual friendship'. The content of reworked female saints' lives that were produced for later medieval patrons, for example those of Osbern Bokenham of Stoke-Clare, tend to put more emphasis than ever before upon close spiritual friendship between men and women. It can be argued that those pious aristocratic ladies of the fifteenth century, of whose private lives we know a little, such as Margaret Beaufort, Cecily, Duchess of York, and Margaret, Duchess of Clarence, 'internalised this ethic of mixed-sex familiarity', developing close relationships with their scribes, priests and ecclesiastical officials.[60] But it could be equally true of ladies below this elevated level. The later medieval household was itself a religious community, with its own chapel and chaplains.[61] [See colour plates] The friendship between a widowed lady and her household chaplain could sometimes cause consternation among members of her family. John Paston III wrote to his elder brother on 8 July 1472 of 'the prowd, pevyshe and evyll dysposyed prest to us all, Syr Jamys', meaning James Gloys, the family chaplain. Many quarrels are picked, he says, to get him and his brother Edmund out of the house: 'Alle that we do is ille doon, and all that Syr James and Pekok dothe is well doon. Syr Jamys and I be tweyn. We fyll owght be-for my modyr wyth "Thow prowd prest" and "thow prowd sqwyer", my modyr takyng hys part.' Such a situation could have practical consequences. Margaret was threatening to make a new settlement of her estate: 'And in thys angyr betwen Syr Jamys and me she hathe promyseid me that my parte shall be nowght.' For the benefit of his elder brother, John Paston II, he adds: 'what your [part] shalbe I can not sey'.[62]

Female networks of association undoubtedly existed, but these did not cut most ladies off from cultural association with men. The evidence as a whole does not support the contention that within gentry families husbands and wives led separate lives, with the wives left at home 'to cultivate those networks of female friendships for which almost the only remaining evidence is to be found in their wills'.[63] Some men, it is true, spent a considerable amount of time away from home, such as John Paston I and John Paston II. But there is no need to postulate any form of cultural apartheid. That would be a distortion of the social reality. Certainly wills do afford glimpses of female networks, and not only in religious matters; they are shown in the distribution of their gowns and jewellery, for example. This hardly makes such networks exclusive. Apart from their servants, to whom else could they give their gowns and jewellery? The will of Margaret Wiltshire, for example, proven in the presence of the Bishop of Worcester on 24 September 1387, first of all arranges for her burial in the church of the Dominicans in London, beneath the stone where her husband, John Wiltshire, rests, and for the disposition of her manor of Bradenham in Buckinghamshire to a group of six men headed by the Earl of Warwick, her son John, and two other knights. She then proceeds to make bequest of her goods. Her psalter goes to 'my most honoured lady of Warwick (*ma treshonure dame de Warr'*)', and her best houpland to Avis Biblesworth. All her kerchiefs of Paris are to be divided between Avis, Agnes Stoke, Alison Spernore, Alison Rusell, Margaret Thynton and Margaret Vanney, at the discretion of 'my very honoured lady', of Roger Tangeley and of the said Avis. Furthermore, Agnes de Whitenhale and Lucy de Lodelowe, who are presumably her servants, are to be rewarded from her coats, kirtles and unlined hoods, again according to the discretion of her executors. The remainder of her goods and chattels, however, are to be divided among a group of the most favoured men and women. They include the Countess of Warwick and Avis de Biblesworth, to be sure, but the others are Sir Roger Tangeley, Thomas Barentyn, brother of Avis, Sir John, parson of Bradenham Church, Nicholas Trymmel, W. Wanney and John Warmeley. The same features are to be found in the fuller list of bequests made by Margaret Legat of Wotton under Edge in her will, proven before the same bishop on 8 January 1385. Having specified her place of burial, disposed of her land and tenements and made various pious bequests, she turns to her goods. The list is headed by a mortar and pestle to the lord of Berkeley and her best ring to his wife. We then have gold rings to Elizabeth, daughter of Margaret, and to Katherine de Berkeley. Joan Bristowe is to have her best piece of Paris kerchief and Claricia Wyggestowe another gold ring. The wife of John

Winter is to have a ring, while Joan Bounde is to have an ivory comb. The three daughters of Roger Duynysh' are each to have half a mark and one of them a kerchief of Paris. Her own sister, Katherine Stonhouse, is to have a blue tabard lined with fur, a piece of Paris kerchief, a table cloth and towel, a cooking pot of best quality, a green bed with canopy, a blanket and one pair of linen sheets. There are bequests to Katherine's three daughters. Katherine, presumably the eldest, is singled out. She is to have a bed of Norwich worsted with canopy, a blanket and a pair of linen sheets, a chest, a posnet (a metal pot) and a copper pan as well as a kirtle. Each of the other two daughters is to have 20s, a cooking pot, a Paris kerchief, a tunic, a fur or lining, a hose and a kirtle. Alice Prestes is to have a tunic of rabbit fur, a caul, a fillet and a pair of black beads. Margaret, her servant, is to have a smock and a caul. John Winter is to have a copper pan, while Hugh Bisseley is to have her best cooking pot. W. Legat is to have a green girdle with golden harness, a pair of amber beads, and a beautiful chest. Finally, Elizabeth Blees, her sister, is to have half a mark and W. her brother is to have forty pence. In other words, her friends and relatives are to have what is most appropriate to them.[64]

What, then, did their reading suggest to ladies about themselves? We have already noted that contemplation of the Virgin reinforces certain aspects of female behaviour as exemplary. Devotional literature, whatever else it does, also tends to stress women's subordinate role in the world. The *Speculum devotorum*, for example, glosses the story of Jesus at the Temple as follows: 'Take heed how our meek lady defers to Joseph, saying here to Jesus, "your father and I", and not "I and your father have sought you, sorrowing . . .". By this example of our meek lady, let women learn to be meek and not to place themselves before men in anything, and this applies especially to those women who have husbands.'[65]

With this in mind let us return to the question of romance and its effects. Both of the great literary genres that arose in the French-speaking lands during the later half of the twelfth and the early thirteenth centuries were decidely male-centred.[66] The epics or *chansons de geste* were obviously so in that most of the action took place on the battlefield. The ladies were present as nurturers – as providers of food and rest – and as counsellors. Their advice, however, showed that they were very much integrated into the value-system of the warrior nobility, supporting loyalty to lineage and to feudal lord. They are also portrayed with responsibility for the running of the household, but essentially they figure as the encouragers of male participants, and they are located on the sidelines. Despite the love theme and the attention focused on the lady, the romance is even more fundamentally male-centred. Whereas the epic is about the communal interest, the romance centres on the individual knight's quest for identity. Although it often involves the attainment of a woman, and despite the fact that she serves as inspiration, her feelings are relatively unimportant. As has been said, whereas the *chanson de geste* represents woman 'as the companion of man, as his spouse, as his constant helper and adviser even in military and political matters', the romance represents her as 'a romantic object'.[67] The lady alone is portrayed as a helpless figure, requiring male protection for her person and her estates. This is shown startlingly in *Yvain* where the hero, having killed Laudine's husband, proceeds to marry her. The ideologically charged text assures the reader that marriage is necessary to her survival while at the same time showing that she is perfectly capable of running the household with the advice of her knights, like any feudal lord. While the lady in romance acquires her identity through marriage, she also recognises that there is another world which her lord must inhabit, the world of adventure and tournament. If she figures at all in these, she figures as observer. Moreover, the romance often centres on a fundamental tension between love and prowess, between the private world centred on the woman and the public world centred on the court and its concerns. The tension is essentially experienced by men; it is a tension which in the extreme examples of Lancelot and Tristan has tragic consequences as love conflicts with feudal loyalty. As Penny Schine Gold puts it, 'The attitude which unites the two genres is the attitude that women's importance rests in their relationship to men, whether as active helpmate or passive object.'[68]

French romances were well known in England but there were also, of course, home-grown romances in Anglo-Norman and later in Middle English. These possessed their own characteristics and, indeed, evolved considerably during the thirteenth and fourteenth centuries. Although they tend to be 'sceptical of courtly poetics', as Susan Crane puts it,[69] and the later romances in Middle English in particular are increasingly didactic, stressing social and sexual propriety and frequently ending in marriage, the emphasis upon the hero remains throughout. A lady's standing is shown to be contingent upon marriage. There are spirited damsels indeed – Guy of Warwick's Felice and Ipomedon's la Fière, for example – but it is the knight who invariably comes out on top. Although a lady can be capable of exemplary love, women's frivolity, wiles and shifting affections are frequently encountered. As far as the fundamental values of society are concerned, the romances are clear: 'men should engage in chivalry to be worthy of love, and women should accord their love only to the chivalrous'.[70]

In reading or hearing romances women could recognise their role and internalise what was expected from them; but, more significantly still, they could recognise, and absorb uncritically, what they could expect from the men. This included social violence in certain circumstances; even violence against them. A particularly powerful example comes from the French romance of *Yder* which survives in one manuscript in Anglo-Norman dialect from the second half of the thirteenth century.[71] Early in the romance Yder encounters the noble and courteous King Ivenant who promises to knight him if he passes a test which the king customarily offers to young aspirants to knighthood. This is to resist the charms of the king's seductive wife. Naturally, Yder passes the test, a task made easier by the fact that he is already in love. After resisting a series of verbal advances, Yder replies that he is not interested in her love; instead he advises her to go away and to be careful that he does not strike her. He draws away from her as much as possible, but she draws closer immediately. Yder then kicks her in the belly so that she falls backwards and her colour drains away. 'I cannot criticise him for this', says the poet, 'as he was unable to defend himself in any other way.' The people playing games in the hall had seen the kick and heard the words; they laughed a lot and were very pleased about it, for they knew all about the custom.

The queen left angrily, upset because she knew she had been humiliated. Meanwhile, a spokesman for the knights who were in the hall told the king that Yder had defended himself valiantly: 'The queen had kept caressing him,' they said. 'She would have kissed him if he had agreed; he called her a loose-living whore.'[72]

Of course, ideology does not impact upon the reader in a necessarily straightforward or uniform way. Pre-existing cultural influences are at work which affect the text's message as we read; such influence is likely to occur as social experience when texts are read in groups, emphasising or de-emphasising the messages that come across. Altogether, however, the ideology surrounding medieval woman was an extremely powerful one. On the face of it, women were encouraged to see themselves as potentially foolish and fickle, loquacious and lascivious, as passive and subsidiary, as inspiring or inhibiting their men, and it is hard to doubt that many women did absorb uncritically elements of the patriarchal ideology that was inherent in their culture. But there were other possibilities. There was the possibility of outright resistance. The most famous resister was the French writer, Christine de Pisan, who, in the prologue to *La Cité des Dames*, tells how she was reading the *Lamentations* of Matheolus, a strikingly misogynistic text, and wondering why her own sense of herself and her own observations of women did not accord with the views of the learned men. At first she accepted the traditional arguments, however, on the grounds they could not all be wrong:

> And, finally, I decided that God formed a vile creature when He made woman and I wondered how such a worthy artisan could have deigned to make such an abominable work which, from what they say, is the vessel as well as the refuge and abode of every evil and vice. As I was thinking this, a great unhappiness and sadness welled up in my heart, for I detested myself and the entire feminine sex, as though we were monstrosities in nature.[73]

Her painful thoughts were interrupted by a vision of three crowned ladies – Reason, Rectitude and Justice – who inspired her to write a work in defence of women. But Christine might be regarded as the exception which proves the rule. Although we should not necessarily take her prologue at face value, the point is that she was a privileged, talented and highly educated woman who enjoyed the mental resources to resist centuries of misogynistic thought. Even she had needed to fight to resist the strong ideological influences upon her.

There are, however, alternative ways of reading texts. As far as later medieval devotional literature is concerned, Anne Clark Bartlett has detected a shift away from the traditional tendency to reorientate the female reader in order to negate her femininity, which was seen as very largely a barrier to successful religious experience. The later texts, she maintains, contain three distinct 'counter discourses'. One is that of spiritual friendship. A second is the discourse of courtesy, where the Christ lover is depicted as a courtly knight actively pursuing the romance heroine who is no longer the lascivious daughter of Eve but a worthy creature in her own right.[74] 'Such conventions', she argues, 'offer readers a validation (albeit an ambivalent one) of female power, agency and beauty.'[75] The third discourse is that of nuptial and Passion contemplation with its vivid representations of the maternal body of the Virgin Mary, of Christ's sufferings on the cross and of his ardour as the divine bridegroom. This type of mystical or quasi-mystical experience, with its peculiar variety of morbid eroticism, is deeply distasteful to many modern readers. But there is no doubt of its appeal to some women who were desirous of deeply moving religious experiences. There is no doubt, too, that it could turn some women, like the English visionary Margery Kempe, who publicised their experiences, into figures of significance; that it could 'empower' them, to use the current idiom.

But how much validation there was in these 'counter discourses' must remain a matter of debate. The discourse of spiritual familiarity, despite overtones of equality, nevertheless firmly reinforces the role of the male as instructor and the female as recipient of instruction. Nor is it free from misogynistic observations. The narratives of nuptial and Passion contemplation are patently predicated upon repression of natural female desires, or at least of their natural outlets. As for the theme of Christ the lover-knight, its effects are indeed ambivalent, as Bartlett herself notes. Like the romances on which it draws, it stresses qualities such as meekness, humility, chastity and, above all, passivity as the most desirable female characteristics. It should also be pointed out that Bartlett's three counter discourses are not female readings of the older devotional texts, but reworkings by male authors in which they accommodate broad cultural changes. The courtly discourse, for instance, quite obviously reflects the general pervasiveness of the romance genre in later medieval culture. They may, indeed, incorporate elements of female resistance to traditional paradigms, but they should not be seen, at least not in any straightforward way, as the direct product of such resistance. None the less, these 'counter discourses' open up the possibility of interpreting texts in different ways.

Another possible response, however, was that of the semi-literate Margery Kempe, who seems to have accepted those influences upon her which she could assimilate and simply by-passed those which she could not.[76] Margery was born around 1373, the daughter of John Brunham of King's Lynn, a man at the apex of urban society, five times mayor and twice MP. Technically illiterate, she was semi-literate in the sense that she had access to a considerable range of devotional literature through being read to, often in fact by the religious men who belonged to her spiritual circle. In her intense emotionalism, characterised by uncontrollable fits of weeping, in her bond of mutual chastity with her husband (in his case, unwillingly), and in many other ways, Margery was in the tradition of later medieval female visionaries and mystics that included figures like the beguine Marie of Oignies, St Bridget of Sweden, the 'heretic' Marguerite Porete, and the Blessed Angela of Foligno. The point here is that Margery was able to side-step constraints upon her behaviour simply by refusing to countenance them, and by concentrating upon those elements of doctrine and advice which she found congenial.

This brings us back to Chaucer and to his portrait of Dame Alice, the Wife of Bath, who has also been seen in this way.[77] Dame Alice is a compendium created from the stereotypes of misogynist literature. She is, in fact, 'the embodiment and living exponent of all that male clerical writers most feared'.[78] She is all those things that the knight of la Tour Landry warns his daughters against being. They would recognise her sartorially:

> Hir coverchiefs ful fyne weren of grounde;
> I dorste swere they weyeden ten pound.
> That on a Sunday weren upon hir heed.
> Hir hosen weren of fyn scarlet reed,
> Ful streite ytyed, and shoes ful moyste and newe. . . .
>
> Ywympled wel, and on hir heed an hat
> As brood as is a bokeler or a targe.
>
> (*General Prologue*, ll. 453–71)

And also behaviourally:

> 'Sire olde kaynard, is this thyn array?   [dotard]
> Why is my neighebores wyf so gay?
> She is honoured over all ther she gooth;
> I sitte at hoom, I have no thrifty clooth . . .'.
>
> (*Wife of Bath's Prologue*, ll. 235–8)

But the Wife of Bath is also recognisable as a feminist. The vast panoply of works on women and women's vices, from the ancient world through St Paul and the early fathers to medieval estates satire, denies woman an authentic voice.[79] They are silent; they are the Other. Chaucer's embodiment gives the Other a voice, and allows her to speak. In doing so, he lays bare the roots of anti-feminism. In the works she cited, Geoffrey de la Tour Landry's daughters could have perceived clearly the origins of what was being preached to them. Much depended upon the glossing of texts, the interpretations and extrapolations of which medieval writers were so fond. The Wife of Bath does some glossing of her own, reinterpreting St Paul and St Jerome to suit her own purposes.[80] She then gives us an antagonistic view of the relations between the sexes in showing us in

79. '*Upon an amblere esily she sat, Ywympled wel, and on her heed an hat*': Chaucer's Wife of Bath (from the Ellesmere manuscript)

detail how she manipulates, feigns and contrives to get the better of her husbands. But what she also shows us is that her actions are inspired by the need to counter male institutional power and her husbands' desire to control her, her activities and her associations. It is little wonder that she reacts against the idea of inherited gentility, of *gentillesse* passed from father to son. It was this that did so much to dictate that a woman's status was dependent upon her husband's. In support of her position she creates her own discourse, much dependent upon the patriarchal tradition within which she is suffering, but drawing in counter-authorities, including proverbs, astrology and the supernatural, as well as her own experience.[81] In other words she reinterprets cultural symbols and representations to subvert the prevailing orthodoxy, much as Caroline Walker Bynum has shown pious women manipulating medieval lore relating to food – distribution of alms, fasting, eucharistic devotion and miracles – in pursuit of self-determination and empowerment.[82]

But there is another reading of the Wife of Bath beyond the feminist. If we turn from the prologue of her tale to the tale itself, the story of the Knight and the Loathly Lady, another possibility emerges. The action begins with an act of rape by one of King Arthur's knights:

> And so bifel it that this kyng Arthour
> Hadde in his hous a lusty bachelor,
> That on a day cam ridynge fro ryver;
> And happed that, alone as he was born,
> He saugh a mayde walkynge hym biforn,
> Of which mayde anon, maugre hir heed,
> By verray force, he rafte hir maydenhed.
>
> (*Wife of Bath's Tale*, ll. 882–8)

The law of Arthur's realm was that the knight should automatically lose his life for this crime.[83] However, at her instigation, the matter was put into the queen's hands. Her judgement was this: if the knight could return in twelve months' time with the answer to a single question, then his life would be spared. The question was this: 'What thyng is it that woomen most desiren?' The knight searched high and low and was given a whole series of possible answers – richness, honour, merriment, rich array, 'lust abedde', to be flattered, to be free both in action and from criticism, to be told – falsely – that they could keep a secret. None of these carried conviction. Finally, close to despair, the knight was riding through a forest when he came upon a fairy ring. Just as he purposed to ask the ladies his question, they disappeared leaving an old hag. She promised to give him the answer to his question if he, in return, would plight her his troth to do the very next thing she required of him, if it lay within his power.

When the knight came to hold his day, at a court composed entirely of noble wives, maidens and widows, with the queen herself presiding as justice, he had his answer ready:

'My lige lady, generally,' quod he,
'Wommen desiren to have sovereynetee
As wel over hir housbond as hir love,
And for to been in maistrie hym above.
This is youre moost desir, thogh ye me kille . . .'

(Wife of Bath's Tale, ll. 1037–41)

It was, of course, the correct answer, and the knight was spared his life; but at a price. The old hag now claimed her prize – his hand in marriage. After the marriage, conducted privately on the morrow, the knight finds it difficult to pay his marriage debt. The old hag asks him why this should be so. The reason is threefold: her ugliness, her age, and her low birth. Having lectured him on the true nature of *gentillesse*, she comes to the crucial point. He can choose one of two alternatives. She can remain 'foul and old' but true, or she can become young and fair but with all the probable consequences in terms of cuckoldry. Faced with an impossible decision, he puts himself in her hands:

'My lady and my love, and wyf so deere,
I put me in youre wise governance;
Cheseth yourself which may be moost plesance,
And moost honour to yow and me also . . .'.

(Wife of Bath's Tale, ll. 1030–3)

Now, at last, she really does have mastery. In consequence, she grants him both his desires. Henceforth she becomes fair *and* true:

And whan the knyght saugh verraily al this,
That she so fair was, and so yong therto,
For joye he hente hire in his armes two,
His herte bathed in a bath of blisse.
A thousand tyme a-rewe he gan hire kisse,
And she obeyed hym in every thyng
That myghte doon hym plesance or likyng.

(Wife of Bath's Tale, ll. 1050–6)

The knight has been forced to recognise women not as objects but as creatures with feelings in their own right. He has been forced to ask himself for once what it is that a woman wants. Once the institutional supports of a male-dominated world are taken from him, the knight is brought face to face with his double standards and his narcissistic egocentricity. The court which passes initial sentence upon him and the court to which he returns in twelve months and a day is a female one. Neither is he protected by the discourse itself. The *Wife of Bath's Tale* is a romance certainly, but a romance with a difference. The knight's quest in this instance is woman-centred in a way that it has not been before. His self-realisation becomes, in effect, the realisation of the content and consequences of patriarchy.

As has been pointed out, the tale has features in common with the famous lays of the late twelfth-century writer Marie de France.[84] They have a supernatural setting, the teller is a woman and, above all, they centre upon the gratification of female desires. But there is more to it than this. Ultimately, it is not that male desires have simply yielded to female ones, but rather that they have been integrated. When the lady has true mastery over her man and her life she yields it. Why? Because what she wants is not sovereignty at all but recognition. She wants love and fulfilment. The dénouement of the tale is mirrored in the Wife of Bath's prologue, where Alice reaches an accommodation with her fifth husband, the clerk Jankyn.

Here, however, it is an accommodation resulting from conflict. Their marriage began as a raunchy but stormy one, with Jankyn habitually reading to his wife from his book of wicked wives. Here were all the stock characters from the Bible and from the classical world so beloved of the clerks. Not surprisingly, Jankyn's book has a great deal in common with Geoffrey de la Tour Landry's, a large section of which deals with Eve and with other female perpetrators of enormities drawn from misogynistic tradition. One evening, the Wife of Bath relates, Jankyn was reading to her from his book as was his wont, when she could stand it no more. Seeing that he was going to continue reading from it all night, she suddenly tore three leaves from the book and hit him with such force on the cheek that he fell back into the fire. Getting up like a mad lion he smote her on the head so that she was 'somdel deef' on that side thereafter. As she feigned dying, Jankyn broke down and repented of his action, whereupon she hit him again. The process was different but the result was the same as in the tale. He yielded sovereignty to her, but she declined to exercise it:

> But atte laste, with muchel care and wo,
> We fille accorded by us selven two.
> He yaf me al the bridel in myn hond,
> To han the governance of hous and lond,
> And of his tonge, and of his hond also;
> And made hym brenne his book anon right tho.   [burn]
> And whan that I hadde geten unto me,
> By maistrie, al the soveraynetee,
> And that he seyde, 'Myn owene trewe wyf,
> Do as thee lust the terme of al thy lyf;
> Keep thyn honour, and keep eek myn estat'-
> After that day we hadden never debaat.
> God helpe me so, I was to hym as kynde
> As any wyf from Denmark to Ynde,
> And also trewe, and so was he to me.

(*Wife of Bath's Prologue*, ll. 811–25)

For all Chaucer's imaginative leap, the Wife of Bath remains a male creation and both the prologue's ending and the tale's dénouement belong to the world of male fantasy. It would be quite wrong to see the result as one of sexual equality. Bliss may ensue, but the Wife has done no more than temper male sovereignty. It remains intact, but by mutual agreement. In both her prologue and her tale the Wife of Bath works largely, although not exclusively, from within the dominant male discourse.[85] The one hinges particularly on the traditional texts, even if differently glossed, while the other is still formally a romance. However, these fictive explorations do point to the theoretical possibility, and hence to the practical probability, of a genuine *modus vivendi*, as the partners negotiate the social and institutional world they inhabit; in doing so, they employ whatever resources they have at their disposal. One cannot negotiate without ideas, but it is not essentially on the level of interpreting texts that real relationships are negotiated, whatever some literary theorists might think. Real women in real situations, and no doubt many men, ignored the excesses of misogynistic doctrine but were none the less influenced by the weight of opinion that gave women, formally at least, a subsidiary role. For most people then, as now, their lives were not ones of perpetual conflict, even latent conflict, but of accommodation within institutional and ideological parameters.

CHAPTER 7

Conclusion: the Role of the Lady in Later Medieval England

And so we return to the Pastons. It has been convincingly argued recently, on the basis of the Paston evidence, that honour or 'worship' in the provincial gentry society of the fifteenth century was bound up more with mundane matters than with chivalric display.[1] Local society was the true arena in which worship was lost or earned, and matters such as arranging marriages, handling lawsuits, dealing with neighbours, supporting tenants and associates, and generally participating in local society, were the real stuff of reputation. As we have seen, ladies played a significant part in all of this. To be sure, it was the men who held office and who went to court. But the broad participation of the women in noble society outside of household and home makes the distinction between public and private spheres an unreal one. It was not just that the Paston women are found advising their menfolk on conduct likely to ease or impede them in the pursuit of worship, but that they themselves frequently intervened. Ladies, of course, inherited a reputation as intercessors and peacemakers. The practical results of this can be observed not only in family matters but also on the wider public scene in the defence of family interests. One quite famous occasion in the Paston letters is the initiative taken to neutralise Elizabeth Mowbray, the Duchess of Norfolk, in a long-running dispute between John Paston III and his uncle William. Margery Paston wrote to her 'swete hert', that is her husband John Paston III, with the following plan, suggested to her by her cousin, William Gourney:

> and he seyd if I wold goo to my lady of Norffolk and besech hyr good grace to be youre good and gracyous lady, she wold so be; for he seyd that on word of a woman shuld do more than the wordys of xx men, yiffe I could rewyll my tonge and speke non harme of myn unkyll. And if ye comaund me so for to do, I trist I shuld sey nothyng to my ladys displesure . . .

She continued:

> I understond by my seyd cosyn Gornay that my lady is nere wery of hyr
> parte, and he seyth my lady shal come on pylgremage in-to this towne, but he
> knowyth not wheder afore Cristmes or aftyr; and if I wold thanne gete my
> Lady Calthorp, my moder in law, and my moder and my-selfe, and come
> before my lady besychyng hyr to be youre good and gracyous lady, he
> thynkyth ye shull have an ende, for fayne she wold be redde of it, wyth hyr
> onowre (honour) savyd, but yette money she wold have.[2]

As one commentator has said, the 'trio of elderly women that Margery assembled'
– that is, Margaret Paston, Elizabeth Brews and Elizabeth Calthorp – 'must have
been formidable'.[3] It is important not to take this wholly at face value, however.
There is an element of role play here. After all, the plan was devised by a male
relative and friend to the Pastons, who also appears to have done some preliminary
'softening-up'. It is evidence of a female network in operation, but it is a network
which was operating in the interests of a shared male and female concern.

In any case, intercession was only one aspect of the female involvement in the
furtherance of family interests. The important point is the one made by Philippa
Maddern that 'the power of these women derived not from their husbands'
frequent absences nor their own individual strength of character, but from the
peculiar nature of the system of honour, which rewarded behaviour appropriate to
women as well as men'.[4]

It is extremely unlikely that any of this was new in the fifteenth century; what
are new are the sources which enable us to see the women's full involvement more
clearly than ever before. The other collections of fifteenth-century letters reveal
the same role for the lady. As the recent editor of the Plumpton letters has
reminded us, what the male landowner needed was 'not patient Griselda, but a
vigorous, loyal helpmate', whose 'counsel was undimmed by lack of knowledge'.
'Like the Pastons', she concludes, 'the women we meet in the Plumpton
Correspondence were as sensitive to the honour of the family as the men, and
could defend it fiercely.'[5] We should not make too strong a distinction, however,
between chivalric culture and the rather civilian sense of honour presented in
fifteenth-century letters. Although the Paston men, for example, participated
only rarely in full chivalric display, chivalry nevertheless remained a significant
element in their culture, as indeed their books show. Mundane concerns must
always have been of paramount importance in local society. This is not to say,
however, that chivalric culture was merely a veneer. What linked chivalry with the
honour system were the two-fold notions of lineage and gentility, and here the
women were heavily involved. Gentility mattered greatly, and it mattered on both
sides of the family. In a letter to Margaret in July 1461 John Paston I thundered
against 'that knavyssh knyght', Sir Miles Stapleton: 'he and hys wyfe and other
have blaveryd here of my kynred in hodermoder, but be that tyme we have reknd
of old dayes and late dayes myn shall be found more worchepfull thanne hys and
hys wyfes.' Notwithstanding the colloquial language in which it is couched, John
Paston's meaning is clear enough.[6]

80. 'for above al the erthe my singuler trust is most in her': Alice de la Pole (née Chaucer), Duchess of Suffolk

By way of conclusion, a few details from the life of a lady who figures from time to time in the Paston letters may serve to underline the themes of this book. She is Alice, daughter of Thomas Chaucer and ultimately Duchess of Suffolk.[7] Around 1444 James Gresham reported to his master, the judge William Paston, that he and Drue Barantyn had argued over the feasibility of approaching the duchess direct. Even before she had sole direction of the Suffolk estates, Alice was a formidable figure.[8] During the 1440s, moreover, she participated in the unruly behaviour of the Suffolk faction. On one occasion she went to Norwich with Sir Thomas Tuddenham and two other persons, all of them in disguise. She herself was disguised 'lyke an huswyf of the countre'. From Norwich they went to Lakenham woods 'to tak the ayr and disport theymself'. In his will, the duke made her his sole executrix, 'for above al the erthe my singuler trust is moost in her'. Facing the possibility of his death in April 1450, the duke wrote a letter of advice to his son:

> I charge you, my dere sone, alwey, as ye be bounden by the commaundement of god to do, to love, to worshepe your lady and moder, and also that ye obey alwey hyr commaindements, and to beleve hyr councelles and advises in alle youre werks . . .

Alice, in fact, had a jointure of all the Suffolk estates, and was now a powerful lady indeed. After her husband's murder on 3 May 1450, she moved quickly to secure the Suffolk lands. By early June she was already appointing officials. She acquired the wardship of her son and eventually married him to a daughter of the Duke of York. The accounts of her receiver-general survive for the year 1453–4. They reveal her strong control over her administration – handling receipts, authorising payments, appointing to offices, arranging for her husband's memorial, and consulting her council. Like Margaret Paston, but on a diffferent social level, she demanded, deserved and received respect as a gentle woman.

Notes

1. Introduction

1. Norman Davis (ed.), *Paston Letters and Papers of the Fifteenth Century*, 2 vols (Oxford, 1971 and 1976), ii, no. 897.
2. *Paston Letters*, i, no. 73. Here and elsewhere I have modernised the spelling in the letters where necessary in the interest of clarity.
3. *Paston Letters*, i, no. 226.
4. This sentiment occurs in one of the letters which the devious John Paston III had prepared for his mother to send: *Paston Letters*, i, no. 378.
5. *Paston Letters*, ii, no. 861.
6. *Paston Letters*, ii, nos 715–16.
7. *Paston Letters*, ii, no. 745.
8. Joan Kelly, 'The Social Relations of the Sexes', *Signs: Journal of Women in Culture and Society*, i, no. 4 (Summer, 1976), pp. 809–23; repr. in *Women, History and Theory: The Essays of Joan Kelly* (Chicago, 1984), pp. 1–18.
9. *Ibid.*, p. 8.
10. See, for example, Gisella Bock, 'Challenging Dichotomies: Perspectives on Women's History', in K. Offen, R.R. Pierson and J. Rendall, *Writing Women's History: International Perspectives* (London, 1991), pp. 1–17, and Joan Wallach Scott, 'Gender: A Useful Category of Historical Analysis', published most recently in Joan Wallach Scott (ed.), *Feminism and History* (Oxford, 1996), pp. 152–80, and originally published in *American Historical Review*, 91/5 (Dec. 1986).
11. Bock, 'Challenging Dichotomies', pp. 16–17.
12. Scott, 'Gender: A Useful Category', pp. 161–5.
13. Gerda Lerner, *The Creation of Patriarchy* (Oxford, 1986), p. 238.
14. See Amanda Vickery, 'Golden Age to Separate Spheres? A Review of the Categories and Chronology of English Women's History', *The Historical Journal*, 36, 2 (1993), pp. 383–414. This offers a powerful critique of the use of separate spheres by historians of the nineteenth century in particular.

15. L. Kerber, 'Separate sphere, female worlds, woman's place: the rhetoric of women's history', *Journal of American History*, lxxv (1988), pp. 9–39.
16. Joan Kelly, 'The Doubled Vision of Feminist Theory', in *Women, History and Theory*, p. 57. This essay first appeared in *Feminist Studies*, 5, no. 1 (Spring, 1979), pp. 216–27.
17. The classic study is Lerner, *The Creation of Patriarchy*.

2. The Origins of the English Lady

1. For what follows see David Crouch, *The Image of Aristocracy in Britain 1000–1300* (London, 1992), which provides an excellent précis of developments. I have drawn especially upon chapter one, 'The Earl and the Count'.
2. *Ibid.*, p. 2.
3. Marjorie Chibnall (ed.), *The Ecclesiastical History of Orderic Vital*, 6 vols (Oxford, 1969–80), vi, p. 16; Crouch, *op. cit.*, pp. 5–6.
4. *Ibid.*, p. 4.
5. *Ibid.*, p. 3.
6. See footnote to Crouch, *op. cit.*, p. 47.
7. *Early Yorkshire Charters*, 3 vols, ed. W. Farrer (Edinburgh, 1914–16), ii, no. 780.
8. Quoted by Crouch, p. 76.
9. For what follows see Marjorie Chibnall, *The Empress Matilda: Queen Consort, Queen Mother and Lady of the English* (Oxford, 1991), pp. 97–102.
10. For the terms themselves see William of Malmesbury, *Historia Novella*, ed. and trans. K. Potter (London, 1955), pp. 50–6.
11. J.H. Round, *Geoffrey de Mandeville* (London, 1892), pp. 70–5.
12. Christine Fell, *Women in Anglo-Saxon England* (Oxford, 1984), pp. 91–3.
13. Domesday Book, fo. 179v; quoted by Ann Williams, 'A Bell-house and a Burh-geat:

Lordly Residences in England before the Norman Conquest', in C. Harper-Bill and Ruth Harvey, *Medieval Knighthood IV* (Woodbridge, 1992), p. 236.

14. Pauline Stafford, 'Women in Domesday' in *Reading Medieval Studies*, xv (Reading, 1989), pp. 75–6; Domesday Book, fo. 373a–b.

15. For what follows see Williams, 'A Bell-house and a Burh-geat', pp. 221–40.

16. See, especially, John Blair (ed.), *Minsters and Parish Churches: The Local Church in Transition 950–1200* (Oxford, 1988), pp. 1–19. See also the same author's *Early Medieval Surrey* (Stroud, 1991), chs 4–6.

17. See Richard Gem, 'The English Parish Church in the Eleventh and Early Twelfth Centuries: A Great Rebuilding?', in Blair, *Minsters and Parish Churches*, pp. 21–30.

18. John Blair, *Anglo-Saxon Oxfordshire* (Stroud, 1994), pp. 138–9.

19. R.A. McKinley, *The Surnames of Oxfordshire* (London, 1977), p. 68. The figures for Norfolk and Suffolk are similar: R.A. McKinley, *Norfolk and Suffolk Surnames in the Middle Ages* (London, 1974), pp. 141–2.

20. See J.C. Holt, *What's in a name? Family Nomenclature and the Norman Conquest* (University of Reading, 1982).

21. McKinley, *The Surnames of Oxfordshire*, pp. 7–17. The foregoing remarks are based substantially on McKinley's Oxfordshire material.

22. There are, in fact, some instances of locative names in Anglo-Saxon England, for example among the witnesses to Tova's lease (Blair, *Oxfordshire, loc. cit.*), although they were not hereditary and their significance remains unclear. See also Ann Williams, 'A Bell-house and a Burh-geat', p. 237.

23. I.J. Sanders, *English Baronies: A Study of their Origin and Descent, 1086–1327* (Oxford, 1960), p. 81.

24. *Victoria County History of Warwickshire*, vol. VI, p. 276.

25. Charles R. Young, *The Making of the Neville Family 1166–1400* (Woodbridge, 1996), p. 49. For other instances see Scott L. Waugh, *The Lordship of England: Royal Wardships and Marriages in English Society and Politics, 1217–1327* (Princeton, 1988), p. 20.

26. A different view is taken by John Gillingham who appears to see chivalry as a fully developed elite mentality by the time of Gaimar if not before. See his 'Thegns and Knights in Eleventh-Century England: Who

was then the Gentleman?', *TRHS* 6th ser., v (1995), pp. 129–53, and his '1066 and the introduction of chivalry into England', in G. Garnett and J. Hudson (eds), *Law and Government in Medieval England and Normandy* (Cambridge, 1994), pp. 31–55.

27. For a good summary of these issues and for recent work on the subject see Janet Burton, *Monastic and Religious Orders in Britain 1000–1300* (Cambridge, 1994), ch. 10. And see, in particular, C. Harper-Bill, 'The piety of the Anglo-Norman knightly class', in *Proceedings of the Battle Conference on Anglo-Norman Studies II* (Woodbridge, 1979), pp. 63–77, and Emma Mason, 'Timeo barones et dona ferentes', in *Religious Motivation: Biographical and Sociological Problems for the Church Historian*, Studies in Church History, 15 (Oxford, 1978), pp. 61–75.

28. For burials see Brian Golding, 'Burials and benefactions: an aspect of monastic patronage in thirteenth-century England', in W.M. Ormrod (ed.), *England in the Thirteenth Century: Proceedings of the 1984 Harlaxton Symposium* (Woodbridge, 1986), pp. 64–75, and C. Harper-Bill, 'Anglo-Norman knightly burials', in C. Harper Bill and R. Harvey (eds), *The Ideals and Practice of Medieval Knighthood* (Woodbridge, 1986), pp. 35–48.

29. See J.C. Ward, 'Fashions in monastic endowment; the foundations of the Clare family, 1066–1314', *Journal of Ecclesiastical History*, 32 (1981), pp. 427–51.

30. C.D. Ross (ed.), *The Cartulary of Cirencester Abbey*, vol. I (London, 1964), p. xxiii.

31. *Victoria County History of Warwickshire*, vol. II, pp. 59, 61, 82.

32. *Paston Letters*, ii, no. 897.

33. Crouch, *op. cit.*, p. 12.

34. Most particularly, by Pauline Stafford, 'Women and the Norman Conquest', *TRHS* 6th ser., iv (1994), pp. 221–49. See also A. Klinck, 'Anglo-Saxon women and the law', *Journal of Medieval History*, 8 (1982), pp. 107–21: 'There is a much closer resemblance between the situation obtaining in late Anglo-Saxon England and post-Conquest England than there is between the early and late Anglo-Saxon period. Thus to describe Anglo-Saxon England as a time when women enjoyed an independence which they lost as a result of the changes introduced by the Norman Conquest is misleading.'

35. For what follows I am much indebted to Fell, *Women in Anglo-Saxon England*. Fell is a

strong defender of the traditional view: 'away from the feuds of the court we are entitled to assume that the average Anglo-Saxon wife was valued and respected, enjoying economic and marital rights, her independence safe-guarded and her interests protected' (*ibid.*, pp. 72–3).

36. *Ibid.*, p. 75; Dorothy Whitelock (ed.), *Anglo-Saxon Wills* (Cambridge, 1930), no. 19.
37. Fell, *Women in Anglo-Saxon England*, p. 95.
38. *Ibid.*, pp. 95–6; Whitelock, *Anglo-Saxon Wills*, no. 3.
39. Fell, *Women in Anglo-Saxon England*, p. 84; Whitelock, *Anglo-Saxon Wills*, no. 21. See also Dorothy Whitelock, *The Will of Aethelgifu* (Oxford, 1968).
40. See A.J. Robertson, *Anglo-Saxon Charters* (Cambridge, 1956), no. 78, and the comments by Doris Stenton, *The English Woman in History* (1956), pp. 26–7. See also Fell, *Women in Anglo-Saxon England*, p. 78.
41. For what follows see Fell, *Women in Anglo-Saxon England*, pp. 56–9.
42. *Ibid.*, p. 98.
43. *Ibid.*, p. 61.
44. For what follows see Stafford, 'Women and the Norman Conquest', pp. 241–2.
45. See Whitelock, *The Will of Aethelgifu*, pp. 14–16, 36–7.
46. See Stafford, 'Women and the Norman Conquest', p. 231 and the reference to her other work given there.
47. For what follows see the invaluable essay by Marc A. Meyer, 'Women's Estates in Later Anglo-Saxon England: The Politics of Succession', *Haskins Journal*, 3 (1991), pp. 111–29.
48. See Ian W. Walker, *Harold: The Last Anglo-Saxon King* (Stroud, 1997), pp. 127–30.
49. For Godgifu see also Joan C. Lancaster, *Godiva of Coventry* (Coventry, 1967).
50. For what follows see Eleanor Searle, 'Women and the legitimisation of succession at the Norman Conquest', in R. Allen Brown (ed.), *Proceedings of the Battle Conference on Anglo-Norman Studies III* (Woodbridge, 1981), pp. 159–70.
51. *Ibid.*, p. 165.
52. *Ibid.*, pp. 168–9, citing W.E. Wightman, *The Lacy Family in England and Normandy 1066–1194* (Oxford, 1966), pp. 40–2.
53. The case is discussed in detail by R.W. Southern, *St Anselm and his Biographer* (Cambridge, 1983), pp. 185–93, where a rather different view is taken from Searle's.
54. *Ibid.*, p. 188.

55. Searle, 'Women and the legitimisation of succession', p. 168.
56. Quoted by Stafford, 'Women and the Norman Conquest', p. 227 and by Marjorie Chibnall, 'Women in Orderic Vitalis', *Haskins Journal*, 2 (1990), pp. 107–8.
57. For what follows see, especially, J.C. Holt, 'Feudal Society and the Family in Early Medieval England: IV. The Heiress and the Alien', *TRHS* 5th ser., xxxv (1985), pp. 1–28, and Judith A. Green, 'Aristocratic Women in Early Twelfth-Century England' in C. Warren Hollister (ed.), *Anglo-Norman Political Culture and the Twelfth-Century Renaissance* (Woodbridge, 1997), pp. 59–82.
58. J.C. Holt, 'Politics and Property in Norman England', *Past and Present*, 57 (1972), pp. 7–8.
59. See especially J. Hudson, *Land, Law and Lordship in Anglo-Norman England* (Oxford, 1994), Part Two: Heritability.
60. P. Stafford, 'Women and the Norman Conquest', pp. 237–40. For a European perspective on the move away from the morning-gift towards *maritagium* see D. Owen Hughes, 'From brideprice to dowry in Mediterranean Europe', *Journal of Family History*, iii (1978), pp. 262–96.
61. Holt, 'The Heiress and the Alien', p. 4.
62. Jane Martindale, 'Succession and Politics in the Romance-Speaking World, *c.* 1000–1140', in Michael Jones and Malcolm Vale (eds), *England and her Neighbours 1066–1453: Essays in Honour of Pierre Chaplais* (London, 1989), pp. 19–41. On the question of inheritance customs see also Stephen D. White, *Custom, Kinship and Gifts to Saints: The 'Laudatio Parentum' in Western France, 1050–1150* (Chapel Hill, N.C. and London, 1988); Jean Yver, *Egalité entre héritiers et exclusion des enfants dotés* (Paris, 1966), and Emily Z. Tabuteau, *Transfers of Property in Eleventh-Century Norman Law* (Chapel Hill and London, 1988).
63. For the text of Henry's coronation charter see W. Stubbs, *Select Charters*, 9th edn (Oxford, 1913), p. 118. It is translated in *English Historical Documents*, ii, ed. D.C. Douglas and G.W. Greenaway (London, 1953), no. 19.
64. William T. Reedy (ed.), *Basset Charters, c. 1120–1250*, Pipe Roll Society, lxxxviii (1995), no. 47.
65. For Richard Basset see Judith A. Green, *The Government of England under Henry I* (Cambridge, 1986), pp. 231–2.
66. Reedy, *Basset Charters*, pp. xi–xii.
67. Sir Frank Stenton, *The First Century of*

English Feudalism, 2nd edn (Oxford, 1961), pp. 34–7.

68. Sally Thompson, *Women Religious: The Founding of English Nunneries after the Norman Conquest* (Oxford, 1991), ch. 9.

69. Judith Green, on the other hand, has recently argued that the *statutum decretum* may not have been a royal decree after all, but a local provision which emanated from the court of Archbishop Theobald and which reflected a general trend: 'Aristocratic women', pp. 74–5, 79–82. For a broader discussion of the problems arising from multiple heiresses see Scott L. Waugh, 'Women's Inheritance and the Growth of Bureaucratic Monarchy in Twelfth- and Thirteenth-Century England', *Nottingham Medieval Studies,* xxxiv (1990), pp. 71–92.

70. J.C. Holt, *Magna Carta,* 2nd edn (Cambridge, 1992), p. 53.

71. J.H. Round, *Rotuli de Dominabus et Pueris et Puellis,* Pipe Roll Society, 13 (1913), pp. 21–30. Round's genealogical footnotes are invaluable.

72. Holt, *Magna Carta,* especially pp. 53–5.

73. *Ibid.,* p. 453.

74. Green, 'Aristocratic Women', p. 67, citing D. Crouch, 'Oddities in the Early History of the Marcher Lordship of Gower', *Bulletin of the Board of Celtic Studies,* 31 (1984), pp. 133–41.

75. G. Barraclough (ed.), *The Charters of the Anglo-Norman Earls of Chester, c. 1071–1237,* Record Society of Lancashire and Cheshire (Gloucester, 1988), nos 102, 119–23, 127–9, 145–6.

76. For what follows see Thompson, *Women Religious,* pp. 167–77.

77. For what follows see P. Stafford, 'The Portrayal of Royal Women in England, Mid-Tenth to Mid-Twelfth Centuries', in John Carmi Parsons (ed.), *Medieval Queenship* (Stroud, 1994), pp. 144–67, especially pp. 156–60.

78. Chibnall, 'Women in Orderic Vitalis', pp. 105–21.

79. For the empress see also M. Chibnall, *The Empress Matilda* (Oxford, 1991).

80. See Betty Blandel, 'The English Chroniclers' Attitude Toward Women', *Journal of the History of Ideas,* 16 (1955), pp. 113–18. This pioneering study argues that the Anglo-Saxon sources show women in a great range of activities but do so in a more positive and a more casual way than do their twelfth-century counterparts, implying that the active role of women was more natural and accepted than it later became.

81. For Aethelflaed see Fell, *Women in Anglo-Saxon England,* pp. 91–3.

82. Stafford, 'The Portrayal of Royal Women', pp. 157–8.

83. For what follows see Chibnall, 'Women in Orderic Vitalis'.

84. *Ibid.,* p. 114.

85. *Ibid.,* p. 115.

86. See, for example, G. Duby, 'Women and Power', in Thomas N. Bisson (ed.), *Cultures of Power: Lordship, Status and Process in Twelfth-Century Europe* (Philadelphia, 1995), pp. 69–85.

87. See Lois L. Huneycutt, 'Female Succession and the Language of Power in the Writings of Twelfth-Century Churchmen', in Parsons (ed.), *Medieval Queenship,* pp. 189–201.

88. R.C. Johnston (ed.), *Jordan Fantosme's Chronicle* (Oxford, 1981), verses 99–100, 105–6.

89. See Kate Norgate, *The Minority of Henry III* (London, 1912), p. 37. See also Doris M. Stenton, *The English Woman in History* (1957), p. 37.

90. E. King (ed.), 'Estate Records of the Hotot Family', in *A Northamptonshire Miscellany,* Northamptonshire Record Society, xxxii (1983), p. 45.

91. See Rowena E. Archer, '"How ladies . . . who live on their manors ought to manage their households and estates": Women as Landholders and Administrators in the Later Middle Ages', in P.J.P. Goldberg, *Woman is a Worthy Wight: Women in English Society, c. 1200–1500* (Stroud, 1992), p. 160 and references given there.

92. On concubinage see P.A. Stafford, *Queens, Concubines and Dowagers, the King's Wife in the Early Middle Ages* (Athens, Ga., 1983).

93. Peter Dronke, *Medieval Latin and the Rise of the European Love Lyric,* 2nd edn (Oxford, 1968), i, pp. 1–56. See also C.N.L. Brooke, *The Medieval Idea of Marriage* (Oxford, 1989), p. 57.

94. For ambivalence see Penny Schine Gold, *The Lady and the Virgin: Image, Attitude, and Experience in Twelfth-Century France* (Chicago, 1985).

95. See, for example, Elizabeth Williams, 'After 1066: The Literary Image', in Fell, *Women in Anglo-Saxon England,* pp. 172–93, and Holt, 'Feudal Society and the Family', p. 20.

96. For this argument see J. Gillingham, 'Love, Marriage and Politics in the Twelfth Century', *Forum for Modern Language Studies,* 25 (1989), pp. 292–303. See also Roberta Krueger, 'Love, Honor and the Exchange of Women in' *Yvain:* Some Remarks on the Female Reader', *Romance Notes,* 25 (1985), pp. 302–17, and Jocelyn Wogan-Browne, 'Saints' Lives and the Female

Reader', *Forum for Modern Language Studies*, 27 (1991), pp. 314–32.

97. S.S. Walker, 'Free consent and marriage of feudal wards in medieval England', *Journal of Medieval History*, 8 (1982), pp. 123–34.

98. Holt, 'Feudal Society and the Family', p. 26.

99. For comment see Fell, *Women in Anglo-Saxon England*, pp. 69–70, and Bandel, 'The English Chroniclers' Attitude Toward Women', pp. 113–14.

100. Chibnall, 'Women in Orderic Vitalis', pp. 118–19.

101. For the debate on continuity see, in addition to works already cited, Jo Anna McNamara and Suzanne Wemple, 'The Power of Women through Family in Medieval Europe, 500–1100', in Mary Erler and Maryanne Kowaleski (eds), *Women and Power in the Middle Ages* (Athens, Ga., 1988), pp. 81–101; Lois L. Huneycutt, 'Images of Queenship in the High Middle Ages', *Haskins Journal*, 1 (1989), pp. 61–71, and with reference to Anglo-Saxon England Klinck, 'Anglo-Saxon women and the law', pp. 107–21, and M.A. Meyer, 'Land charters and the legal position of Anglo-Saxon women', in B. Kanner (ed.), *The Women of England from Anglo-Saxon time to the present* (London, 1980), pp. 57–82.

3. Gentility and Social Position

1. For what follows see the fascinating discussion in Crouch, *The Image of Aristocracy*, pp. 150–1, drawing on L. Foulet, 'Sir, messire', *Romania*, lxxi (1950), pp. 1–48.

2. M.J. Franklin (ed.), *The Cartulary of Daventry Priory*, Northampton Record Society, xxxv (Northampton, 1988), no. 12.

3. See, for example, Peter Coss, *The Knight in Medieval England 1000–1400* (Stroud, 1993), pp. 49–50 and the references given there.

4. For a recent and extremely helpful discussion of Gaimar see Ian Short, 'Gaimar's Epilogue and Geoffrey of Monmouth's *Liber Vetustissimus*', *Speculum*, 69 (1994), pp. 323–43.

5. Crouch, *The Image of Aristocracy*, p. 151, citing Foulet.

6. For a more extensive treatment see *The Knight in Medieval England*, ch. 3, 'Angevin Knighthood and its Transformation'. David Crouch has also expressed dissatisfaction with the precise contours of the Duby model. See *The Image of Aristocracy*, p. 153.

7. For what follows see, in particular, P.D.A. Harvey and Andrew McGuinness, *A Guide to British Medieval Seals* (London, 1996), especially ch. 3. More work has been done on the seals of women in France. See, in particular, B. Bedos-Rezak, 'Women, Seals and Power in Medieval France, 1150–1350' in Erler and Kowaleski (eds), *Women and Power in the Middle Ages* (Athens, Ga., 1988), pp. 61–82 and the same author's 'Medieval Women in French Sigillographic Sources' in J.T. Rosenthal (ed.), *Women and Sources of Medieval History* (Athens, Ga., 1990), pp. 1–36. Both essays are reprinted in her *Form and Order in Medieval France: Studies in Social and Quantitative Sigillography* (Aldershot, 1993). See also C.H. Hunter Blair, 'Armorials on English Seals from the Twelfth to the Sixteenth Centuries' in *Archaeologia*, 89 (1943).

8. See T.A. Heslop in G. Zarnecki *et al.* (eds), *English Romanesque Art 1066–1200* (London, 1984).

9. For the date see Hunter Blair, 'Armorials on English Seals', p. 22.

10. W. de G. Birch, *Catalogue of Seals in the Department of Manuscripts in the British Museum*, vol. II (London, 1892), no. 6658. Another (de Birch no. 6691) has a lady's feet resting on a hound couchant and a lap dog in her left hand.

11. N. Crossley–Holland, *Living and Dining in Medieval Paris: The Household of a Fourteenth-Century Knight* (Cardiff, 1996), p. 56. Guy is the famous ménagier of Paris, whose work is translated by Eileen Power, viz. *The Goodman of Paris* (London, 1928).

12. See *The Knight in Medieval England*, pp. 79–80.

13. de Birch, *Catalogue of Seals*, no. 6645; Harvey and McGuinness, *Guide to British Medieval Seals*, pp. 51–2.

14. For the details see *The Knight in Medieval England*, pp. 79–80, and the references given there.

15. A field *crusily* is one powdered with *cross crosslets*.

16. *Fusils* are tall lozenges.

17. A *cinquefoil* is a leaf with five petals.

18. For the details on which these cases are based see my essay 'Heraldry and Monumental Effigies in the North East', in T.E. Faulkner (ed.), *Northumbrian Panorama: Studies in the History and Culture of North-East England* (London, 1996).

19. For what follows and a fuller discussion of the Lumleys see Coss, 'Heraldry and Monumental Effigies', pp. 7–14.

20. The obverse was the standard portrayal of a

standing female figure in a gown girt at the waist with long manches, fleur-de-lis in the right hand and bird in the left. See R.B. Patterson, *Earldom of Gloucester Charters* (Oxford, 1973), pp. 24–5 and plates XXXI d & e. See also Harvey and McGuinness, *Guide to British Medieval Seals*, pp. 58–9.

21. A field *vairy* is one composed of two tinctures arranged in the manner used to denote vair (squirrel-fur).

22. *Party* indicates a vertically divided field.

23. See C.H. Hunter Blair, *Durham Seals*, no. 2537, *Archaeologia Aeliana*, 3rd ser., xi (1914), depicted on plate 29. The charter confirms her husband's grant of grain to the monks of Farne Island. It is printed in J. Raine, *The History and Antiquities of North Durham* (London, 1852), Appendix p. 123, no. 700. For the genealogy see Sanders, *English Baronies*, p. 103. The lady's husband died in 1253. W. de Birch (6726) gives another example of this seal, which he wrongly ascribes to the wife of Eustace de Vesci (d. 1216). The counterseal is broken in exactly the same place, which may suggest a weakness in the construction.

24. Illustrations in Hunter Blair, 'Armorials on English Seals', plate XV g & h, and discussion p. 21.

25. Men seemed to do so only to emphasise succession to titles and estates. See Adrian Ailes, 'Heraldic Marshalling in Medieval England' in *Proceedings of VIII Colloquium at Canterbury, Académie Internationale D'Héraldique* (1995), p. 20. I have learned a great deal from this invaluable essay.

26. An alternative way of dimidiating was *per fess*, that is to say by placing the one set of arms horizontally above the other on the shield. For an example see the seal of Eleanor de Bohun, wife of Robert Ferrers, Earl of Derby (1273) in R.C. Fowler, *Seals in the Public Record Office* (Oxford, 1925), no. 54. The Ferrers arms are above and the Bohun arms below.

27. Hunter Blair, 'Armorials on English Seals', XVI v; discussed p. 23.

28. See James Blundell, 'Husbands galore', *The Coat of Arms*, new series, iii, no. 105 (1978), pp. 11–12, where line drawings are given.

29. Hunter Blair, 'Armorials on English Seals', p. 23 and plate XVI ff.

30. The seal is depicted in Fowler, *Seals in the Public Record Office*, no. 53.

31. Ailes, 'Heraldic Marshalling in Medieval England', p. 16.

32. *Paston Letters*, i, pp. 383–4.

33. See John Cherry, 'Heraldry as Decoration in the Thirteenth Century' in M. Ormrod (ed.), *England in the Thirteenth Century* (Stamford, 1991), p. 131 and plate 27.

34. Thorlac Turville-Petre, 'The Relation of the Vernon and Clopton Manuscripts', in D. Pearsall (ed.), *Studies in the Vernon Manuscript* (Cambridge, 1990), pp. 29–44. See also Felicity Riddy, '"Women talking about the things of God": a late medieval sub-culture' in Carol M. Meale (ed.), *Women and Literature in Britain 1150–1500* (Cambridge, 1993), pp. 110 and 122 note 43. It is difficult to follow her, however, in her assertion that 'it may have been they [the women] who read the book while their husbands were running the country'.

35. For an interesting discussion of the social significance of dress see D. Roche, *The Culture of Clothing: Dress and Fashion in the 'Ancien Régime'* (Cambridge, 1994).

36. W. Dugdale, *The Antiquities of Warwickshire* (London, 1656), rev. W. Thomas (London, 1730), i, p. 445.

37. For a description of the tomb see *Victoria County History of Warwickshire*, vol. VII, pp. 527–8. For the earl's will see *Calendar of Patent Rolls 1436–41*, p. 574, and Dugdale, i, pp. 445–7.

38. T.M. Felgate, *Ladies on Suffolk Brasses* (Ipswich, 1989), p. 63.

39. For descriptions see Felgate, *Ladies on Suffolk Brasses*, pp. 24–67 and the same author's *Suffolk Heraldic Brasses* (Ipswich, 1978), pp. 106–11.

40. Incidentally, the engraver has displayed simple crosses not the *paty* (splayed) cross of the Francys arms; they are correct on the shield.

41. The engraver has omitted the *cotises* of the Harleston arms.

42. In addition to the Clopton chapel, there is also a Clopton chantry. Here there is a monument to John Clopton himself (d. 1497) with the kneeling figures of John and his wife. A frieze of shields is along the wall. There is much decoration and writing, including a poem by Lydgate. The Clopton chapel has a monument to Sir William Clopton (d. 1446), in addition to the brasses.

43. For a recent sociological study of sumptuary legislation in general see Alan Hunt, *Governance of the Consuming Passions: A History of Sumptuary Law* (London, 1996). The English situation is dealt with specifically in ch. 12, which also references recent work on the subject. The standard authority is Frances

Baldwin, *Sumptuary Legislation and Personal Regulation in England* (Baltimore, 1926).

44. Statute 11 Edward III: c.4 (1337), *Statutes of the Realm* 1: 280.

45. W.F. Carter (ed.), *The Lay Subsidy Roll for Warwickshire of 6 Edward III (1332)*, Dugdale Society Publications, vi (London, 1926), pp. 19, 20, 42, 53. Sir (*Dominus*) was also used as a courtesy title for five clerics, in accordance with normal usage.

46. Dorothea Oschinsky (ed.), *Walter of Henley and Other Treatises on Estate Management and Accounting* (Oxford, 1971), p. 403.

47. Statute 37 Edward III cc.8–14, *Statutes of the Realm* 1: 380–1.

48. On these subjects see my essays, 'The Formation of the English Gentry', *Past and Present*, 147 (1995), pp. 38–64 and 'Knights and Esquires and the Origins of Social Gradation in England', *TRHS* 6th ser., v (1995), pp. 155–78.

49. Hunt, *Governance of the Consuming Passions*, pp. 150–6, 304–5.

50. Parliament did not return to sumptuary regulation until the act of 1463. There were six further statutes between then and 1553.

51. For a recent discussion see Nigel Saul, 'Chaucer and Gentility', in Barbara Hanawalt (ed.), *Chaucer's England: Literature in Historical Context* (Minneapolis, 1992), pp. 41–55.

52. For a summary of developments see *The Knight in Medieval England*, pp. 127–34. Particularly important essays are R.L. Storey, 'Gentlemen-Bureaucrats', in Cecil Clough (ed.), *Profession, Vocation and Culture in Later Medieval England* (Liverpool, 1982), pp. 90–129, and Rosemary Horrox, 'The Urban Gentry in the Fifteenth Century', in J.A.F. Thomson (ed.), *Towns and Townspeople in the Fifteenth Century* (Gloucester, 1988), pp. 22–44. See also C. Carpenter, *Locality and Polity: A Study of Warwickshire Landed Society* (Cambridge, 1992), ch. 3.

53. Banneret, for long signifying an experienced knight who commanded his own contingent in the field or his own troop on campaign, seemed for a time in the second half of the fourteenth century to be solidifying into a social rank.

54. For what follows I am indebted to Felicity Riddy, 'Mother Knows Best: Reading Social Change in a Courtesy Text', *Speculum*, 71 (1996), although I differ from her in my interpretation.

55. For courtesy literature in general see Jonathan Nicholls, *The Matter of Courtesy: Medieval Courtesy Books and the 'Gawain' Poet*

(Woodbridge, 1983), and Diane Borstein, *The Lady in the Tower: Medieval Courtly Literature for Women* (Hamden, Conn., 1983).

56. It may, however, reflect its different purpose. *Urbain le Courtois* seems designed to prepare boys for service in the great households (Riddy, 'Mother Knows Best', p. 78).

57. See below, ch. 6.

58. Christine Carpenter (ed.), *Kingsford's Stonor Letters and Papers 1290–1483* (Cambridge, 1996), no. 260.

59. *Ibid.*, nos. 211, 216.

60. *Ibid.*, no. 172.

61. *Ibid.*, no. 166; *Paston Letters*, ii, no. 745.

62. The sheriff's returns are published in F. Palgrave (ed.), *Parliamentary Writs*, 2 vols in 4 (London, 1827–34), vol. II, div. 2, pp. 288–90, drawing on BL MSS Harley 1192 fo. 8b and Cott. claud. C.II fo. 56.

63. For Denise see *Complete Peerage*, vol. IV, p. 424, and vol. IX, p. 421. For the question of her legitimacy see below, p. 71.

64. *Complete Peerage*, vol. XI, p. 384.

65. For Clemencia see John Carmi Parsons, *Eleanor of Castile: Queen and Society in Thirteenth-Century England* (London, 1994),p. 219. For the history of Foxton see *Victoria County History of Northamptonshire*, vol. IV, p. 168.

66. *Calendar of Close Rolls 1288–96*, p. 144.

67. William himself died without heir in 1297. See *Complete Peerage*, vol. XII, pt 2, pp. 281–3.

68. *Victoria County History of Northamptonshire*, vol. IV, p. 96.

69. *Ibid.*, p. 267.

70. See below, pp. 131–8.

71. *Placita de Quo Warranto*, 2 vols, ed. W. Illingworth (London, 1818), ii, p. 671.

72. *Victoria County History of Northamptonshire*, vol. IV, p. 96.

73. For what follows I have relied heavily upon the excellent recent work by Jennifer C. Ward and Frances A. Underhill: Jennifer C. Ward, *English Noblewomen in the Later Middle Ages* (London, 1992), *passim* and especially pp. 99–112, 153–9, and 'Elizabeth de Burgh, Lady of Clare (d. 1360)', in Caroline M. Barron and Anne F. Sutton (eds), *Medieval London Widows, 1300–1500* (London, 1994), pp. 29–45; Frances A. Underhill, 'Elizabeth de Burgh: Connoisseur and Patron', in June Hall McCash (ed.), *The Cultural Patronage of Medieval Women* (Athens, Ga., 1996), pp. 266–87.

74. For this summary of her early life see Ward, 'Elizabeth de Burgh', and the references given there.

75. Underhill, 'Elizabeth de Burgh', p. 268.
76. *Ibid.*
77. See George Holmes, *Estates of the Higher Nobility in Fourteenth-Century England* (Cambridge, 1957), pp. 58–9. For further details on the households of Elizabeth de Burgh and other ladies see Ward, *English Noblewomen*, ch. 3. For households more generally, see Kate Mertes, *The English Noble Household, 1250–1600* (Oxford, 1988).
78. Underhill, 'Elizabeth de Burgh', p. 279.
79. For a summary see Ward, *English Noblewomen*, pp. 158–9.
80. Underhill, 'Elizabeth de Burgh', p. 268, citing Marjorie Boyer, 'Medieval Suspended Carriages', *Speculum*, 34 (1959), pp. 360–1.
81. For what follows see Ward, 'Elizabeth de Burgh', pp. 37–40.
82. *Ibid.*, p. 38.
83. For the economy of Elizabeth's estates see Ward, *English Noblewomen*, ch. 6, especially pp. 117–27, and also Holmes, *Estates of the Higher Nobility*, ch. 4 and pp. 143–57, 161–3.
84. Holmes, *Estates of the Higher Nobility*, p. 58.
85. J.R. Maddicott, 'Law and Lordship: royal justices as retainers in thirteenth- and fourteenth-century England', *Past and Present* Supplement 4 (1978), pp. 20–3; quoted by Ward, *English Noblewomen*, p. 136.
86. N. Pevsner, *The Buildings of England: Suffolk*, 2nd edn, revised by E. Radcliffe (London, 1974), p. 341.
87. See John Salmon, *Saints in Suffolk Churches* (Bury St Edmunds, 1981), p. 47.
88. PRO C47/8/A. These are published as *The Household Book of Dame Alice de Bryene*, ed. Marion K. Dale and trans. Vincent B. Redstone, Suffolk Institute of Archaeology and Natural History (Ipswich, 1931).
89. PRO A.C.51/24. The letters are transcribed and discussed by Edith Rickert in 'A Leaf From A Fourteenth-Century Letter Book', *Modern Philology*, 25 (1927–8), pp. 249–55.
90. Similar advice was given by a relative to William Stonor on the death of his wife, Elizabeth. See below, p. 55.
91. He wrote another short letter to Philippa, which repeats the same bald facts.
92. *Calendar of Patent Rolls 1280*, p. 428; D.J. Stagg (ed.), *New Forest Documents AD 1244–AD 1334*, Hampshire Record Series, iii (1979), no. 74; R.B. Turton (ed.), *Honour and Forest of Pickering*, North Riding Record Society, NS ii (1895), pp. 63–7. I owe these references to the kindness of Miss Jean Birrell.

93. William F. Skene (ed.), *Johannis de Fordun: Chronica Gentis Scotorum*, vol. II (Edinburgh, 1872), p. 299. I owe this reference to the kindness of Professor A.A.M. Duncan.
94. See, especially, Sue Sheridan Walker, 'Litigation as Personal Quest: Suing for Dower in the Royal Courts, circa 1272–1350', in S. Sheridan Walker (ed.), *Wife and Widow in Medieval England* (Ann Arbor, 1993), pp. 81–108.
95. For what follows see Nigel Saul, 'Murder and Justice Medieval Style: the Pashley case, 1327–8', *History Today* (August 1984), pp. 30–5.
96. For what follows I am much indebted to the splendid essay by Rowena Archer, 'How ladies . . . who live on their manors ought to manage their households and estates', pp. 149–81.
97. Christine de Pisan, *The Treasure of the City of Ladies or the Book of the Three Virtues*, ed. & trans. S. Lawson (Harmondsworth, 1985), pp. 76, 128, 130.
98. Archer, 'How ladies', pp. 150, 158.
99. *Ibid.*, p. 150.
100. Oschinsky (ed.), *Walter of Henley and Other Treatises*, pp. 388–91, 398–9.
101. *Ibid.*, p. 49. See also Archer, 'How ladies', p. 157.
102. See, in particular, M.T. Clanchy, *From Memory to Written Record: England 1066–1307*, 2nd edn (Oxford, 1993), pp. 188–96, and Susan Groag Bell, 'Medieval Women Book Owners: Arbiters of Lay Piety and Ambassadors of Culture', in Judith M. Bennett *et al.*, *Sisters and Workers in the Middle Ages* (Chicago, 1989), pp. 135–61.
103. For what follows see Clanchy, *From Memory to Written Record*, pp. 197–200.
104. Bell, 'Medieval Women Book Owners', pp. 148–9.

4. Visual Representation and Affective Relations

1. See P. Binski, *The Painted Chamber at Westminster*, Society of Antiquaries Occasional Paper 9 (London, 1986).
2. For a good introduction to such matters see Veronika Sekules, 'Women and Art in England in the Thirteenth and Fourteenth Centuries', in J. Alexander and P. Binski, *Age of Chivalry* (London, 1987), pp. 41–8. See also Chiara Frugoni, 'The Imagined Woman', in C. Klapisch-Zuber (ed.), *A History of Women in*

the West I: Silences of the Middle Ages (Cambridge, Mass. and London, 1992), pp. 336–422.

3. For the several phases in the iconography of the Virgin and their significance see Gold, *The Lady and the Virgin*, ch. II, 'Religious Image'. See especially the successive late twelfth- and thirteenth-century statues at Amiens, pl. 8 and 9.

4. For this idea see Emile Mâle, *L'Art religieux de la fin du Moyen Age en France* (Paris, 1949; first publ. 1908), 1949, pp. 400–2.

5. See Derek Brewer, 'The Ideal of Feminine Beauty in Medieval Literature, Especially "Harley Lyrics", Chaucer and Some Elizabethans', *Modern Language Review*, 50 (1955), pp. 257–69. This study is extended by Kevin S. Kiernan, 'The Art of the Descending Catalogue, and a Fresh Look at Alisoun', *Chaucer Review*, 10 (1975), pp. 1–16.

6. Sekules, 'Women and Art', p. 43.

7. H.A. Tummers, *Early Secular Effigies in England: The Thirteenth Century* (Leiden, 1980). The earliest, on his dating, are: a lady in Worcester Cathedral belonging to the mid-thirteenth century, a lady at Monkton Farleigh, Wiltshire, from the third quarter of the century, and the lady at Romsey, Northants, from 1270–80.

8. For a classic discussion see Lawrence Stone, *Sculpture in Britain: The Middle Ages* (Harmondsworth, 1955), ch. 4, 'The Age of Elegance', and for the most recent discussion P. Binski, *Westminster Abbey and the Plantagenets: Kingship and the Representation of Power 1200–1400* (New Haven and London, 1995), ch. 3. A European perspective is given by E. Panofsky, *Tomb Sculpture. Its changing aspects from Ancient Egypt to Bernini* (London, 1964).

9. Tummers discusses costume on ladies' effigies on pp. 54–9.

10. Pictured in Tummers, pl. 159.

11. For further details see Coss, 'Heraldry and Monumental Effigies in the North East', p. 19, and references given there. This effigy is not noticed by Tummers.

12. Binski, *Westminster Abbey and the Plantagenets*, pp. 179–80.

13. Coss, 'Heraldry and Monumental Effigies', pp. 20–1.

14. For what follows see, in particular, Paul Binski, 'The Stylistic Sequence of London Figure Brasses', in John Coales (ed.), *The Earliest English Brasses: Patronage, Style and Workshops 1270–1350* (London, 1987), pp. 69–131. See also, in the same volume, John

Blair, 'English Monumental Brasses before 1350: Types, Patterns and Workshops', pp. 133–74. Concentrating on the full-length figures gives a false impression of the early history of brasses in England. Blair's study encompasses the full range of brasses, including crosses, crosses with or without figures and half figures, shields and inscriptions. English brasses owed much to their earlier development in France and the Low Countries. The first appearance of brass in England appears to have been Henry III's great mosaic pavement in the presbytery of Westminster Abbey dated 1268, with bands of Purbeck marble bearing long inscriptions in brass letters. Also in the abbey are two simple brasses for Margaret and John de Valence who died in 1276 and 1277 respectively. They have long-stemmed crosses and marginal inscriptions in separate letters which are identical to those on the pavement. Cross brasses were very popular and came from an English prototype, the carved relief cross slab, well known since the twelfth century. One of the earliest marble slabs with brass inscriptions was that of Isabel de Pleci at Hook Norton, Oxfordshire (d. 1272–8). The most compendious modern study, however, is by the late Malcolm Norris: *Monumental Brasses: The Memorials*, 2 vols (London, 1977), and *Monumental Brasses: The Craft* (London, 1978).

15. Binski, 'Stylistic Sequence', p. 80.

16. The dating of the earliest brasses remains problematic and controversial.

17. The Lisles held the manor of the Isle in Sedgefield parish. Their arms are not known for sure, but Sir Walter de Lisle who conveyed the manor of Edmundbyers, County Durham, in 1325 was very likely a relative. His seal shows that he bore the charges that figure on the shield alongside the lady. The tinctures are not known. Further details are in Coss, 'Heraldry and Monumental Effigies', pp. 26–8.

18. Binsky and Blair, on the other hand, believe that it was made in a northern workshop, under southern influence, on the grounds that the London trade did not reach so far (*op. cit.*, pp. 90, 134). But if the lady were connected with Hertfordshire and Cambridgeshire – as would be the case if she were married to a Bassingbourne – then she would have been associated with the heartland of the London trade.

19. Tummers, *Early Secular Effigies*, p. 22.

20. For further discussion of this device and its consequences see below, p. 146.

21. See, for example, pl. 9 and fig. 40 in Coss, *The Knight in Medieval England*, depicting the Langleys of Siddington and the Ruyhales of Birtsmorten, respectively, in precisely this pose. Alternatively, they might be depicted side by side holding a shield. See the portrayal of Sir John de Hartshill and his wife, Margaret, *c.* 1350, in Richard Marks, *Stained Glass in England during the Middle Ages* (London, 1993), p. 11. The glass was once at Merevale, Warwickshire. The arms are his.

22. See Marks, *Stained Glass in England*, p. 15.

23. There is a good summary, with a range of apposite cases, in Ward, *English Noblewomen*, ch. 2. For a general discussion of marriage see C.N.L. Brooke, *The Medieval Idea of Marriage* (Oxford, 1989). For canon law see J.A. Brundage, *Law, Sex and Christian Society in Medieval Europe* (Chicago, 1987). A wealth of learning on the subject of medieval marriage is contained in the works of the late Michael Sheehan: James K. Farge (ed.), *Marriage, Family and Law in Medieval Europe: Collected Studies of Michael M. Sheehan* (Cardiff, 1996).

24. See, for example, K.P. Wentersdorf, 'The clandestine marriages of the Fair Maid of Kent', *Journal of Medieval History*, v (1979), pp. 203–31.

25. See, in particular, S.L. Waugh, *The Lordship of England: Royal Wardships and Marriages in English Society, 1217–1327* (Princeton, 1988), ch. 1, especially pp. 37, 53–4.

26. J.W. Willis Bund (ed.), *Register of Bishop Godfrey Giffard, September 23rd 1268 to August 15th 1301*, Worcestershire Historical Society, 2 vols (1902), i, p. 110.

27. *Ibid.*, pp. 359–60.

28. 'Handfasting' at the church door can be found in depictions of the seven sacraments on fonts, in stained glass and in wall paintings. A good example of the last is at Kirton in Lindsey, Lincolnshire.

29. *Ibid.*, pp. 367–8.

30. I owe this reference to Mark Page, *Royal and Comital Government and the Local Community in Thirteenth-Century Cornwall*, Oxford D. Phil. (1996), p. 140, citing F.C. Hingeston-Randolph (ed.), *The Register of John de Grandisson, Bishop of Exeter*, ii (London and Exeter, 1897), ii, pp. 701–2, 721–2, 727; see also L.E. Elliott-Binns, *Medieval Cornwall* (London, 1955), p. 240.

31. H. Nicholas (ed.), *Testamenta Vetusta* (London, 1826), p. 52. Sir William Dugdale, *The Baronage of England* (London, 1675), i, p. 229.

32. *Calendar of Inquisitions Post Mortem*, v, no. 67.

33. Quoted by P.P.A. Biller, 'Marriage Patterns and Women's Lives: A Sketch of Pastoral Geography', in Goldberg (ed.), *Woman is a Worthy Wight*, p. 70. For William de Pagula see W.A. Pantin, *The English Church in the Fourteenth Century* (Cambridge, 1955), pp. 195–202.

34. See Michael Sheehan, 'Choice of Marriage Partner in the Middle Ages: Development and Mode of Application of a Theory of Marriage', in his *Collected Studies*, p. 109.

35. Tummers gives another early example, at Charlton Mackrell, Somerset. The earliest German example seems to be dated around 1300 (*Early Secular Effigies*, p. 153).

36. William Fraser, *The Red Book of Menteith*, 2 vols (Edinburgh, 1880), i, facing p. 75. I am extremely grateful to Professor A.A.M. Duncan for bringing this effigy to my attention.

37. Careby does not stand alone. At South Stoke (or Stoke Rochford) in the same county a couple are shown under a blanket with their feet, and two lap dogs, beneath. They belong to a tradition, particularly strong in the north and north-east Midlands, of depicting only the head and shoulders and the feet of an effigy, the rest of the bodies being concealed in one way or another. See Brian Kemp, *English Church Monuments* (1980), pp. 38–40, where these matters are discussed and the South Stoke effigy is shown. See also the same author's *Church Monuments* (Shire Album, 1985). I am extremely grateful to Professor Kemp for discussing these matters with me.

38. See P. Binski, 'Monumental Brasses', in *The Age of Chivalry*, p. 172.

39. I owe this information to the late Dr Malcolm Norris who, with characteristic generosity, supplied me with photocopies of known examples.

40. See Christa Grössinger, *The World Upside-Down: English Misericords* (London, 1997), p. 134.

41. *Paston Letters*, i, no. 212.

42. The dates on some brasses were left blank to be filled in later. There are examples where this was never done.

43. F.J. Furnivall, *The Fifty Earliest English Wills*, Early English Text Society, lxxviii (1882), pp. 116–19.

44. See, for example, J. Roger Greenwood, 'Wills and Brasses: Some Conclusions from a Norfolk Study', in Fr. Jerome Bertram (ed.),

Monumental Brasses as Art and History (Stroud, 1996). This contains instances of testators specifying that brasses should contain images of themselves and their wives, but none expressing views on the precise content of those images.

45. Norris, *The Craft*, p. 90 and pl. 72. The will is published in Somerset Archaeological Collections, II, p. 169.

46. See Binski, *Westminster Abbey and the Plantagenets*, pp. 200–1 and the references given there. This contract is subsequent to that made with the marblers on 1 April.

47. Northamptonshire Record Office, Stopford Sackville collection, no. 4239.

48. Norris, *The Craft*, pp. 97–8. The indenture is published in the Thoroton Society Record Series, 21 (1962), pp. 1–2.

49. Nicolas (ed.), *Testamenta Vetusta*, p. 87; cited Ward, 'Elizabeth de Burgh', p. 44.

50. The drawings are shown in Marks, *Stained Glass in England*, p. 24. See also Norris, *The Craft*, p. 93.

51. *Paston Letters*, i, no. 72.

52. *Ibid.*, no. 77.

53. Margery's letters are i, nos 415–20.

54. Elizabeth's letters are nos 168–170, 172, 172–3, 175–6, 180, 204, 208, 226, 229 and 237. The language of the Stonor letters has been somewhat modernised and the punctuation of the published texts modified as necessary in the interests of clarity.

55. *Stonor Letters*, no. 169.

56. *Ibid.*, no. 175.

57. *Ibid.*, no. 172.

58. *Ibid.*, no. 91.

59. Lawson (ed.), *The Treasure of the City of Ladies*, p. 130.

60. Documentary evidence for these matters is rather slight for the medieval period. P.J.P. Goldberg has provided a good example from the York consistory court, in the depositions (dated 1365) relating to the birth of Alice de Rouclif, a child of minor gentry. (P.J.P. Goldberg, (ed.), *Women in England c. 1275–1525* (Manchester, 1995), no. 4.) The depositions confirm what one would have expected, that childbirth was an almost exclusively female affair. See also Carol Rawcliffe, *Medicine and Society in Later Medieval England* (Stroud, 1995), ch. 9: 'Women and Medicine: the Midwife and the Nurse'. There is inevitably more evidence for later periods. See Valerie Fildes (ed.), *Women as Mothers in Pre-Industrial England* (London, 1990).

61. On this see Margaret Aston, 'Segregation in Church', in W.J. Sheils and Diana Wood (eds), *Women in the Church* (Oxford, 1990), pp. 237–94.

62. See below, pp. 131–7.

63. M.K. Dale and V.B. Redstone (eds), *The Household Book of Dame Alice de Bryene*, Suffolk Institute of Archaeology and Natural History (Ipswich, 1931). For what follows see pp. 7–8, 14, 19, 27–8, 30–1, 33, 39–40, 65–6, 76, 87.

64. *Paston Letters*, i, no. 226.

65. *Ibid.*, no. 378.

66. *Stonor Letters*, no. 176.

5. Lady Versus Lord: Antagonistic Relations

1. For what follows see Sheridan Walker, 'Free consent and marriage of feudal wards', pp. 123–34. The quotation comes from p. 125.

2. *Calendar of Patent Rolls 1358–61*, p. 278; quoted by Sheridan Walker, 'Free consent', p. 128.

3. The evidence comes from a Chancery inquisition couched in the form of a proof of age: PRO C.132/45/8. It is published in two parts in *Calendar of Inquisitions Post Mortem*, vol. I, no. 875, and vol. XIII, no. 313. Strictly speaking, marriage was a matter for the ecclesiastical courts. The documents are badly damaged in places. The case is noted by Sheridan Walker, 'Free consent', p. 126.

4. The reference to Longespée is obscure at this date, but see below, p. 129.

5. The document is illegible at this point.

6. *Victoria County History of Warwickshire*, vol. III, p. 28 and vol. IV, pp. 106, 198.

7. See *Victoria County History of Warwickshire*, vol. II, p. 64; *Calendar of Patent Rolls, 1272–81*, p. 188. She was living in 1285. A successor was elected in 1291.

8. What follows is based on the following sources: *Close Rolls 1231–34*, pp. 276, 363; *Close Rolls 1237–42*, pp. 393–4; *Ex e Rotuli Finium*, ii, p. 431; *Victoria County History of Oxfordshire*, vol. V, pp. 57, 160, and vol. VI, pp. 20–1; *Complete Peerage*, vol. XII, pt 2, pp. 364–5; Sanders, *English Baronies*, pp. 51–2. For Richard Siward see David Crouch, 'The Last Adventure of Richard Siward', *Morgannwg*, xxxv (1991), pp. 7–30.

9. This benefaction was made for her soul and those of her ancestors and children. She appears to have been the mother of Richard Siward II, who was brought up in Scotland. Her heirs,

however, were found to be Margery, Ela and Isabel, the daughters of Philippa's sister, Alice, and her husband, John Bisset.

10. For what follows see *Complete Peerage*, vol. XII, pt 2, pp. 366–7 and Emma Mason, 'The Resources of the Earldom of Warwick in the Thirteenth Century', *Midland History*, iii, no. 2 (1975), pp. 67–75, and the references given there.

11. *Calendar of Patent Rolls 1232–47*, p. 61.

12. *Calendar of Patent Rolls 1247–58*, p. 76.

13. For these quotations see Paul Brand, 'Family and Inheritance, Women and Children', in C. Given-Wilson (ed.), *An Illustrated History of Late Medieval England* (Manchester, 1996), pp. 63 and 65.

14. See R.H. Helmholz, 'Married Women's Wills in Later Medieval England' in Sheridan Walker (ed.), *Wife and Widow in Medieval England*, pp. 165–82.

15. This was true even if she had been a party to the grant, except if the grant had been made in a royal court by final concord. See Brand, *op. cit.*, p. 65.

16. *Op. cit.*, p. 65.

17. For what follows I have relied heavily upon R.H. Helmholz, *Marriage Litigation in Medieval England* (Cambridge, 1974), especially ch. III.

18. *Ibid.*, p. 74.

19. *Ibid.*, pp. 88–9.

20. See Brand, 'Family and Inheritance', p. 58.

21. J.B. Post, 'Ravishment of Women and the Statutes of Westminster', in J.H. Baker (ed.), *Legal Records and the Historian* (London, 1978), pp. 150–64.

22. *Ibid.*, p. 157, citing *Year Books 33–35 Edward I*, Rolls Series (London, 1879), pp. 533–5; *Calendar of Inquisitions Post Mortem*, vol. iii, no. 391.

23. See S. Sheridan Walker, 'Punishing convicted ravishers: statutory strictures and actual practice in thirteenth- and fourteenth-century England', *Journal of Medieval History*, 13 (1987), pp. 237–50, especially p. 239.

24. F. Pollock & F.W. Maitland, *The History of English Law*, reissued with new intro. by S.F.C. Milsom (Cambridge, 1968), ii, pp. 395–6, citing *Rotuli Parliamentorum*, i, p. 140.

25. *Complete Peerage*, vol. V, p. 642; *Calendar of Patent Rolls 1266–72*, pp. 520–1.

26. For what follows see P.R. Coss, *The Langley Family and its Cartulary: A Study in Later Medieval Gentry*, Dugdale Society Occasional Paper no. 9 (Oxford, 1974), pp. 14–18.

27. The translation is from J.B. Post, 'Sir Thomas West and the Statute of Rapes, 1382', *Bulletin of the Institute of Historical Research*, 53 (1980), pp. 24–30, where the details of the case can be found.

28. Furnivall (ed.), *The Fifty Earliest English Wills*, pp. 4–10.

29. *Victoria County History of Warwickshire*, vol. V, p. 58.

30. *Calendar of Inquisitions Post Mortem*, v, no. 555.

31. The principal evidence on which the following account is based is published in Hon. G. Wrottesley (ed.), *Extracts from the plea rolls of the reign of Edward II*, William Salt Archaeological Society, vol. 10, pt 1 (1889), pp. 27–8, 34–9; Hon. G. Wrottesley (ed.), *Extracts from the Coram Rege Rolls of Edward III and Richard II*, William Salt Archaeological Society, vol. 14, pt 1 (1893), pp. 4, 18–19; and D.W. Sutherland (ed.), *The Eyre of Northamptonshire 3–4 Edward III*, Selden Society, i (London, 1983), pp. 216–18.

32. On approvers see, most recently, Jens Röhrkasten, 'Some Problems of the Evidence of Fourteenth-Century Approvers', *Journal of Legal History*, v (1984), pp. 14–22.

33. The statute of 1352 confined 'high treason' to treason against the Crown. Treason against one's lord was now invariably 'petty treason'. See J.G. Bellamy, *The Law of Treason in the Later Middle Ages* (Cambridge, 1970), pp. 225–31.

34. See R.I. Moore, *The Formation of a Persecuting Society: Power and Deviance in Western Europe, 950–1250* (Oxford, 1987), pp. 23–7.

35. See N. Vincent, 'Simon of Atherfield (d. 1211), a martyr to his wife', *Analecta Bollandiana*, 113 (1995), pp. 349–61. I am grateful to Dr David Crook for drawing this essay to my attention.

36. R. Curtis (ed.), *Le Roman de Tristan en Prose*, vol. I (Cambridge, 1985), p. 116. I owe this reference to the kindness of Dr Helen Nicholson.

37. *Calendar of Inquisitions Miscellaneous*, ii, no. 657; *Calendar of Close Rolls 1313–18*, p. 471, and *1323–7*, p. 413.

38. See L.C. Gabel, *Benefit of Clergy in the Later Middle Ages* (repr. New York, 1969), especially pp. 87–90.

39. For attitudes towards spousal murder in early modern England see, for example, Garthine Walker, "Demons in female form': representations of women and gender in murder

pamphlets of the late sixteenth and early seventeenth centuries', in William Zunder and Suzanne Trill (eds), *Writing and the English Renaissance* (London, 1996), pp. 123–39.

40. See Albert Hartshorne, 'Monumental Effigies', in *Victoria County History of Northamptonshire*, vol. I, (London, 1902), pp. 399, 401.

41. The arms borne by Sir Thomas Murdak and by his son John were *or, fretty sable*. The arms depicted on the effigy show *a fess between six fleur-de-lis* and *a fess, in chief three roundels*.

42. Sir Philip de Gayton himself bore *argent, crusily and three fleurs de lis azure*. Sir John de Gayton, however, bore *argent a fess between six fleurs de lis gules*.

43. For this case see R. Sillem (ed.), *Records of Some Sessions of the Peace in Lincolnshire, 1360–1375*, Lincoln Record Society, xxx (1936), pp. lxv–lxxiv. It is also discussed in John Bellamy, *Crime and Public Order in England in the Later Middle Ages* (London and Toronto, 1973), pp. 54–5. The Cantilupe case should be contrasted, however, with a series of instances cited by Paul Strohm in *Hochon's Arrow: The Social Imagination of Fourteenth-Century Texts* (Princeton, 1992), pp. 128–30, where the woman was invariably burned.

44. G.D.G. Hall (ed.), *The Treatise on the Laws and Customs of the Realm of England Commonly called Glanvill* (Oxford, 1965), p. 3.

45. G.E. Woodbine (ed.), trans. (with revision and notes) by Samuel E.Thorne, 'Bracton' (*Bracton de legibus et consuetudinibus Angliae: Bracton on the Laws and Customs of England*), 4 vols (Oxford, 1968–77), pp. 394, 403, 414–19.

46. C.A.F. Meekings (ed.), *Crown Pleas of the Wiltshire Eyre, 1249*, Wiltshire Archaeological and Natural History Society, xvi (1961), p. 80.

47. Two examples are cited, from the 1241 and 1255 Surrey eyre rolls respectively. Both are of instigation, but neither carries any suggestion that the girl herself was acting maliciously. Nor, in fact, is there any suggestion that the instigator was related to the girl: C.A.F. Meekings (ed.), and prepared for the press by David Crook, *The 1235 Surrey Eyre*, vol. I, Surrey Record Society (1979), pp. 123–41.

48. A case at the Shropshire eyre of 1256 shows a girl having been beaten and tied up in order to force her to make an appeal: Alan Harding (ed.), *The Roll of the Shropshire Eyre of 1256*, Selden Society, 96 (London, 1980), no. 672. At the Warwickshire eyre of 1221 a girl brought a case seemingly for reasons of revenge but the motive

was not sexual: D.M. Stenton (ed.), *Rolls of the Justices in Eyre for Gloucestershire, Warwickshire and Shropshire, 1221 and 1222*, Selden Society, 59 (London, 1940), no. 751. See also, Post, 'Ravishment of Women', pp. 152–3 for a less sceptical view of the likelihood of revenge accusations.

49. For analyses see Meekings, *Crown Pleas of the Wiltshire Eyre, 1249*, pp. 79–80, and *The 1235 Surrey Eyre*, vol. I, p. 121.

50. J.S. Brewer (ed.), *Giraldi Cambrensis opera: Gemma Ecclesiastica*, Rolls Series (London 1861–91), vol. ii, section II, xi, pp. 219–20. Quoted by J. Wogan-Browne, 'Saints' Lives and Female Readers', pp. 21–2.

51. Glanvill, p. 176.

52. The exception of malicious accusation may reflect male fears rather than reality.

53. Post, 'Sir Thomas West and the Statute of Rapes', p. 24.

54. For example, that she had failed to specify by which door her attacker had entered. See Post, 'Ravishment of Women', pp. 155–6. The belief that the justices were generally worried by the malicious nature of appeals is hard to sustain.

55. Justice Thurkleby apparently argued in 1244 that a woman can only appeal rape of her virginity. See Post, 'Ravishment' p. 153. For a case brought by a widow, however, see Meekings, *Crown Pleas of the Wiltshire Eyre, 1249*, no. 296. She failed to prosecute her appeal; the jurors said that he did in fact lie with her by force and that they had reached a compromise.

56. Post, 'Ravishment of Women', p. 160. For a very recent discussion of the legislation and legal procedures in cases of rape and abduction see J.G. Bellamy, *The Criminal Trial in Later Medieval England* (Stroud, 1998), Appendix 1, pp. 162–86. Professor Bellamy's study appeared too late to be used in the body of this chapter. It should be noted, however, that he confirms the relatively low incidence of rape among the felonies coming to court and the miniscule rate of conviction. See also J.L. Carter, *Rape in Medieval England: An Historical and Sociological Study* (Lanham, 1985). For study of rape narratives in court in early modern England see Miranda Chaytor, 'Husband(ry): Narratives of Rape in the Seventeenth Century', *Gender and History*, 7, no. 3 (1995), pp. 378–407, and Garthine Walker, 'Rereading Rape and Sexual Violence in Early Modern England', *Gender and History*, 10, no. 1 (forthcoming 1998).

57. See A.W.B. Simpson, *An Introduction to the History of the Land Law* (Oxford, 1961), p. 65.
58. Glanvill, pp. 65–6.
59. For what follows see, especially, Janet S. Loengard, '*Rationabilis Dos*: Magna Carta and the Widow's "Fair Share" in the Earlier Thirteenth Century', in Sheridan Walker (ed.), *Wife and Widow in Medieval England*, pp. 59–80. See also J. Biancalana, 'Widows at Common Law: The Development of Common Law Dower', *Irish Jurist*, new series, xxiii (1988), pp. 255–329.
60. Loengard, '*Rationabilis Dos*', p. 72.
61. For what follows see, in particular, Mason, 'The Resources of the Earldom of Warwick', pp. 67–75, and David Crouch, 'The Local Influence of the Earls of Warwick, 1088–1242: A Study in Decline and Resourcefulness', *Midland History*, xxi (1996), pp. 1–22.
62. For the difficulties faced by Earl Thomas see Crouch, 'The local influence of the Earls of Warwick', especially pp. 11, 13. The litigation between Earl Thomas and Countess Philippa and Richard Basset is in *Close Rolls 1234–37*, pp. 220, 367, *Close Rolls 1237–42*, p. 1, *Curia Regis Rolls*, vol. XV, pp. 55, 60–1, 185, *Curia Regis Rolls*, vol. XVI, p. 58.
63. See *Calendar of Close Rolls 1264–68*, pp. 461, 468–70, 515–16, 561.
64. Mason, 'The Resources of the Earldom of Warwick', p. 74.
65. Coss, *Lordship, Knighthood and Locality*, pp. 290–1.
66. This is a matter which has caused some confusion. To be precise, a widow with a jointure was entitled to a third of her husband's remaining land. See below, notes 67 and 71.
67. For what follows see, in particular, the important essay by Rowena Archer, 'Rich Old Ladies: The Problem of Late Medieval Dowagers' in A.J. Pollard (ed.), *Property and Politics: Essays in Later Medieval English History* (Gloucester, 1984), pp. 16–35.
68. K.B. McFarlane, *The Nobility of Later Medieval England* (Oxford, 1973), p. 66.
69. Eileen Spring, *Law, Land and Family: Aristocratic Inheritance in England 1300–1800* (Chapel Hill and London, 1993), especially ch. I.
70. *Ibid.*, p. 35.
71. The fullest treatment of these issues is by Simon Payling, 'The Politics of Family: Late Medieval Marrriage Contracts' in R.H. Britnell and A.J. Pollard (eds), *The McFarlane Legacy: Studies in Late Medieval Politics and Society* (Stroud, 1995), pp. 21–47.
72. See Simon Payling, 'Arbitration, Perpetual Entails and Collateral Warranties in Late Medieval England', *Journal of Legal History*, xiii (1992), p. 33.

6. *Literature, Gender and Ideology*

1. Ruth Kelso, *Doctrine for the Lady of the Renaissance* (Urbana, 1956), p. 1.
2. *Ibid.*, p. 3.
3. J.J. Parry (ed.), *The Art of Courtly Love by Andreas Capellanus* (New York, 1990), i, p. 36.
4. *Op. cit.*, p. 30.
5. On the education of girls in the early modern period see Martine Sonnet, 'A Daughter to Educate' in Natalie Zemon Davis and Arlette Farge (eds), *A History of Women in the West III: Renaissance and Enlightenment Paradoxes* (Cambridge, Mass., and London, 1993), pp. 101–31, and Merry E. Wiesner, *Women and Gender in Early Modern Europe* (Cambridge, 1993), part 2, and references given there.
6. For what follows see the introduction to M.Y. Offord (ed.), *The Book of the Knight of the Tower* translated by William Caxton, Early English Text Society, supplementary series no. 2 (London, 1971).
7. The examples are taken from Thomas Wright (ed.), *The Book of the Knight of La Tour-Landry*, Early English Text Society (OS 1906, repr. New York, 1969), chs X–XIII. I have modernised the spelling.
8. Wright's text has 'vessell', which he believed to be a scribal error. Vane, that is weathercock, is from Caxton's text, p. 25.
9. F.J. Furnivall and I. Gollancz (eds), *Hoccleve's Works: the Minor Poems*, Early English Text Society, Extra Series nos 61 and 73 (repr. in one vol., London, 1970), p. 164 (verse 98).
10. Parry, *The Art of Courtly Love*, p. 67.
11. I have employed Caxton's text here (p. 26), as Wright's is clearly defective.
12. This is actually Caxton's chapter heading, p. 127.
13. Wright, ch. XV.
14. For various critical commentaries on the prioress see Larry D. Benson (ed.), *The Riverside Chaucer* (Oxford, 1987), pp. 803–6. One of the most effective treatments of the prioress in contemporary context remains Eileen Power, 'Madame Eglentyne: Chaucer's Prioress in Real Life', in her *Medieval People* (London, 1924; repr. with introduction by Richard Smith, Bristol, 1986).

15. M. Oliva's study of 542 nuns from the diocese of Norwich shows 64 per cent of them as definitely drawn from the local gentry: M. Oliva, 'Aristocracy or meritocracy? Office-holding patterns in late medieval English nunneries', in Sheils and Wood (eds), *Women in the Church*, pp. 197–208, and the same author's *The Convent and the Community in the Diocese of Norwich from 1350 to 1450* (Woodbridge, 1994). See also Roberta Gilchrist, *Gender and Material Culture: the Archaeology of Religious Women* (London, 1994), p. 50. Chaucer himself was acquainted with the aristocratic Barking, where his sister or daughter, Elizabeth, was a nun, and with St Leonard's near Stratford atte Bowe, which he had visited as a boy and where the fictive Madame Eglentyne was prioress.

16. Wright, ch. XCVI.

17. *Ibid.*, ch. LXXII.

18. Caxton, p. 103.

19. What follows is from Wright, chs XVIII–XIX.

20. This is clear from Caxton's text (p. 37). The translation in Wright's manuscript is unclear.

21. For this image see Grössinger, *The World Upside-Down*, pp. 87–92 with illustrations.

22. Wright, ch. XCVII.

23. Sharon Farmer, 'Persuasive Voices: Clerical Images of Medieval Wives', *Speculum*, 61 (1986), pp. 517–43.

24. *Ibid.*, p. 541.

25. J.R. Maddicott, *Simon de Montfort* (Cambridge, 1994), pp. 38–59.

26. See, most recently, John Carmi Parsons, 'The Intercessionary Patronage of Queens Margaret and Isabella of France', in M. Prestwich, R.H. Britnell and R. Frame (eds), *Thirteenth Century England VI* (Woodbridge, 1997), pp. 145–56, and references given there. See also P. Strohm, 'Queens as Intercessors', in his *Hochon's Arrow: The Social Imagination of Fourteenth-Century Texts* (Princeton, 1992), pp. 95–119.

27. The sermon is in Wright, chs XLVII–XLIX.

28. *Ibid.*, ch. XXI.

29. *Ibid.*, chs XLVII–XLIX; Caxton, pp. 70, 77–8.

30. See above, pp. 50–1.

31. Wright, chs CXXII–CXXXIII.

32. *Paston Letters*, i, nos 18, 203, 332, and ii, no. 446.

33. C.H. Talbot (ed.), *The Life of Christina of Markyate, A Twelfth-Century Recluse* (Oxford, 1959, repr. 1987), especially pp. 14, 43, 74. See also J. Wogan-Browne, 'Saints' Lives and the Female Reader', in *Forum for Modern Language Studies*, 27 (1991), pp. 316–21.

34. See Susan Crane, *Gender and Romance in Chaucer's Canterbury Tales* (Princeton, 1994), pp. 10–11. See also Jennifer R. Goodman, '"That wommen holde in ful greet reverence": Mothers and Daughters Reading Chivalric Romances', in L.Smith and J.H.M. Taylor (eds), *Women, the Book and the Worldly* (Woodbridge, 1995), pp. 25–30.

35. For the evidence upon which the following argument is based see Carol Meale's thorough study '". . .alle the bokes that I have of latyn, englisch, and frensch": laywomen and their books in late medieval England', in *Women and Literature in Britain*, and the same author's '"Gode men/Wiues maydnes and alle men": Romance and its Audiences', in Carol M. Meale (ed.), *Readings in Medieval English Romance* (Woodbridge, 1994), pp. 209–25.

36. Meale, *Women and Literature*, p. 140.

37. For the debate on this manuscript see the references given by Meale, 'Gode men', p. 222.

38. For the traffic in the Paston books see P.R. Coss, 'Aspects of Cultural Diffusion in Medieval England: the Early Romances, Local Society and Robin Hood', *Past and Present*, 108 (August 1985), pp. 54–6.

39. *Ibid.*, p. 44–6.

40. For a description of this manuscript and notes on the families who figure in its marginalia see B.D.H. Miller, 'The Early History of Bodleian Ms. Digby 86', *Annuale medievale*, ii (1961), pp. 23–55. See also J. Tschann and M.B. Parkes, *Facsimile of Oxford, Bodleian Library, Ms Digby 86*, Early English Text Society, Supplementary Series 16 (1996). For comment on the contents see J. Frankis, 'The Social Context of Vernacular Writing in Thirteenth-Century England: the Evidence of the Manuscripts', in P.R. Coss and S.D. Lloyd (eds), *Thirteenth Century England I* (Woodbridge, 1986), pp. 182–4.

41. See Lynne S. Blanchfield, 'The romances of MS Ashmole 61: an idiosyncratic scribe', in M. Mills, J. Fellows and C.M. Meale (eds), *Romance in Medieval England* (Woodbridge, 1991), pp. 65–87. Another good example is Cambridge University Library Ff.2.38 which contains ten romances in addition to saints' lives, courtesy books, and a wide variety of items for spiritual guidance. For a description

see M.B. Parkes, 'The Literacy of the Laity', in David Daiches and Anthony Thorlby (eds), *The Medieval World* (London, 1973), pp. 568–9.

42. By Felicity Riddy in an unpublished paper. See Meale, *Readings in Medieval English Romance*, pp. 221–2.

43. Crane, *Gender and Romance*, p. 6.

44. Riddy, 'Women talking about the things of God', pp. 104–27.

45. On this Riddy cites A.I. Doyle, *The Vernon Manuscript: A Facsimile of Bodleian Library, Oxford, MS Eng. Poet.a.1.* (Cambridge, 1987), pp. 14–15, and the essays by N.F. Blake and Carol Meale in Derek Pearsall (ed.), *Studies in the Vernon Manuscript*, pp. 45–59 and pp. 115–36.

46. Eileen Power, *Medieval English Nunneries* (Cambridge, 1922), pp. 317–22.

47. Gilchrist, *Gender and Material Culture*, p. 123.

48. *Ibid.*, p. 109.

49. Riddy goes further than this, in fact, and suggests that the cultures were indistinguishable. For her, Chaucer's portrait of the prioress with her refined table manners, etc. is a representation of this phenomenon: *Ibid.*, pp. 109–10.

50. Sometimes these professions were copied into bishops' registers. For the details see Mary C. Erler, 'Three Fifteenth-Century Vowesses', in Barron and Sutton (eds), *Medieval London Widows*, pp. 165–7.

51. In some cases, the woman associated herself with a religious house, as for example did Elizabeth de Burgh, lady of Clare, who was associated with the Minoresses (the Franciscan nuns) of Aldgate outside London. In 1343 she received a papal indulgence allowing her to enter their enclosure with two ladies. She had earlier taken a vow of chastity. See Ward, 'Elizabeth de Burgh', pp. 37–41.

52. Riddy, 'Women talking about the things of God', p. 108.

53. For Cecily, Duchess of York, see also C.A.J. Armstrong, 'The Piety of Cecily, Duchess of York', in Douglas Woodruff (ed.), *For Hilaire Belloc. Essays in Honour of his 72nd Birthday* (London, 1942), pp. 73–94.

54. See above, pp. 111–12.

55. E. Panofsky, *Early Netherlandish Painting* (Cambridge, Mass., 1953), I, p. 68. It is quoted by Sandra Penketh in a splendid essay to which I am much indebted for what follows: Sandra Penketh, 'Women and Books of Hours', in Lesley Smith and Jane H.M. Taylor (eds), *Women and the Book: Assessing the Visual Evidence* (London and Toronto, 1997), pp. 266–81.

56. See Penketh, *op. cit.*, p. 6, quoting the much-cited thesis of Susan H. Cavanaugh: 'A Study of Books Privately Owned in England 1300–1450' (unpubl. Ph.D. thesis, University of Pennsylvania, 1980).

57. See J.A.F. Thomson, 'Knightly Piety and the Margins of Lollardy', in Margaret Aston and Colin Richmond (eds), *Lollardy and the Gentry in the Later Middle Ages* (Stroud, 1997), pp. 95–111.

58. See Anne Clark Bartlett, *Male Authors, Female Readers: Representation and Subjectivity in Middle English Devotional Literature* (Ithaca and London, 1995), ch. IV, '"Ghostly Sister in Jesus Christ": Spiritual Friendship and Sexual Politics'. I am very much indebted to this fascinating study.

59. See Bartlett, *op. cit.*, pp. 86–9 for the relationship between James Greenhagh, of the Carthusian house at Sheen, and Joanna Sewell of the nearby Bridgittine nunnery of Syon.

60. *Op. cit.*, pp. 112–13 and references given there. For Margaret Beaufort, see in particular, Michael K. Jones and Malcolm Underwood, *The King's Mother: Lady Margaret Beaufort, Countess of Richmond and Derby* (Cambridge, 1992).

61. On this point see R.G.K.A. Mertes, 'The Household as a Religious Community', in Joel Rosenthal and Colin Richmond (eds), *People, Politics and Community in the Later Middle Ages* (New York, 1987), pp. 123–39, and Diana Webb, 'Woman and Home: The Domestic Setting of Late Medieval Spirituality', in Sheil and Wood (eds), *Women in the Church*, pp. 159–74.

62. *Paston Letters*, i, no. 353. See also no. 355.

63. Riddy, 'Women talking about the things of God', p. 109.

64. Warwick Paul Marett (ed.), *A calendar of the register of Henry Wakefield, Bishop of Worcester, 1375–95*, Worcestershire Historical Society (1972), pp. 15, 119–20, 229–32.

65. Bartlett, *Male Authors, Female Readers*, p. 109, and references given there.

66. For what follows see, in particular, Gold, *The Lady and the Virgin*, ch. 1, 'Secular Image: Women in Chanson de Geste and Romance', and works cited there. Some writers, however, have been arguing for a more positive female role in the birth of romance. See above ch. 2, note 96. Jocelyn Wogan-Browne takes a more

optimistic view of the cultural significance of female saints' lives and women's likely responses to them (Wogan-Browne, 'Saints' Lives and the Female Reader', pp. 314–32).

67. W.W. Comfort, in 'The Character Types in the Old French Chansons de Geste', *Publications of the Modern Language Association*, 21 (1906), pp. 375–6 (quoted by Gold, *op. cit.*, pp. 37–8).

68. *Ibid.*, p. 42. For an especially damning indictment of romantic love, born at a particular moment in the history of misogyny, see R. Howard Bloch, *Medieval Misogyny and the Invention of Western Romantic Love* (Chicago, 1991): 'Although the discourse of courtliness, which places the woman on a pedestal and worships her as the controlling *domna* [lady], seems to empower women along with an enabling femininity, it is yet another ruse of sexual usurpation thoroughly analogous to that developed in the early centuries of our era by the fathers of the church. No less than the discourse of misogyny does that of courtly love reduce woman to the status of a category. . . . Misogyny and courtly love are co-conspiring abstractions of the feminine whose function was from the start, and continues to be, the diversion of women from history by the annihilation of the identity of the individual woman . . . and thus the transformation of woman into an ideal', pp. 196–7. See also Gayle Rubin, 'The Traffic in Women: Notes on the "Political Economy" of Sex', in Rayna Reiter (ed.), *Toward an Anthropology of Women* (New York, 1975), pp. 157–210; repr. in Scott (ed.), *Feminism and History*, pp. 105–51.

69. Susan Crane, *Insular Romance: Politics, Faith, and Culture in Anglo-Norman and Middle English Literature* (Berkeley and London, 1986), p. 12. This is an excellent recent study of romance in England.

70. *Ibid.*, p. 163.

71. Alison Adams, ed. and trans, *The Romance of Yder* (Cambridge, 1983). The manuscript is Cambridge University Library Ee.4.26. Although the manuscript is Anglo-Norman, suggesting that the romance was circulating in England, it was composed in western France in the late twelfth or early thirteenth century.

72. I have closely followed Alison Adams' translation, pp. 40–1.

73. *The Book of the City of Ladies by Christine de Pizan*, trans. Earl Jeffrey Richards (New York, 1982), pp. 4–5.

74. See also Rosemary Woolf, 'The Theme of Christ the Lover-knight in Medieval English Literature', *Review of English Studies*, n.s. 13 (1962), pp. 1–16.

75. Bartlett, *Male Authors, Female Readers*, p. 3.

76. *Ibid.*, pp. 22–3. The literature on Margery Kempe is by now considerable. See the bibliography in the Penguin edition of her (dictated) work: B.A. Windeatt, trans., *The Book of Margery Kempe* (London, 1985).

77. Bartlett, *Male Authors, Female Readers*, p. 22 citing Susan Schibanoff, 'Taking the Gold Out of Egypt: The Art of Reading as a Woman', in Elizabeth Flynn and Patrocinio Schweickart (eds), *Gender and Reading: Essays on Readers, Texts, and Contexts* (Baltimore, 1986), pp. 83–106.

78. Peter Brown and Andrew Butcher, *The Age of Saturn: Literature and History in the Canterbury Tales* (Oxford, 1991), p. 26. Ch. One of this book brings together a good deal of recent work on the subject of the Wife of Bath.

79. For the Wife of Bath in relation to medieval estates satire see Jill Mann, *Chaucer and Medieval Estates Satire* (Cambridge, 1973), pp. 121–7. For the basic misogynist texts see Alcuin Blamires, *Woman Defamed and Woman Defended: An Anthology of Medieval Texts* (Oxford, 1992).

80. See Carolyn Dinshaw, *Chaucer's Sexual Poetics* (Madison, 1989), ch. 4.

81. See Lee Patterson, '"For the Wyves love of Bathe": Feminine Rhetoric and Poetic Resolution in the Roman de la Rose and the Canterbury Tales', *Speculum*, 58, 3 (1983), pp. 656–95.

82. Caroline Walker Bynum, 'Fast, Feast, and Flesh: The Religious Significance of Food to Medieval Women', *Representations*, 11 (1985), pp. 1–25.

83. This was very different, of course, from the reality of fourteenth-century England. See above, pp. 139–43. There is an irony here in that Chaucer himself was accused of rape. It is a matter which has caused much debate among Chaucer specialists over the years. See, most recently, C. Cannon, '*Raptus* in the Chaumpaigne Release and a Newly Discovered Document Concerning the Life of Geoffrey Chaucer,' *Speculum*, 68 (1993), pp. 74–94.

84. See Brown and Butcher, pp. 54–7, who also describe the tale as a 'black romance'.

85. On this basis, Elaine Tuttle Hansen has recently castigated all those who see either Chaucer's fictive character or his treatment of her as an expression of a proto-feminist

position. (*Chaucer and the Fictions of Gender* (Berkeley, 1992), ch. 2) Jill Mann, on the other hand, commends Chaucer for his vision of mutuality in relationships. (*Geoffrey Chaucer* (Hemel Hempstead, 1991), pp. 87–93.) The ambiguities in Chaucer's dénouement are highlighted by Corinne J. Saunders, 'Women Displaced: Rape and Romance in Chaucer's *Wife of Bath's Tale*' in Susan Deacy and Karen F. Pierce (eds), *Rape in Antiquity: Sexual Violence in the Greek and Roman Worlds* (London, 1997), pp. 115–31, which examines the Tale in the context of the contemporary law and legal procedure.

7. Conclusion – The Role of the Lady in Later Medieval England

1. Philippa Maddern, 'Honour among the Pastons: gender and integrity in fifteenth-century English provincial society', *Journal of Medieval History*, 14 (1988), pp. 357–71.

2. *Paston Letters*, i, no. 418. The date of this letter is uncertain, but it is generally ascribed to 1481.

3. Riddy, 'Women talking about the things of God', p. 126.

4. Maddern, 'Honour among the Pastons', pp. 365–6.

5. Joan W. Kirby, 'Women in the Plumpton Correspondence: Fiction and Reality', in Ian Wood and G.A. Loud (eds), *Church and Chronicle in the Middle Ages: Essays presented to John Taylor* (London, 1991), pp. 219–32. For the letters themselves see Joan Kirby (ed.), *The Plumpton Letters and Papers*, Royal Historical Society, Camden 5th ser., vol. 8 (Cambridge, 1996).

6. *Paston Letters*, i, no. 58.

7. For what follows see Archer, 'Women as Landholders and Administrators', pp. 153–6, where full references are given.

8. *Paston Letters*, ii, no. 432.

Further Reading

The notes contain full citations to the scholarly works consulted in the writing of this book. Readers wishing to explore aspects of the subject further might wish to begin with the following books:

Bartlett, Anne Clarke, *Male Authors, Female Readers* (Cornell University Press, 1995)

Crane, Susan, *Gender and Romance in Chaucer's Canterbury Tales* (Princeton University Press, 1993)

Crouch, David, *The Image of Aristocracy in Britain 1000–1300* (Routledge, 1992)

Dinshaw, Carolyn, *Chaucer's Sexual Poetics* (University of Wisconsin Press, 1989)

Fell, Christine, *Women in Anglo-Saxon England* (Blackwell, 1984)

Gilchrist, Roberta, *Gender and Material Culture: The Archaeology of Religious Women* (Routledge, 1994)

Gold, Penny Schine, *The Lady and the Virgin: Image, Attitude, and Experience in Twelfth-Century France* (University of Chicago, 1985)

Helmholz, R.H., *Marriage Litigation in Medieval England* (W.M.W. Gaunt & Sons, 1986; repr. from Cambridge University Press, 1975)

Kelly, Joan, *Women, History and Theory* (University of Chicago Press, 1984)

Lerner, Gerda, *The Creation of Patriarchy* (Oxford University Press, 1986)

Mann, Jill, *Geoffrey Chaucer* (Harvester Wheatsheaf, 1991)

Meale, Carol M. (ed.), *Women and Literature in Britain, 1150–1500* (Cambridge University Press, 1993)

Scott, Joan Wallach (ed.), *Feminism and History* (Oxford University Press, 1996)

Shahar, Shulamith, *The Fourth Estate* (Methuen, 1983)

Walker, S. Sheridan (ed.), *Wife and Widow in Medieval England* (University of Michigan Press, 1993)

Ward, Jennifer, *The English Noblewoman in the Middle Ages* (Longman, 1992)

Queens have been receiving considerable attention lately. A good introduction to the subject is John Carmi Parsons (ed.), *Medieval Queenship* (Alan Sutton, 1994)

Fine studies of individual queens include:

Chibnall, Marjorie, *The Empress Matilda: Queen Consort, Queen Mother and Lady of the English* (Blackwell, 1991)

Howell, Margaret, *Eleanor of Provence: Queenship in Thirteenth-Century England* (Blackwell, 1997)

Jones, Michael K. & Underwood, Malcolm G., *The King's Mother: Lady Margaret Beaufort, Countess of Richmond and Derby* (Cambridge University Press, 1992)

Parsons, John Carmi, *Eleanor of Castile: Queen and Society in Thirteenth-Century England* (MacMillan, 1995)

Stafford, Pauline, *Queen Emma and Queen Edith: Queenship and Women's Power in Eleventh-Century England* (Blackwell, 1997)

For the correspondence of medieval queens see:

Crawford, Anne (ed.), *Letters of the Queens of England 1100–1547* (Alan Sutton, 1994)

For written sources see:

Blamires, Alcuin, *Woman Defamed and Woman Defended: An Anthology of Medieval Texts* (Oxford University Press, 1992)

Carpenter, Christine (ed.), *Kingsford's Stonor Letters and Papers 1290–1483*, Royal Historical Society (Cambridge University Press, 1996)

Dale, Marion K. (ed.), *The Household Book of Dame Alice de Bryene* (Suffolk Institute of Archaeology and Natural History, 1931)

Davis, Norman (ed.), *Paston Letters and Papers of the Fifteenth Century*, 2 vols (Oxford University Press, 1971 and 1976)

Goldberg, P.J.P., *Women in England, 1275–1525* (Manchester University Press, 1995)

Kirby, Joan (ed.), *The Plumpton Letters and Papers*, Royal Historical Society (Cambridge University Press, 1996)

Ward, Jennifer, *Women of the English Nobility and Gentry, 1066–1500* (Manchester University Press, 1995)

Wright, Thomas (ed.), *The Book of the Knight of La Tour-Landry*, Early English Text Society (repr. Greenwood Press, 1969; originally publ. 1906)

For visual sources see:

Coales, John (ed.), *The Earliest English Brasses: Patronage, Style and Workshops 1270–1350* (Monumental Brass Society, 1987)

Grössinger, Christa, *The World Upside-Down: English Misericords* (Harvey Miller Publishers, 1987)

Harvey, P.D.A. & McGuinness, Andrew, *A Guide to British Medieval Seals* (The British Library and Public Record Office, 1996)

Kemp, Brian, *English Church Monuments* (Batsford, 1980)

Marks, Richard, *Stained Glass in England during the Middle Ages* (Routledge, 1993)

Norris, Malcolm, *Monumental Brasses: The Memorials*, 2 vols. (Phillips and Page, 1977)

—, *Monumental Brasses: The Craft* (Faber and Faber, 1978)

Tummers, H.A., *Early Secular Effigies in England: The Thirteenth Century* (E.J. Brill, 1980)

General works on women in medieval England include:

Barron, Caroline & Sutton, Anne (eds), *Medieval London Widows, 1300–1500* (Hambledon Press, 1994)

Bennett, J.M., *Women in the Medieval Countryside: Gender and Household in Brigstock before the Plague* (Oxford University Press, 1987)

Goldberg, P.J.P. (ed.), *Woman is a Worthy Wight* (Alan Sutton, 1992; reissued as *Women in Medieval English Society, c. 1200–1500*)

—, *Women, Work, and Life Cycle in a Medieval Economy: Women in York and Yorkshire* (Oxford University Press, 1992)

Jewell, Helen, *Women in Medieval England* (Manchester University Press, 1996)

Leyser, Henrietta, *Medieval Women: A Social History of Women in England 450–1500* (Weidenfeld & Nicolson, 1995)

Index